# AFFIRMATIVE ACTION, THE SUPREME COURT, AND POLITICAL POWER IN THE OLD CONFEDERACY

**Ronnie Bernard Tucker**

**University Press of America,® Inc.**
Lanham • New York • Oxford

**Copyright © 2000 by**
**University Press of America,® Inc.**
4720 Boston Way
Lanham, Maryland 20706

12 Hid's Copse Rd.
Cumnor Hill, Oxford OX2 9JJ

**Library of Congress Cataloging-in-Publication Data**

Tucker, Ronnie Bernard.
Affirmative action, the Supreme Court, and political power in the old
Confederacy / Ronnie Bernard Tucker.
p.    cm.
Includes bibliographical references and index.
1.  Affirmative action programs—Southern States. 2.
Affirmative action programs—Law and legislation—United
States. I. Title.
HF5549.5.A34T83    1999    331.13'3'0975—dc21    99-049063 CIP

ISBN 0-7618-1547-3 (cloth: alk. ppr.)

♾™ The paper used in this publication meets the minimum
requirements of American National Standard for Information
Sciences—Permanence of Paper for Printed Library Materials,
ANSI Z39.48—1984

# DEDICATION

I must first give thanks, praises, and adoration to God and my Lord and Savior Jesus Christ. Without the guidance and the ability given by God, I would have never made it! I shall always praise His Holy Name and thank him for his goodness. I would like to dedicate this book, first of all to my mother, Bertha T. Hewing in appreciation for her parental guidance. I appreciate and thank you very much for being there during the difficult days as well as the good days. Thank you Mother, for believing in me and instilling in me the proper work ethic. May God always continue to richly bless you. I love you very much and words can never express my gratitude.

This book is also dedicated to Clara, Kristie, and Ron II who allowed me the time, love, and space required to complete this project. I'm especially grateful to Ron and Kristie who sacrificed time with their father in order for me to complete this book.

Certainly, this project must be dedicated to my loving and supporting baby sister, Lanee. Thank you for all of the library books, encouraging e-mail, and your listening ear when the chips were down. Truly, a portion of this work is attributed to your continuous support. And, of course, thanks to Danny and Andrea for being who you are and what you've been in my life. I would also like to express my gratitude to the remainder of my family. I cannot forget those who have gone on to eternity, but in some way, shaped my life personally, spiritually, or as humanitarians. I cannot forget Lee and Della, my grandparents, who planted the seeds that shaped and molded my existence. The journey would not have been complete without the influence of other family members who have gone home. They include: Marcelous and Beulah Hutchins, Frank Green, Doshie Batts, Ramos Tucker, and Earl Hewing. Those who crossed my path in which I served as their pastor include the trio of Deacons, LeRoy Wert, J.D. Hammond, and Ladelle Morris, Thelma Hammond, Ethel McCoy, and Dorothy Flakes. They are gone, but not forgotten. Thanks for making me a better person and human being. Special thanks goes to Artee Williams, State Personnel Director, State of Arkansas, for supplying me with the information that was used to collect the data for this book.

Last, but not least, this book would not have been completed without the aid of Trina M. Smith. Thank you for your hard work and patience.

Thanks must also be given to Rev. and Mrs. Tyrone Ellis and their support in the publication of this book. May God Bless you for your willingness to support my effort. I must also give thanks to the Philadelphia Baptist Church, Menifee, Arkansas, along with the Bethel Baptist Church, Starkville, Mississippi.

# TABLE OF CONTENTS Page

# LIST OF TABLES

# COURT CASES CITED

COURT CASES                                          Page

COURT CASES                                          Page

# PREFACE

The book assessed the impact of affirmative action on employment, hiring, and the advancement of African Americans in the southern states as the result of the 1964 Civil Rights Act and the 1965 Voting Rights Act. The book explored African American progress in state government in the Old Confederacy. In part, the book is an impact assessment of employment diversity from 1964 to 1995, which analyzes employment patterns of African Americans in administrative and managerial positions.

The book analyzed the employment and hiring practices for seven southern states in the Old Confederacy. These included: Arkansas, Georgia, Mississippi, North Carolina, Oklahoma, South Carolina and Tennessee. The research in this book examined affirmative action decisions and the United States Supreme Court, and the potential impact of these decisions on recruitment, hiring, and protection of African Americans in southern state government.

The research revealed that the number of African American elected officials demonstrated a relationship with the increase of African Americans in state government. The analysis revealed that as the number of African American elected officials increase, the number of African Americans in state government increased as well as the result of the 1965 Voting Rights.

The higher the percentage of African Americans in the overall state population, increased the potential size of the labor pool . Those states with a higher percentage of African Americans in the state population also had a larger labor pool that was African American. Conversely, states with a lower percentage of African Americans in the state population had a smaller state government population that was African American.

The litigation of cases by the United States Supreme Court and other Federal Courts of Appeal did not have a direct relationship on the pattern of employment in the southern states. This was explained, in part, as the result of incremental policy implementation and the fact that none of these cases did not have a direct relationship with the hiring and promotion of African Americans in the southern states under study.

# ACKNOWLEDGMENTS

The author expresses gratitude to all of those individuals without whose unselfish assistance this book would have never been completed. I would like to express my sincere appreciation to Dr. Mfanya D. Tryman, my major professor and dissertation director. The author expresses gratitude to the other members of my dissertation committee which include, Dr. Stephen D. Shaffer, Dr. W. Martin Wiseman, Dr. Diane E. Wall, and Dr. Melvin C. Ray. Thanks to each of you for sharing your areas of expertise during the dissertation process.

The author must express a deep and heartfelt appreciation for his colleagues at the University of Central Arkansas, Conway, Arkansas. Thank you Dr. Michael Kelley for believing in me and pursuing the avenues by which this academic endeavor began and was completed. I shall always remember all that you've done for me. I also want to thank the rest of the staff and faculty in the Political Science Department for your assistance and support. My thanks goes to Dr. Gary Wekkin, Dr. John Passe` Smith, Dr. Tom McGinnis, Dr. Lani Malysia and Dr. Don Whistler.

The author must also acknowledge and thank Mrs. Marlene LaDouc, especially since it was she who taught me how to utilize and operate that "dreadful monster," known as the computer. I shall always remain grateful for your assistance. There are many others who have made contributions in their own ways, Mary Richardson, Dorris Baggett, Dr. Connie Baird, Melissa Heitzler, Reverend Henry Anderson and the officers and members of the Union Baptist Church, Morrillton, Arkansas, the late Reverend T. S. Skipper and the officers and members of the Morning Star Baptist Church, the seven other Public Administration graduates who blazed the trail for me, Dr. Ethel Ambrose, Denise Moore, Anita Anderson, and Zennettie Black for your support in the pursuit of my Ph. D. I would also like to express my thanks to the women basketball officials and the supervisor, Mr. James Waites, of the Southwestern Athletic Conference, Reverend Luke Hawkins, Reverend Henry Harris, my brothers of Silver Trowel Lodge #9, Morrillton, Arkansas, the pastor, officers, and members of Mt. Pelier Baptist Church, Starkville, Mississippi, the office workers in the Department of Political Science at Mississippi State University, and the Ice Cold Brothers of Alpha Phi Alpha (Pi Lambda and Kappa Beta), Dr.

Sonetra Howard, and all of the professors in the Department of Political Science and Public Administration at Mississippi State. Thanks also, to anyone I may have forgotten.

# CHAPTER I

# INTRODUCTION

Affirmative action policies, it could be argued, are a natural extension of the long struggle for equal rights in the United States. The struggle for equality of opportunity has included African Americans, women, and other racial and ethnic groups. This effort has affected practically all aspects of the lives of these groups that have historically encountered ongoing gender, racial, and ethnic discrimination. A vital component of the quest for equality is that of equal treatment in the workplace. More specifically, the campaign for economic equality contends with issues that pertain to jobs, pay, and promotions.

Affirmative action, as it relates to economic parity, is a policy that advocates special efforts to hire protected groups (i.e., those who historically have suffered from discrimination) as a means of compensating for past discriminatory practices. One of the goals of affirmative action is to develop a workforce reflective of the racial and sexual composition of the population (Burnstein, 1994). However, affirmative action programs are viewed by some as programs that go well beyond "mere" equality of opportunity and provide not only remedial assistance, but also preferential compensatory action in special instances and particular contexts, especially in the areas of employment and education (Abraham, 1980). In this context, affirmative action programs are distinguished from "neutrality" programs, in that affirmative action programs were instituted to bring about increased employment opportunities of protected groups, job promotions, and admission to colleges and universities (Karst, 1989). Neutrality programs, by design, merely eliminate consideration of race as a factor and does not include a mechanism for preferential treatment.

This research assesses the impact of affirmative action on employment, hiring, and advancement of African Americans in the southern states affected by the implementation of the 1964 Civil Rights Act and the 1965 Voting Rights Act. It explores the extent to which a diversified workforce exists in the Old Confederacy as a result of state governments' responses to affirmative action. It is, in part, an impact assessment of employment diversity from 1964-1995, as patterns and trends related to progress in administrative and managerial positions of African Americans are examined. Employment diversity is explored within the context of the history of job or employment/workplace equity and Supreme Court decisions addressing affirmative action since *DeFunis* (1974) and *Bakke* (1978). Data collected by the State Personnel Boards of Arkansas, Georgia, Mississippi, North Carolina, Oklahoma, South Carolina and Tennessee are examined to determine the extent and the range of modifications in employment practices as they relate to African Americans. Findings from the analysis will be used to discuss whether there is a continued need for affirmative action practices in the area of human resource personnel. Additionally, public policy recommendations regarding affirmative action and its retention or abolishment will be proposed.

Southern states are the focus of the research because they have historically been the bastions of *de jure* race discrimination and job inequality (Karst, 1989). This region is of particular significance since the "Old Confederacy" overtly resisted any and all attempts at racial equality for African Americans. It is commonly accepted that northern states presented greater opportunities for economic and job advancement for African Americans (Burnstein, 1994). This study, then, examines the barriers and progress of African American workers in what many consider to be the historical bastions of *de jure* racism and oppression in the United States. It is generally acknowledged that African Americans have made some advances into mid-level, upper level and executive positions of management and authority. The question, from a research perspective, is why and how much?

This study focuses on the composition of the administrative personnel of the seven southern states of Arkansas, Georgia, Mississippi, North Carolina, Oklahoma, South Carolina and Tennessee in examining affirmative action. Descriptive longitudinal data will be analyzed to determine the movement of African Americans in hiring and promotions since the 1964 Civil Rights Act. The research will assess whether administrative personnel in southern states reflect the qualified racial population within the workforce of each state, and to what extent they represent the state as a whole.

Oklahoma is not typically considered a part of the Old Confederacy, however, there is justification for incorporating it into the analysis. This inclusion is supported by Daniel Elazar (1972), in *American Federalism: A View From the States.* Elazar presents a categorization of the "Greater South" which suggests that this region includes the southern states east of the Mississippi plus Missouri, Arkansas, Louisiana, Oklahoma and Texas (Elazar 122, 1972). In the *"The American Mosaic,"* Elazar includes Oklahoma in his "Western South" (Elazar 188, 1984). Elazar states that the Western South experienced the same antagonistic relationship with the federal government as the confederate southern states. According to Elazar, in politics, most of the Western South was born in the solid South. He also points out that the Western South was characterized by the same problems of racism and federal intervention.

There is further evidence for including Oklahoma as part of the southern states. Oklahoma is contiguous to Arkansas, which was a part of the Old Confederacy. While Oklahoma was a territory, it was administered by Arkansas from Fort Smith, Arkansas. Moreover, the political culture of Oklahoma paralleled the political culture of the other six selected states. Oklahoma practiced the doctrine of "separate-but-equal" as evidenced by the case of *McLaurin v. Oklahoma State Regents* 339 U.S. 637 (1950). The *McLaurin* case addressed the issue of African American legal inequality, a common denominator with the other selected states. It can, therefore, be argued that Oklahoma has geographical, cultural (social), political, and legal attributes similar to those of Arkansas, Georgia, Mississippi, North Carolina, South Carolina, and Tennessee. Hence, it can be justly characterized as a southern state.

**Organization of the Book**

This research is structured into eight chapters. A conceptual definition of affirmative action is presented in Chapter II. The chapter discusses the importance of affirmative action and its relationship to and impact upon a diversified work force. A discussion is presented focusing on what the courts have outlined in an affirmative action plan that passes constitutional muster.

Another key issue analyzed in Chapter II is the constitutionality of affirmative action as it relates specifically to the "Equal Protection Clause" of the Fourteenth Amendment to the United States Constitution. Given the history of discrimination, particularly the resistance to racial equality in the employment of African Americans in the South, the discussion of this issue is essential in overcoming the legacy of inequality. The issue of "reverse discrimination" is also addressed in Chapter II. Reverse discrimination has become a key policy issue related to affirmative action. The concept of reverse discrimination relates to the issues or problems of set-asides, quotas, job recruitment and job employment, as well as promotion of individuals and groups that constitute a "protective class." Continuous charges of reverse discrimination have stifled, and in some instances, even led to the abolishment of affirmative action programs.

Chapter II also discusses the pros and cons of affirmative action and the current political climate for the debate. This political climate includes the California Civil Rights Initiative, commonly known as Proposition 209, which California voters recently approved, that eliminates all preferential treatment in hiring, promoting, and education. Congressional initiatives designed to totally eliminate affirmative action are addressed as well. The chapter devotes discussion to the issue of a "color-blind" society as it relates to the issue of affirmative action and affirmative action programs. The chapter highlights and analyzes Titles VI and VII of the 1964 Civil Rights Act, the origin of affirmative action, and its public policy evolution in the executive and congressional branches of government. A summary of the 1965 Voting Rights Act (VRA) is also included. The VRA is important because increases in black elected officials and voting black constituencies in the seventies and eighties paralleled the increases in black employment gains in state governments during this time. It could be argued that the increased number of black elected officials put additional pressure on state governments to hire and promote African Americans.

Chapter III addresses the history of job, economic and workplace inequality. This chapter takes a historical look at the issues and problems African Americans have confronted in their plight for racial equality in employment. The struggle for employment equity and equality began with the United States Constitution, which in its conception did not provide racial equality for African Americans. This section provides an overview of the key struggles that have been encountered and the ongoing problem in creating a workplace reflective of the general population. This chapter provides the foundation for examining the legal inequality that affirmative action and employment diversification policies have attempted to remedy.

Chapter III also provides the historical framework for assessing whether there exists an inherent need for affirmative action in the southern states. This becomes even more significant given the fact that southern states have consistently offered strong resistance to any quest for racial equality in the past. Employment diversity, like other civil rights efforts, has continually faced obstacles.

The United States Supreme Court has played a pivotal role in issues related to affirmative action. Chapter IV analyzes court decisions relating to affirmative action. Cases beginning with *Griggs* (1971), *DeFunis* (1974), and *Bakke* (1978) through 1988 are discussed. The policy implications for affirmative action based on the decisions of the Rehnquist Supreme Court are analyzed. Prior to *Bakke*, the United States Supreme Court had been viewed as the champion for protecting the rights of African Americans. However, since 1978 a number of Supreme Court decisions have gone against proponents of affirmative action. This has been due, in part, to the appointment of more conservative judges to the Supreme Court during the Reagan-Bush administrations. Justices Rehnquist, Kennedy, Scalia and O'Connor were appointed by Reagan and Justices Souter and Thomas were appointed by Bush. These appointments had strong ideological overtones by Presidents opposed to affirmative action. The inclusion of these court cases reflects the fact that the United States Supreme Court has an important impact in the formation of public policies, laws, statues, legislation, rules and regulations.

In addition to *DeFunis* and *Bakke* this chapter analyzes Supreme Court decisions related to affirmative action and civil rights since the late sixties. The format for analyzing these cases consists of a discussion of what issues led to the Court deciding the case, the role of the government in the case, the legal arguments on both sides, the majority opinion, concurring opinion, and the dissenting opinion handed down. This section of the research will also assess the impact of those Supreme Court decisions for affirmative action and a diversified workforce in American society.

Chapter V presents the Supreme Court and federal court cases pertaining to affirmative action from 1989 through 1996. The cases in this chapter demonstrate how the courts have change their judicial philosophy regarding affirmative action. During the earlier terms of the courts as discussed in Chapter IV, the court's appeared to have been employee friendly. However, the court's during the 1990s appeared to have change directions philosophically and ruled in favor of the employer. These cases are included to give an idea of which direction society and the federal government are moving in the 1990s. The format for Chapter V is the same as previously mentioned in Chapter IV.

Chapter VI is important because it provides empirical data related to affirmative action. The data are utilized to evaluate the extent to which the South, which had *de jure* racism and discrimination, has progressed in diversifying a traditionally all white male workforce. The data assist in determining the extent to which affirmative action and black political power has allowed African Americans to obtain managerial and professional positions and the extent to which they reflect the available black labor force and the general black population of each state.

Chapter VII also examines data related to the Voting Rights Act of 1965 and the election of African American elected officials. This includes data on voting, percent of state population that is African American, and the population of the states in the study. Assessment of the VRA is important because the 1964 Civil Rights Act cannot be examined apart from the political pressure brought to bear by African American politicians for more jobs for their constituents.

Chapter VIII, the concluding chapter, provides an assessment of affirmative action in state government. In the summary chapter the actual recommendations for affirmative action and employment diversity in the seven states are presented.

## Rationale for the Book

### Previous Research Related to Affirmative Action

Studies that have heretofore been conducted in the arena of affirmative action have approached the subject from a myriad of perspectives including gender, academia, unemployment rates, white males before and after affirmative action, the glass ceiling, higher education, affirmative action policies and African American women, and minority representation. The most enduring and dominant areas of research have been in the areas of education and employment. Within the last decade, however, a number of different angles have emerged. Hudson (1994), for example, examines issues relating to white males and how they have been impacted by affirmative action programs. He specifically explores the employment of white males before and after the implementation of affirmative action initiatives. Minority representation in state legislatures is another aspect of affirmative action that has received some attention. Odezah (1993) presents a study reviewing representative bureaucracy in Oklahoma state government.

Although these treatises do show some diversity evolving with the research of affirmative action, a significant amount of the inquiry that has focused on state and federal government has remained with the institution of education, including both public school systems and colleges and universities. Studies that examine affirmative action and education can be characterized according to one of two basic divisions: employment practices and admission's policies. Those that pertain to employment practices are discussed first. In "The Impact of Affirmative Action on the Employment Practices In Pennsylvania's State System of Higher Education," Connor (1985) examines affirmative action in the state's higher educational system. Mitchell (1982) discusses affirmative action and equal employment opportunity on Virginia's public school system. The focus is on the perception of affirmative action by school personnel officials. Nava (1982) provides an assessment of affirmative action employment programs in selected California School Districts. This study includes environmental factors that affect the implementation of affirmative action programs in California public schools. Bowen (1981) does include an analysis of Mississippi and affirmative action, however, the focal point of this study is affirmative action employment programs in Mississippi public universities. The issue of affirmative action and equal employment at the University of Arizona is studied longitudinally from 1966 to 1976 by Goodwin (1979). In the area of government employment and the state, McClelland-Cooper (1977) reviews employee trends (1973-1976) and employee perceptions of the impact of equal employment opportunity and affirmative action. A study conducted by Johnson (1976) discusses affirmative action and employment programs regarding African Americans employed at Michigan State University and their perception of how affirmative action programs affected their careers (Johnson, 1976).

The second concentration in education and affirmative action research addresses admission's policies. Brown (1996) provides an analytical view of affirmative action programs and the impact of recent court orders on Alabama colleges and universities. Diubaldo (1991) presents an interesting study regarding affirmative action four year plans and their effect on gender attitudes relating to women in academia and urban school boards. A study presented by Manifold (1980) presents research focusing on the implementation of affirmative action plans for equal employment opportunity in public school districts in Pennsylvania. The development of a model for establishing and maintaining an affirmative action employment program for public institutions of higher education is presented in Whitehead's work (1972). His model focuses on the implementation of affirmative action programs that will benefit employment programs in public institutions of higher learning.

An equally significant amount of affirmative action research has been in the arena of employment and employment practices. A study by Edmond (1990) researches the effect of federal equal employment opportunity and affirmative action policies on the employment of black women in the higher grades. The area of recruitment and selection in affirmative action is the focal point of a research design by Higgins (1974). The research design centers on an inventory model of a social audit of equal employment opportunity programs applied to selected commercial firms in urban settings emphasizing recruitment, selection, and affirmative action (Higgins, 1974). Espinosa (1991) presents a study of affirmative action from the perspective of studying the link between changing work arrangements and changing employment outcomes, whereas Badgett (1990) discusses the racial differences in unemployment rates and employment opportunities with an emphasis on affirmative action. Relative black male employment among business establishments, with a focus on the relation to management orientation toward affirmative action, organizational context, and organizational characteristics is the theme of Walker's (1990) work. Anderson (1988) examined the effect of affirmative action programs on female employment and earnings. Phillips (1987) conducted a case study on Detroit, Michigan, analyzing equal employment opportunity, affirmative action, mayoral initiatives and bureaucratic responses. The development and transformation of federal equal employment opportunity law with an historical analysis into the evolution and politics of affirmative action in the subject of Andritzky's (1984) research.

## The Current Research

This study expands the current body of knowledge on affirmative action in that it focuses on the impact of affirmative action and voting in seven specific southern states.   There are currently no academic studies comparing the seven southern states utilizing data supplied by the State Personnel Boards. This research is unique in that state government in the "New South" is being examined.  In order to assess the effects of affirmative action, an academic study is needed that encompasses the analysis of longitudinal data. The study provides an opportunity to study whether the New South is progressing in the area of employment hiring and promotion practices.  By studying the seven selected southern states, this study will provide the missing link in the existing literature in the area of affirmative action and state government in states making up the Old Confederacy.

This study reviews the issue of southern resistance to federal mandates in the area of employment.  The results of this research will provide an analysis that will contribute to a more comprehensive understanding of the progress African Americans have made in state government since the inception of Title VI and Title VII.

## Justification for the Book

The seven selected states of Arkansas, Georgia, Mississippi, North Carolina, Oklahoma, South Carolina and Tennessee responded to the request for data for this study. These states are representative of the Old Confederacy. Table 1 demonstrates how these states are representative in a number of ways.  Southern states have an average of twenty percent African American population, compared to a twenty-two percent average African American population for the selected states. The average percent of African Americans in the state legislature for the selected states is 14% compared to 12% for the states of the Old Confederacy. There is a 2% difference in average population for the selected states and the Old Confederacy as a whole. In comparing the average percent of Republican presidential votes for the Old Confederacy and those of the study, it revealed a two percent difference. The Old Confederacy had an average Republican presidential vote of 45% whereas the selected states had an average Republican presidential vote population of 47%. The median age for both the Old Confederacy and the selected seven states was thirty-three years.  In examining the average percent of rural population in the

Old Confederacy, it was revealed that the Old Confederacy had an average of 38% compared to the selected states which had an average rural population of 43%.

Table 1

A Comparison of Old Confederacy States
and the Representative Sample of Selected States

| State | Percent African American Population | Percent African Americans in State legislature | Percent Republican Presidential Votes | Median Age | Percent Rural Population | Party of the Governor |
|---|---|---|---|---|---|---|
| Alabama | 25% | 2% | 50% | 33 | 40% | Republican |
| Arkansas * | 16% | 10% | 37% | 33.8 | 46% | Republican |
| Florida | 14% | 13% | 42% | 36.4 | 15% | Democrat |
| Georgia * | 27% | 18% | 47% | 31.6 | 37% | Democrat |
| Louisiana | 31% | 23% | 40% | 31 | 32% | Republican |
| Mississippi * | 36% | 25% | 49% | 31.2 | 53% | Republican |
| North Carolina * | 22% | 16% | 49% | 33.1 | 50% | Democrat |
| Oklahoma * | 7% | 4% | 48% | 33.2 | 32% | Republican |
| South Carolina * | 30% | 15% | 50% | 32 | 45% | Republican |
| Tennessee * | 16% | 12% | 46% | 34 | 39% | Republican |
| Texas | 12% | 10% | 49% | 30.8 | 9% | Republican |
| Virginia | 19% | 10% | 47% | 32.6 | 31% | Republican |
| West Virginia | 3% | .007% | 37% | 35.4 | 64% | Republican |
| Average of Confederate States | 20% | 12% | 45% | 33 | 38% | Republican |
| Average of Sample States | 22% | 14% | 47% | 33 | 43% | Republican |

* Indicates those states selected for the study.
Data collected from Statistical Abstract- 1998.
Data collected from Congressional Quarterly-1998.

This demonstrated only a 5% difference in the amount of rural population for the Old Confederacy as a whole in comparison to the seven selected states of the study. A further review of the data revealed that the Old Confederacy as well as the selected states had mostly Republican governors.

The representativeness of the selected states, is also borne out by assessing the geographical location of them in the study, it was shown that the selected states were composed of those states in both the deep south and rim south states. The states of Georgia, Mississippi, and South Carolina are located in the deep south. While the states of Arkansas, North Carolina, Oklahoma, North Carolina and Tennessee are located on the southern rim. Thus, the seven states of the study are representative of the Old Confederacy as a whole in a number of ways.

**The Objectives of the Book**

The following objectives are pursued in this study:

1.  To review the history of racial inequality in order to provide the context and setting for the discussion of affirmative action.
2.  To review theoretical and empirical studies of affirmative action and assess the impact on human resource personnel.
3.  To examine the controversies associated with affirmative action and its relationship to employment.
4.  To assess how far the seven southern state governments of the Old Confederacy have progressed with regards to affirmative action and equal employment in personnel hiring and promotions utilizing longitudinal data.
5.  To determine numerical trends of African Americans in hiring and promoting since the series of Supreme Court cases starting in 1989, began to reverse the legal standards for the business and employment sector.
6.  To analyze major Supreme Court decisions starting with *DeFunis* and *Bakke* related to affirmative action and the implications of each case for African Americans in the public sector.
7.  To analyze employment data related to state government jobs in the selected states since the passage of the Civil Rights Act of 1964 to evaluate the extent to which proportional representation has been reached in state governments positions for African Americans.

8.      To determine, based on the data, if there still is a need for affirmative action programs, although the current political climate of states and congressional action regarding affirmative action appears to no longer be supportive of such programs.

9.      To ascertain what variables have the greatest explanatory value in explaining the progress of African Americans in southern state governments.

10.     To investigate what departments and agencies appear to be the most progressive in the respective states in the placement and promotion of African Americans in mid-and upper-level management.

11.     To draw a number of conclusions based on the data and study that provide direction and foresight for the future of affirmative action.

### The Limitations of the Book

1.      For the purpose of this study, descriptive analysis is utilized in examining the data.

2.      This is primarily a qualitative rather than quantitative study, although a significant amount of data has been collected and will be analyzed.

3.      The data collected and analyzed focuses only on the seven states discussed earlier in the South. Although request and follow-up letters and phone calls were made to the directors of the personnel boards of all states constituting the Old Confederacy, only seven responded with data.

4.      It is an examination of affirmative action as a component of civil rights extending only from Title VI and Title VII of the 1964 Civil Rights Act to the present.

5.      The data from Oklahoma covers only 1984, 1994, and 1996.

# CHAPTER II

# THE ORIGIN OF AFFIRMATIVE ACTION

**Historical Overview of Affirmative Action**

The political atmosphere in which affirmative action evolved is key to understanding its definition and impact. The turbulent Civil Rights Movement of the 1950s and 1960s provided the background for the forthcoming legislation. On March 6, 1961, John F. Kennedy signed Executive Order 10925, establishing the President's Commission on Equal Employment Opportunity and defining the obligations of contractors doing business with the federal government. It states, in part, that, "the contractor will take affirmative action to ensure that applicants are employed, and employees are treated during the employment, without regard to their race, creed, color or national origin" (Executive Order 10925, 1961).

In 1964, the United States Congress passed the Civil Rights Act of 1964, (42 U.S.C. Section 2000 et seq.). This legislative package would produce dramatic changes in American society. For African Americans, the Civil Rights Act of 1964 was considered the first major legislative victory since Reconstruction and the most far-reaching civil rights measure in American history. This Act would provide the mechanism to guarantee African Americans access to equal opportunity and would become the backbone for efforts to eliminate discrimination throughout American society. The 1964 Civil Rights Act allowed individuals to sue on the basis of both individual discrimination and systemic (adverse impact) discrimination.

The 1964 Civil Rights Act consists of eleven titles. Titles I (42 U.S.C. Section 2000 et seq.) and VIII (42 U.S.C. Section 2000g et seq.) enforces voting rights provisions of the Civil Rights Act of 1957 and 1960. Titles III (42 U.S.C. Section 2000b et seq.) and IV ( 42 U.S.C. Section 2000c et seq.) authorize court actions by the Attorney General to challenge segregated public facilities and schools. Title V ( 42 U.S.C. Section 2000d-6 et seq.) amends provisions governing the Civil Rights Commission. Title IX (42 U.S.C. 2000h et seq.) authorizes appeals from orders remanding to state courts civil rights cases that have been removed to federal court and authorizes the U.S. Attorney General to intervene in equal protection cases. Title X (42 U.S.C. 2000i et seq.) establishes a Community Relations Service to assist communities in resolving discrimination disputes. Title XI (42 U.S.C. 2000j et seq.) deals with miscellaneous matters.

The key components of the 1964 Civil Rights Act are Titles II ( 42 U.S.C. 2000a et seq.), VI (42 U.S.C. 2000e-4 et seq.), and VII (42 U.S.C. 2000e et seq.) Title II forbids discrimination in public places. Title VI forbids discrimination in federally assisted programs and Title VII forbids employment discrimination. Title VII affects the composition of human resource personnel by prohibiting discrimination predicated on gender. Titles VI and VII of the 1964 Civil Rights Act established the foundation for the term known as "affirmative action."

The landmark Civil Rights Act of 1964, Public Law 88-352, 42 U.S.C. 2000 et seq. (1964), prohibits discrimination in voting, public accommodations, public education, and employment. It also declares that nothing in the act is designed to grant preferential treatment to any group on the basis of race, color, religion, sex, or national origin. Title VII (42 U.S.C. Section 2000e et seq.) prohibits job discrimination and places a priority on equal employment opportunity. Title VII states, "It shall be an unlawful practice for an employer to fail or refuse to hire or to discharge any individual or otherwise to discriminate against any individual with respect to his compensation, terms, conditions, or privileges of employment, because of such individual's race, color, sex, or national origin" (42 U.S.C. Section 2000e et seq). The 1964 Act applied to the federal government and its contractors. Taylor (1991) posits that it is very interesting that the legislators never seriously considered criminal penalties for persons who discriminate, nor was consideration given to the implementation of punitive damages, or compensation as remedies for violation of Title VII. Rather, the legislators established a "conciliation process" through which victims could be restored to the economic status and job situation they would have enjoyed in the absence of discrimination. It can be argued perhaps, that due to the difficulty in getting a civil rights act passed, it became necessary to omit the inclusion of criminal penalties and punitive damages along with compensatory remedies. Another inference is the issue of trying to appease the southern congressional constituency in procuring their support for passage of the legislation. As advocated by the language of the law, victims are to be made whole (economically) and restored to their rightful place (Taylor, 1991). According to Title VII, a court may require a discriminating employer to stop the offending practice and may order "such affirmative action as may be appropriate, which may include, but is not limited to, reinstatement or hiring of employees, with or without back pay, or any other equitable relief as the court deems appropriate" ( Civil Rights Act of 1964, 42 U.S.C. Section 2000e et seq).

Title VII of the 1964 Civil Rights Act also established a new federal agency, the Equal Employment Opportunity Commission (EEOC). The EEOC's role is to facilitate the conciliation process between private employers and plaintiffs and to pressure employers who discriminate into providing victims with back pay, restitution, and equitable relief (Greene, 1989). This provision allows plaintiffs to initiate discrimination complaints and request mediation through the EEOC, through the federal courts, or both.

The language utilized by the legislators in drafting Title VII is ambiguous and thereby open to different interpretations. Title VII of the 1964 Civil Rights Act speaks of intentional discrimination, but does not address the issue of non-intentional (structural or systemic) discrimination. As a result, there are no provisions setting forth guidelines to determine whether intentional or non-intentional discrimination should be treated differently. Taylor (1991) proposes that the rationale for this omission may be the fact that in 1964 most people assumed discrimination was intentional. However, it is the omission of systemic discrimination that affords the Supreme Court the responsibility for determining what to do in the case of discriminatory practices that are "fair in form but discriminatory in operation" (Greenhouse, 1990).

Consequently, the nebulous language in Title VII of the 1964 Civil Rights Act makes it subject to differing interpretations with regards to the remedies it does permit. The language leaves open to debate whether the directive to make victims "whole" permits courts to order preferential treatment benefitting victims. The ambiguous language leaves unclear the issue of compensation for African Americans considered not to have been discriminated against.  According to Fullinwider (1980), three major interpretations regarding the remedies permitted by Title VII of the 1964 Civil Rights Act have been advanced.  The interpretations include:  (1) courts may order only those remedies that benefit (and make whole) the actual victims of discrimination (no preferential treatment is permitted); (2) courts may order preferential treatment that extends beyond demonstrable victims to redress statistical imbalances between the discriminating employer's work force and the available work force; and (3) courts may order preferential treatment as a remedy for social discrimination.  It has been argued that regardless of what was intended in 1964, Congress clearly did not intend to authorize preferential, results-oriented affirmative action (Greene 1989).

One year after the enactment of Title VII, Lyndon Johnson signed Executive Order 11246, which requires federal contractors to "take affirmative action to ensure that applicants are employed, and that employees are treated during employment, without regard to their race, color, religion, sex, or national origin" (Taylor, 1991).  The order specifies that "such action shall include, but is not limited to the following: employment, upgrading, demotion, or transfer, recruitment or recruitment advertising, layoff or termination, rates of pay and selection for training" (Executive Order 11246).  It is important to note that the order left the decision to define the specifics of affirmative action and its enforcement to the Labor Department.  The Office of Federal Contract Compliance Programs (OFCCP) was given enforcement responsibilities over federal contractors and subcontractors, and the EEOC was appointed over private employers.  The Labor Departments guidelines for affirmative action apply to a wide range of protected groups and consists of results-oriented actions, such as goals, timetables, back pay, and retroactive seniority.

Under the Nixon Administration, the Labor Department issued a new set of affirmative action plans.  These plans were more restrictive, and included all government contractors with fifty or more employees (Mead et. al., 1995).  At this time, Nixon defined affirmative action as a set of specific and result-oriented procedures.  He went further to spell out action that was intended to cause discrimination.  One of his key concepts was "underutilization," which referred to having fewer minorities in a particular job class than would reasonably be expected by their availability.  The Nixon guidelines required contractors to design specific goals and timetables to correct any hiring problems.

In 1978, Carter introduced the Uniform Guidelines on Employee Selection Procedures. These guidelines stated that any employer practice that had an adverse impact on any race, sex, or ethnic group was illegal unless justified by business necessity. Adverse impact referred to job selection rates for any race, sex, or ethnic group that fell below four-fifths that of the group with the highest selection rate (Mead et. al., 1995). The guidelines established by Carter allowed employers to justifiably use race, sex, or ethnic consciousness in rectifying past practices that created an adverse impact.

**The Definition of Affirmative Action**

The literature on affirmative action suggests that the concept has no precise, consensual definition. Nevertheless, it has been agreed upon that whether affirmative action takes place through programs in employment, education, housing or electoral policy, the core objective of this initiative is a commitment to fairly integrate traditionally disadvantaged groups into public institutions and processes (Taylor, 1991). In practice, affirmative action may encompass anything from a company advertisement displaying its non-discriminatory employment policies, to organizations setting strict minimum goals or discussing promotion of African Americans. Affirmative action is one aspect of the federal government's efforts to ensure equal employment opportunity. Pursuant to federal regulations, affirmative action plans must consist of an equal opportunity policy statement, an analysis of the current workforce, identification of problem areas, the establishment of goals and timetables for increasing employment opportunities, specific action-oriented programs to address the problem areas, support for community action programs, and the establishment of an internal audit and reporting system (Berkeley California, 1996).

According to Taylor, (1991) affirmative action refers to specific steps beyond ending discriminatory practices that are taken to promote equal opportunity and ensure that "discrimination will not recur." He states that the goal of affirmative action is to eliminate nonlegal barriers to equal employment opportunity, including intentional discriminatory practices and non-intentional (structure or systemic) discrimination. Affirmative action is defined by Swain (1996) as a range of governmental and private initiatives that offer preferential treatment to members of designated racial and ethnic minority groups as a means of compensating for the efforts of

Affirmative action is an attempt to have an overall workforce reflective of the racial and sexual composition of the general population. Affirmative action programs are often viewed as having hidden agendas that go well beyond equality of opportunity and provide not only remedial, but preferential compensatory action, especially in the areas of education and employment. Thus, affirmative action programs must be distinguished from "neutrality" programs in that these programs were instituted to bring about increased minority employment opportunities, job promotions and admission to colleges and universities (Karst, 1989).

According to Mead et. al. (1995), affirmative action is a program or policy designed to reverse past discriminatory patterns or practices. Affirmative action requires employers or institutions to take actions to hire and admit members of the African American population as well as members of the other previously mentioned protected groups. There are two important characteristics differentiating affirmative action from other anti-discrimination measures. One is that affirmative action concentrates not only on the procedures that firms follow, but also on the outcome of the firm's decisions in terms of employment patterns. Secondly, affirmative action requires firms to eliminate the effects of past discrimination from their labor forces (Burnstein, 1994). Affirmative action basically advocates the principle of a structured readjustment and redistribution of economic resources and opportunities to redress inequities among various social and ethnic groups.

Marble (1996), reports that affirmative action constitutes a series of presidential executive orders, civil rights laws and governmental programs regarding the awarding of federal contracts and licenses, as well as the enforcement of fair employment practices. He suggests that affirmative action was designed with the goal of uprooting the practices of bigotry and to compensate victims of slavery and Jim Crow segregation laws. Furthermore, despite the fact that the actual phrase "affirmative action" was not used by a chief executive until Kennedy's Executive Order 10925 in 1961, the fundamental idea of taking pro-active steps necessary to dismantle prejudice has been around for more than a century (Marble, 1996).

Because of the quest by some for preferential and/or compensatory action, affirmative action programs have been considered controversial due to use of "racial quotas," often euphemistically referred to as "goals" or "guidelines" by critics. The argument set forth, according to Karst's citation of Abraham, is that "given the injustices of the past, both

Furthermore, despite the fact that the actual phrase "affirmative action" was not used by a chief executive until Kennedy's Executive Order 10925 in 1961, the fundamental idea of taking pro-active steps necessary to dismantle prejudice has been around for more than a century (Marble, 1996).

Because of the quest by some for preferential and/or compensatory action, affirmative action programs have been considered controversial due to use of "racial quotas," often euphemistically referred to as "goals" or "guidelines" by critics. The argument set forth, according to Karst's citation of Abraham, is that "given the injustices of the past, both preferential and compensatory treatment must be accorded through affirmative action, that all but guarantees numerically targeted" slots or posts based upon membership, in racial groups or upon gender" (Karst, 1989).

Affirmative action programs have also been considered a "lightening rod" leading to charges of "reverse discrimination" primarily by white men who have been denied admissions, hiring, or promotions because of perceived preferential treatment awarded African Americans. The controversial aspects of affirmative action have not led the United States Supreme Court to develop or invoke a concise definition of the concept. The Supreme Court has refused to institute a standard affirmative action plan and even appears inconsistent in some of its rulings. For example, the Supreme Court refused to allow the use of quotas for admission to medical school in the classic reverse discrimination case of *Bakke v. University of California*, 438 U.S. 265, (1978) but would later approve the use of quotas in admission to a training program (*Weber v. Steelworkers*, 443 U.S. 193, 1979) and in admission as a State Police Trooper (see *U.S. v. Paradise*, 107 U.S. 1053, 1987).

## The Parameters of Affirmative Action

Even though the Court has not been willing to establish guidelines for all affirmative action plans, there have been certain requirements applied in most of the cases. As of 1990, voluntary affirmative action plans that have withstood the scrutiny of the Court have incorporated the following characteristics: 1) the plan must be remedial in that it addresses a past or current deficiency; 2) the plan does not unnecessarily trample non-minority interests, i.e., there can be no displacement of current employees; 3) the plan cannot exclude uncovered groups. The plan cannot exclude white males from certain positions; 4) the plan must be flexible. There can be no waivers if no minority candidates are available; 5) the plan must be temporary. The enactment of the plan does not seek to maintain a certain work force, only to obtain it; and 6) the seniority systems are not designed to be discriminatory and cannot be interfered with in order to protect the jobs of newly hired persons (Scott and Little, 1991).

Affirmative action programs have had a dramatic impact on public personnel administration. However, they have also presented administrators with a continuous dilemma. Proponents of affirmative action have advocated that a "bending of the rules" is sometimes necessary and desirable in order to "make up" for past injustices. Those rejecting this argument propose that "lowering" employment standards should not be practiced because doing so would result in inferior service to the public. It must be understood however, that bending the rules is not synonymous with a lowering of standards (Scott and Little, 1991).

In order to comply with the guidelines required of affirmative action programs, inclusion of qualitative as well as quantitative goals becomes important. The inclusion of qualitative and quantitative goals requires that the program give consideration to numerical objectives as well as the actual remedying of past discriminatory practices. In order to achieve qualitative goals, attitudes have to change. This is a vital role that must be exemplified through human resource personnel. To accomplish this task, there has to be a utilization of personnel administrators interacting with community agencies and neighborhood organizations. In order to create a work force reflective of the population, disadvantaged applicants must be recruited. Personnel practices must be revised to incorporate the needs of the applicants. To achieve this type of networking, affirmative action plans must receive intense thought, consideration, and a total team effort in order to enact or implement the intent of the Civil Rights Act of 1964.

There has been continuous debate regarding the efficacy as well as the lawfulness of affirmative action (Burnstein, 1994), and the constitutionality of numerous affirmative action programs that have been struck down in the eighties and nineties by the Supreme Court. This will be addressed in more detail in Chapters IV& V. Nonetheless, consideration must be given to the argument that not only has affirmative action benefitted African Americans, it has benefitted the entire nation as well. Burnstein indicates that affirmative action has enabled African Americans to attain occupational and educational advancements in large numbers and at a rate heretofore viewed as impossible. The advancements gained through affirmative action have provide numerous long term benefits. The benefits include the accumulation of valuable experiences, the expansion and enhancement of a professional class receiving numerous material benefits, and most importantly, the eradication of debilitating stereotypes. Affirmative action has allowed African Americans to become participants in decision making processes which affect the interest, welfare, and values of other African Americans. Without the advent of affirmative action, the plight of African Americans would have been extremely rough and narrow. More importantly, one of the positive externalities that has accompanied affirmative action programs is teaching many culturally bound whites that African Americans, too, have the capacity for handling responsibility, dispensing knowledge, and applying valued skills (Burnstein, 1994).

Regardless of the gains made through affirmative action, there are those who advance the position that this program negatively impacts African Americans. The most powerful argument set forth is the claim that preferential treatment exacerbates racial resentment, entrenches racial divisiveness, and thereby undermines the consensus necessary for effective sound reform (Glazer, 1975). The essence of this argument is that affirmative action stigmatizes African Americans by implying that they simply cannot compete on an equal level with whites. Another related argument maintains that affirmative action programs sap the morals of African Americans. It is argued that these programs lead to creating a vulnerability that causes a disparity in anxiety because there is the feeling of complacency within the African American race. Finally, there are also those who claim that many beneficiaries of affirmative action are those who need it the least. The thrust of the argument is that affirmative action programs benefit mostly middle class African Americans. According to Burnstein (1994) middle class African Americans are the ones having the least plausible claim to suffering from past discrimination.

## The Constitutionality of Affirmative Action

According to Kellough and Kay (1986) the public policy of affirmative action presents two constitutional concerns. The first is whether these programs discriminate against individuals in violation of the Equal Protection Clause of the Fourteenth Amendment. The second issue is whether affirmative action programs discriminate against individual whites in violation of the Civil Rights Act of 1964, particularly Title VI and Title VII. Encompassed in these two issues is the question of whether affirmative action creates "goals or quotas" and gives rise to the concept of "reverse discrimination" (Kellough and Kay, 1986).

In May of 1971, the Civil Service Commission endorsed the use of numerical goals and timetables for minority group employment in federal departments and agencies. Since that time, the use of employment goals and timetables, commonly known as key components of affirmative action, has been a cornerstone of equal employment opportunity programs (Kellough and Kay, 1986). Kellough and Kay postulate that affirmative action, in the form of employment goals and timetables, directed special attention to race and sex in an effort to remove the effects of past prejudices. According to Fleming et. al. (1978), goals and timetables are not interchangeable with the concept of quotas. Goals may not be rigid and inflexible like quotas, which are numerical quantities that must be met. But goals must be targets reasonably attainable by means of applying every good faith effort to make all aspects of the entire affirmative action program work. Moreover, affirmative action programs, when instituted correctly, do not violate the principle of merit. The intention of affirmative action, in part, is to rectify the past practice of utilizing the "good old boy network." Through the expansion of the employee supply pool to include women and African Americans, affirmative action provides the opportunity for all qualified individuals to compete on an equal basis regardless of race or gender. Race and gender only become important when *ceteris paribus* exists with candidates with equal qualifications. Only then does race or gender become factors in employment selection.

The argument that affirmative action creates goals that are really quotas fails to recognize or even yield consideration to the fact that goals are a mechanism by which institutions can measure their rate of progress in providing equal opportunity. The failure to establish goals only maintains the status quo, and continued dominance by the white male. The successful implementation of affirmative action programs has been due to the continuation of goal-oriented programs. Through juxtaposition and faulty analogy, nevertheless, critics argue that goals are quotas (Swanson, 1981). Swanson explains that the constant equating of goals with quotas leads one to believe that the quota argument is a "deliberate attempt to weaken the entire affirmative action program." It must be kept in mind that affirmative action is an attempt to overcome past discrimination. The objective of some affirmative action programs to utilize preferential and compensatory treatment to rectify past discrimination and racial injustice, however, has given rise to the question of the constitutionality of affirmative action.

Kennedy states that the constitutional argument against affirmative action is predicated on the notion, "that all governmental distinctions based on race are presumed to be illegal and can only escape that presumption by meeting the exacting requirements of strict scrutiny" (Kennedy, 1994). In order for an affirmative action program to survive strict scrutiny, it must further a compelling state interest by the most narrowly tailored means available. Some affirmative action programs cannot meet these requirements. Hence, many of these programs are unconstitutional. The Court has argued that approval has never been given to race-conscious remedies absent judicial, administrative, or legislative findings of constitutional or statutory violations (*Fullilove*, 448 U.S. 497, 1980). This, in part, is due to the fact that a distinction between permissible remedial action and impermissible racial preference rests on the existence of a constitutional or statutory violation; the legitimate interest in creating a race-conscious remedy is not compelling unless an appropriate governmental authority has found that such a violation has occurred (*Fullilove*, 448 U.S. 498, 1980).

Kennedy uses a historical analysis to support the constitutionality of affirmative action. It is his contention that in the forties, fifties, and early sixties, against a backdrop of laws that used racial distinctions to exclude African Americans from opportunities available to white citizens, it seemed that racial subjugation could be overcome by mandating the application of race-blind law (Kennedy, 1994). But, in retrospect, it appears that the concept of race-blind policies were simply a proxy for the fundamental demand that racial subjugation be eradicated (Burnstein, 1994). It also appears that those opposing affirmative action have removed the historical context from the demand for race-blind law.

Depending upon interpretation, one person's "affirmative action" may well constitute another's "reverse discrimination." Nevertheless, it is possible to make distinctions. Karst, writing in 1989, argued that affirmative action may be regarded as encompassing the following five criteria, all of which would appear to be both legal and constitutional: 1) both government and private sponsored activities designed to remedy the absence of needed educational preparation by special, even if costly, primary and/or secondary school level preparatory programs or occupational skills development, provided that access to programs is not based upon race or related group criteria or characteristics, but upon educational or economic need; 2) special classes or supplemental training, regardless of costs, on any level of education or training from the pre-nursery school level to the very top of the professional training ladder; 3) scrupulous enforcement of absolute standards of nondiscrimination on the basis of race, sex, religion, nationality, and age; 4) above the table special recruiting efforts to reach out to those members of heretofore under-used, deprived, or discriminated against segments of the citizenry; and 5) provided the presence of explicit or implicit merit of a bona fide demonstration of potential ability, the taking into account of an individual's race, gender, religion as equitable consideration, but only if "all other things are equal" (Karst, 1989).

**Affirmative Action and Equal Employment**

Eliminating discrimination in employment (public and private) was a major objective of federal civil rights legislation and executive orders in the 1960s. The underlying assumption was that racial discrimination played a major role in creating the income and occupational differentials that existed between whites and African Americans (Zashin, 1978). Zashin indicates that, among earlier presidents, John F. Kennedy was the first since World War II to initiate concerted action against employment discrimination. In 1961, Kennedy established a committee on equal employment opportunity to recommend affirmative steps to implement a federal policy of nondiscrimination. In 1965, President Johnson transferred responsibility for federal equal employment opportunity to the Civil Service Commission. Then, in 1969, President Nixon issued an executive order emphasizing the responsibility of each federal agency to develop an affirmative action program (Zashin, 1978).

In assessing the issue of racial equity in employment, data indicate that African American employment gains in the high-status occupational categories of the total work force from 1970-1974 were virtually zero (Zashin, 1978). The equity of goals and preferential selection as compensatory mechanisms has become highly salient political and legal issues. Yet, the argument is made by some that society is not in a position to say that whites have suffered from the use of such devices (Zashin, 1978). The racial equity issue in employment does present at least two interesting queries: (1) Are qualifications imposed by employers job relevant? and (2) Do employers, public and private, have enough information about the presence of presumably qualified African Americans in the relevant work force to determine whether or not sufficient numbers are available to meet the goals set by federal agencies?

Mandelebaum (1983) argues that the problem of employment discrimination is still a serious one, even after the racial neutrality dictums stated in *Brown v. Board of Education of Topeka, Kansas* 394 U.S. 294 (1955) and the passage of Title VII of the 1964 Civil Rights Act. The vestiges of practices that have been in existence for 200 years do not disappear easily. For example, a study cited by Mandelebaum (1983) revealed that an African American male with the same qualifications as a white male would have received much less than typical whites because of racial differences in pay rates. The pay differential in 1969 was $2,800; this decreased slightly in 1974 to $2,300. The racial difference appeared to account for as much as fifty percent of the total difference in earnings between whites and African Americans in the seventies (Farley, 1977).

Mandelebaum (1983) posits that studies have shown that aggressive affirmative action programs of the late 1960s have helped some African Americans achieve better representation in areas previously closed to them. It is also reasonably clear that affirmative action tends to give a competitive edge to trained and educated African Americans. He further argues that affirmative action officials cannot be held responsible for malfunctions in the economy. Even if affirmative action does not produce more jobs, it can work to move African Americans into more skilled leadership positions. It is not clear, however, whether the best vehicle for this strategy is a national policy and program based upon a questionable theory of proportional representation supported by coercion and bureaucracy (Mandelebaum, 1983).

Policy models utilized in American public administration focus on pragmatic and incremental processes. Affirmative action is a fair example of the maturation of policies and programs to meet changing perceptions of a problem. However, an area of concern is present when policy analysis indicates that incremental adjustments require comprehensive planning and program coherence. Affirmative action requires linking job development training programs while monitoring discrimination, together with sensitivity to the needs of those who are not specially favored by a policy of affirmative action (Mandelebaum, 1983).

Zashin (1978) points out that in the early 1960s, racial equality suddenly appeared on the forefront as a national issue. For approximately a decade, there was intense activity to narrow the various socio-economic and political gaps between African Americans and whites. However, not long after the shock of ghetto riots and an armed black rebellion, those efforts subsided. Zashin notes that by the early 1970s, the Civil Rights Movement had passed into American history. He further speculates that one cannot state that African American equality is no longer a major problem in American society, nor can it be said with confidence that the forces set in motion by the developments of the last two decades will eliminate virtually all the handicaps that have been the legacy of racism and discrimination.

According to Norton (1996), national anxiety concerning affirmative action has never been higher. She indicates that the controversy starts with the identification of affirmative action with jobs. Norton suggests that job employment, more than other areas, has given definition to affirmative action. In the public's mind, affirmative action and jobs go together (Norton, 1996). Recognizing the impact of affirmative action, Norton indicates that affirmative action will always have to remain alert to attacks. Conceivably, affirmative action could be wiped out by a single piece of legislation. She stresses that the "attacks" against affirmative action have existed throughout the entire history of the policy (Norton, 1996).

Marable (1996) suggests that during the Nixon era, the goal of affirmative action and equal opportunity was to utilize a liberal reform by conservative means. Conservatives, according to Marable, cultivated the racist mythology that affirmative action was nothing less than a rigid system of inflexible quotas which rewarded the incompetent and the unqualified, who happened to be people of color, at the expense of hardworking, taxpaying Americans, who happened to be white. Since white men dominate the upper ranks of senior management, and constitute 95% of all senior managerial positions at the ranks of vice-president or above, Marable (1996) supports the idea that affirmative action has opened many professional and managerial positions to African Americans. He concludes his argument by suggesting that affirmative action may not have gone far enough in transforming the actual power relations between African Americans and whites in society. If affirmative action is to survive, its permanent fragility must be recognized, respected, and taken into account in the strategies to maintain and expand such programs (Norton, 1996).

## Arguments For Affirmative Action

In support of affirmative action, Swanson (1981) advocates that affirmative action is needed because it has provided enhanced employment opportunities for African Americans. Affirmative action programs are needed because African Americans have historically suffered invidious discrimination, denying them educational and economic opportunities that whites have taken for granted. Therefore, in an effort to eliminate the lasting effects of such discrimination, the public and private sectors must take steps to provide access to good educational and employment opportunities (Berry et. al. 1993; Swanson, 1981; Marable, 1996).

Marable (1996) insists that affirmative action has been largely responsible for a significant increase in the size of the African American middle class and has opened many professional and managerial positions to African Americans. He argues that affirmative action has sought to increase representative numbers of African Americans within the existing structure and arrangements of power, rather than challenge or redefine the institutions of authority and privilege. Affirmative action was always concerned more with advancing remedies related to unequal racial outcomes than with uprooting racism as a system of white power. Institutional racism is real, according to Marable, and the central focus of affirmative action must deal with the continuing burden of racial inequality and discrimination in American life (Marable, 1996).

A 1994 study of the United States Office of Personnel Management found that African American federal employees were more than twice as likely to be dismissed as their white counterparts. African Americans were especially likely to be fired at much higher rates than whites in jobs where they constituted a significant share of the labor force. African American clerk typists were 4.7 times more likely to be dismissed than whites, and African American custodians 4.1 times more likely to be fired than whites (Marable, 1996). If there is a valid criticism of affirmative action, it might be on the grounds that affirmative action did not go far enough in transforming the actual power relations between African Americans and whites within our society (Marable 1996).

According to Norton (1996), affirmative action's monitoring mechanism, numerical goals, is the major source of the controversy, even though goals must by law be tied to the available pool of qualified individuals. Goals keep track of whether the techniques that actually break down the possibility of discrimination, such as posting jobs and recruiting more widely, are working. Norton (1996) states that without goals, eliminating discrimination proceeds blindly, without any way to chart or change course. Ironically, goals can also help employers avoid culpability. If the goals are not met despite the use of these proactive techniques, the employer's good faith effort is sufficient.

Norton (1996) surmises that the opponents of affirmative action are confused. They have stored up fear and resentment of affirmative action, presumably because it has a significant effect, while maintaining at the same time that it has not worked. According to Norton, in the three decades between 1960 and 1990, the percentage of black men in professional and managerial occupations doubled. Norton supports the idea that African Americans have been challenged to make these gains during a period of profound transition, dislocation, and conversion in the American economy. Furthermore, the nation's most stringent anti-affirmative action proposal made its way to California via Proposition 209. The potential fear is that other states will follow the lead of California. Norton suggests that though excluded during the apex of economic growth in the late 1950s and 1960s, African Americans through the advent of affirmative action are trying to catch up. Thus, she suggests that the solution to the problem is the utilization of affirmative action as the remedy.

Current congressional supporters of affirmative action argue that anti-discrimination efforts alone are insufficient to compensate for the effects of bias and intolerance in the past as well as the present. They contend that despite civil rights laws, white males continue to be disproportionately represented in all areas of opportunity. They further maintain that the diversity resulting from affirmative action programs has helped to diminish stereotypes, enlarge the middle class, and strengthen the economy (*Congressional Digest*, 1996).

Continued support for affirmative action is advocated by Swain (1996). She begins her defense of affirmative action by stating that the policies and programs of affirmative action provide African Americans with the resources to succeed in a highly competitive society. She cites statistical evidence that reveals a wide disparity between the socio-economic conditions of African Americans and those of whites, along with the gross inequities of under-representation of African Americans in many leading professions. Swain also theorizes that without affirmative action policies and programs, the plight of African Americans becomes bleaker. In reference to institutions of higher education admitting African American applicants with below average standardized test scores, she indicates that supporters of affirmative action are quick to point out that few people complain about the policy of giving special preference in college admissions to offspring of alumni, who thereby benefit from affirmative action on the basis of their lineage (Swain, 1996).

In assessing the impact of affirmative action, Swain (1996) observes that despite more than two decades of affirmative action, African Americans lag significantly behind white males in the area of employment and promotions. Hacker supports Swain and emphasizes that the issue of equality in employment encumbers a harsher difficulty for African American males than females. Swain (1996) suggests that one of the concerns regarding affirmative action is that there does not exist an agreed upon standard of merit that can be used objectively when making employment recruitment and promotion decisions. She supports affirmative action as a "compensatory device" (Swain, 1996). Her view is predicated on the old proverbial adage that "African Americans never got the forty acres and a mule" that was promised after the Civil War. Therefore, she argues affirmative action should function as a compensatory device designed to rescue the most disadvantaged African Americans from a way of poverty and despair (Swain, 1996). Kinsley (1995) proposes that while some anxiety regarding affirmative action is justifiable, some objections have become self-indulged fantasies. However, he points out that the actual role of affirmative action in denying opportunities to white people diminished in comparison with its role in the public's imagination and debate relative to the effectiveness of affirmative action.

According to Raskin (1995), the assault on affirmative action is the logical culmination of an unpopular campaign against "political correctness," which began in the late 1980s. Those opposed to the concept of correctness have questioned the utility of multi-culturalism for several years. At issue is the resentment toward affirmative action and the closely related concept of "reverse discrimination." Opponents of affirmative action argue that reverse discrimination victimizes the white male and even stigmatizes the intended beneficiaries- African Americans.

The cries of reverse discrimination are akin to the rhetoric designed to prevent uplifting the African American community. Raskin (1995) argues that Reconstruction created a lightning rod for criticism of the African American. It provided programs that unfairly penalized innocent whites and taught African Americans self-destructive habits of indolence and dependence. It is interesting to note, nevertheless, that the hysteria regarding affirmative action continues in the face of massive evidence of continuing white male dominance in society (Raskin, 1995). While African Americans form a greater presence in the public sector, the ranks of top leadership are still almost all-white (Ranskin, 1995). This is true in mid and upper level management in the private as well as public sector. It is important to point out that the opponents of affirmative action have removed the historical context from the demand for race-blind law, thereby removing the foundation and premise which the Fourteenth Amendment was designed to protect.

**Arguments Against Affirmative Action**

There are numerous arguments against affirmative action as well. The chief arguments focus on the issues of "quotas" and "reverse discrimination." According to Benokraitis and Feagan (1978), reverse discrimination arises when the efforts to rectify past discrimination violates the Equal Protection Clause of the Constitution. Thus, it is argued that affirmative action promotes inequality rather than supporting equality (Benokraitis and Feagan, 1978). Regarding the issue of quotas as it relates to affirmative action, Sowell (1972) argues vehemently against them. He states that "actual harm done by quotas is far greater than having a few incompetent people here and there, and the actual harm will affect the African American population." Sowell further argues "that what the arguments and campaigns for quotas are really saying, loud and clear are that African Americans just don't have it and they will have to be given something in order to have that something." He concludes that affirmative action programs were not and are not needed; additionally, affirmative action leads to reverse discrimination and does not benefit African Americans.

Those critical of affirmative action programs find fault with the use of goals and preferential treatment programs. Critics of quotas in higher education argue that numerical goals erode the standards of academic excellence by substituting the ascribed characteristics of race and sex for intellectual ability and performance as the criterion for admissions to colleges and universities. Sowell (1972) charges that quota systems stigmatize African Americans by making it appear that group membership rather than the individual ability of persons within these protected groups accounts for admission. Preferential treatment is also viewed as contributing to racial and ethnic polarization and reinforcing racial stereotypes (Swanson, 1981).

Sowell supports Swanson's view and argues emphatically that racial preferences almost always breed hatred and resentment among members who find themselves in the non-beneficiary group (Sowell, 1990). Loury, a prominent critic of preferential policies, states that "affirmative action policies of preference" may alter the terms on which employers and workers interact with each other to perpetuate, rather than eliminate existing disparities in productivity between the minority and majority population (Loury, 1995). He further states that if workers believe they will be favored by affirmative action, there will be less incentive to work hard and upgrade their skills.

Arguments against affirmative action are also made by Hook and Roche. Hook points out that the application of affirmative action requirements constitutes unwarranted federal intervention in the internal affairs of colleges and universities. Hook describes affirmative action as "wasting time, effort and the taxpayer's money," (Fleming et. al., 1978). Roche's view is that the federal presence in higher education is a threat to all colleges and universities (Fleming et. al., 1978).

Puddington (1995) concurs with the philosophy that affirmative action is simply another name for racial preferences. He postulates that affirmative action, as a policy, is an affront to American values of fairness and individualism. Carter (1993) further supports the contention that affirmative action programs have produced reverse discrimination and increased racial disharmony. Puddington (1995) suggests that the political leaders of America eradicate all federal programs that extend racial preferences, yet, retain anti-discrimination laws that will truly offer equal opportunity. Puddington theorizes that Americans are supportive of a soft form of affirmative action that encompasses special recruitment, training and outreach efforts designed to rectify obvious cases of proven discrimination. In analyzing affirmative action, Kahlenberg (1995) asserts that affirmative action makes sense only to the extent that there is a current-day legacy of past discrimination which new prospective laws cannot reach back and remedy. He further contends that the Civil Rights

Act of 1991 reaffirmed the need to address unintentional discrimination without crossing the line to requiring preferences.

The conservative Republican wing of Congress advocates that by undermining every individual's right to compete on equal terms, affirmative action has done more to divide Americans than to unite them (*Congressional Digest*, 1996). They maintain that affirmative action programs have hurt beneficiaries and society generally by lowering standards, stigmatizing recipients, and causing resentment on the part of qualified individuals who may be passed over in the process. Affording different treatment to different groups essentially amounts to government-sanctioned discrimination (*Congressional Digest*, 1996).

In her work, "Affirmative Action Revisited," Swain (1996) criticizes affirmative action. She argues that affirmative action policies of racial, ethnic and gender preference are contrary to core American values regarding fairness, equality, and respect for the worth of individuals. In support of her position, she cites the ideology of Justice Clarence Thomas. According to Swain, Justice Thomas stresses that he does not believe in quotas. His position is that America was founded on a philosophy of individual rights, not group rights (Swain, 1996). She points out that Thomas does believe in compensation for actual "victims of discrimination," but not for people whose only claim to victimization is that they are members of a historically oppressed group (Swain, 1996). Furthermore, Swain surmises that affirmative action programs confer benefits primarily on the more advantaged segment of the beneficiary group (Swain, 1996).

Additional criticism of affirmative action is presented by Woodson. As cited in Swain (1996), Woodson criticizes affirmative action policies for their failure to target the poorer sections of the African American population. Swain indicates that a serious criticism of affirmative action focuses on the psychological impact it has on African Americans and those benefitting from affirmative action. It is suggested that psychologically, affirmative action is demeaning, degrading and stigmatizes African Americans, and even suggests that African Americans have an inferiority complex with respect to whites (Swain, 1996).

In a critical analysis of affirmative action, Eastland (1996) argues that affirmative action has taken a toll on public discourse. It is his contention that during the late 1960s and 1970s, advocates of affirmative action stated that it was only temporary and would become unnecessary in the near future. Yet, this "temporary" measure continues. Carter (1993) argues that affirmative action policies set up a dichotomy in which employers and admission officers make an invidious distinction between the "best" candidate and the "best African American." Hence, Carter believes that affirmative action programs inevitably make the accomplishments of all African Americans suspect, even those who are well qualified for the position. From his perspective, affirmative action has essentially limited the social mobility and status of African Americans. Hence, Carter (1993) asserts that African American success has been relegated to a phenomenon that must be explained or apologized for. It is his contention that the philosophy of affirmative action implies that African Americans are stupid and primitive people (Carter, 1993). Thus, affirmative action has created an oppressive environment for African Americans and serves to obscure their achievements. Molinari also posits that policies of affirmative action have done more to divide than to unite. According to her thesis, affirmative action presumes that a characteristic such as skin color or even gender should define the amount of governmental assistance and support an individual or group should receive. Consequently, affirmative action as it exists today has strayed from its original intent and has largely become a program to confer special benefits on designated groups that does not involve equal opportunity but equal results. Therefore, affirmative action was a good idea that went bad (Molinari, 1995).

## The Equal Employment Act of 1995 and Affirmative Action

### Proponents of the Legislation

In assessing the issue of affirmative action, a debate has developed over the effectiveness, feasibility, and fairness of affirmative action, with some championing its continuation and others calling for its restriction or abolishment. During the 1995 legislative session, congressional subcommittees considered the Equal Opportunity Act of 1995. The legislation was studied by the Judiciary Committee's Constitution Subcommittee in both houses. The Senate version of the measure was introduced by Senator Dole (S 1085) on July 27, 1995. The House version of the same legislation was introduced by Republican Representative Canady (HR 2128) of Florida. The Dole-Canady plan (the collective name for the legislation) proposed barring the use of racial and gender-based preferences by the federal government in contracts, hiring and programs. The bill was also aimed at barring the government from requiring or encouraging contractors to use such preferences. The Dole-Canady measure endorsed programs aimed at broad recruiting efforts and expanded opportunities for competition. However, it sought to outlaw those that used goals, timetables, and set-asides as tools to remedy discrimination (*Congressional Quarterly Almanac*, 1995). The plan included a prohibition on government employees or agencies basing any hiring or promotion decisions partly or wholly on such factors as race, color, national origin or gender. A proposal barring the federal government from entering into court-ordered consent decrees aimed at requiring any preferences were included (*Congressional Quarterly Almanac*, 1995). However, the recipients of federal grants such as schools and community organizations, including federal contracts with Historical Black Colleges (HBC's) and Indian Tribes were excluded from the Dole-Canady proposal (*Congressional Quarterly Almanac*, 1995). The proposed legislation did not apply to existing anti-discrimination laws that allowed victims of racial and sexual discrimination to sue to recover lost wages or jobs (*Congressional Quarterly Almanac*, 1995).

The Equal Opportunity Act of 1995, according to Molinari, (a Republican United States Representative from New York) contains no provisions that would weaken important protections of the 1964 Civil Rights Act or any similar anti-discrimination laws (*Congressional Digest*, 1996). Thus, Molinari (Rep. N.Y.) supports the Equal Employment Act of 1995 and testified in support of the legislation at the House Judiciary Subcommittee on the Constitution. It's proponents argue that it restores the principle of equal protection for all Americans as embodied in the Fourteenth Amendment. It is suggested that the Fourteenth Amendment represents a basic belief that society should be blind to distinctions based on color, gender, or any other immutable characteristics, and yet provides protection against insidious acts of discrimination. From this perspective, the Fourteenth Amendment expressly prohibits discrimination and preferential treatment based on race, gender, or national origin.

Molinari (Rep. N.Y.) concludes that the Dole legislation restored the original meaning and purpose to Executive Order 11246, which required that a federal contractor not discriminate against any employee or applicant for employment based on race, religion, gender, or national origin (*Congressional Digest*, 1996). Thus, the Equal Employment Act merely prescribed statutory guidelines that the federal government must adhere to. The legislation was designed to preserve nondiscriminatory outreach, recruiting, and marketing efforts.

In a congressional hearing before the House Judiciary Subcommittee on the Constitution during hearings on the Equal Opportunity Act of 1995, Amselle (Communications Director for the Center for Equal Opportunity) argued that treating people differently because of their skin color was formerly referred to as discrimination; however, today it is known as affirmative action. Amselle states "racial discrimination when practiced by the private sector is abhorred; but when practiced by government it becomes more than just repugnant, it becomes dangerous," (*Congressional Digest*, 1996). He suggests that as a multi-ethnic and multi-cultural society, the division that is presented in affirmative action cannot exist without those not included in the preferred groups becoming justifiably bitter. Through it policies of affirmative action the government is creating, preserving and reinforcing division among its citizens.

In his testimony before the House Judiciary Subcommittee, Amselle further argues that there are two fundamental issues embedded in the arguments promoting racial and ethnic preferences. The first is a historical defense for the implementation of affirmative action as a means of restoration for past discrimination. Amselle states that this view ignores the reality that not all African Americans still suffer the effects of America's shameful past (*Congressional Digest*, 1996). The second argument in favor of racial preferences is more inclusive. It maintains that anti-discrimination laws have proven insufficient in fighting current discrimination, as demonstrated by the disproportionate representation of African Americans in all aspects of American society. Implicit in this argument is the presumption that everyone is guilty of discrimination and as a result government-mandated racial, ethnic, and gender preferences are required to ensure non-discriminatory practices among employers. In support of this testimony, Amselle cites a study by Sniderman and Piazza of Berkeley. Sniderman and Piazza in their study found that whites were more likely to identify African Americans as being "lazy" and "irresponsible" if they were first asked a question about affirmative action (*Congressional Digest*, 1996). The authors concluded that many whites disliked the perceived unfairness of racial preferences so much so that they grew to dislike African Americans, associating one with the other.

According to Cohen (Professor of Philosophy, University of Michigan), who also testified before the House Judiciary Subcommittee in support of the legislation, the objective of the Equal Opportunity Act of 1995 is to prohibit the federal government from providing preferential treatment on the basis of race and gender and also to prohibit the government from requiring or encouraging others to extend such preferences (*Congressional Digest*, 1996). Cohen's position is based on issues related to morality. His perspective is that there is a universal understanding of proper conduct that does not depend upon words or clauses of any statute, but develops directly from recognition of the moral obligation to treat persons equally. Hence, to provide favor to males/females or to whites or African Americans because of color or gender is morally wrong and intrinsically unfair. Cohen uses history to justify the implementation of the Equal Opportunity Act of 1995. In presenting his view to the House Judiciary Subcommittee, Cohen begins by stating that the grievous oppression of African Americans in this country has left a stain on history that cannot be denied. Nevertheless, the idea that redress can be provided by giving preference to those persons victimized because of racial classification and historical discrimination is misguided. The logic of this viewpoint suggests that those historically mistreated should now receive some type of payment to rectify these evils. Cohen, however, is of the opinion that moral entitlements are not the solution and should not be provided.

In support of his stance on affirmative action, Cohen presents an interesting query regarding the future of affirmative action. His question is "whether or not affirmative action should be abandoned?" (Cohen, 1996). The reply given by Cohen centers around the conceptualization of affirmative action. He advocates that the original intent of affirmative action was to insure the elimination of racially discriminatory practices. Based on that interpretation, the Equal Opportunity Act does nothing to hinder that precept. However, if by affirmative action one means preferential devices designed to bring about the redistribution of goods to match racial and gender proportions in the population, then affirmative action must be rejected because that ideology and its accompanying practices are inconsistent with the equal treatment of all persons (Cohen, 1996). To support his argument, Cohen cites the guidelines provided by the Fourteenth Amendment to the United States Constitution. As viewed by the Supreme Court, preferences must be eliminated because they are constitutionally unjust. Cohen concludes his testimony before the House Judiciary Subcommittee with the advocation that the Equal Opportunity Act moves in the right direction toward establishing racial equality.

Additional support for the Equal Opportunity Act is provided by Bolick's (Vice-President of the Institute for Justice) testimony before the House Judiciary Subcommittee concerning the Equal Opportunity Act. Bolick believes the Act is crafted to make the principle of nondiscrimination the law of the land once and for all. He strongly suggests that the language of the 1995 Act does nothing to repeal or modify any other civil rights law(s). Instead, the legislation would bring federal policies into conformity with the intent of the federal civil rights laws. Bolick (1996) suggests that the legislation would establish complete prohibition of discrimination by the federal government. He further argues that numerical goals institutionalize the very type of race measures the anti-discrimination laws were designed to eliminate. The legislation does not displace truly voluntary private-sector affirmative action, which it was implemented to protect. In fact, the Equal Opportunity Act expressly provides for nondiscriminative affirmative action. Bolick (1996) believes that the Equal Opportunity Act presents legislation targeting for the first time those individuals who are in fact truly disadvantaged. It is Bolick's conclusion that true affirmative action is not designed to redistribute opportunities on the criteria of race and skin color. It is, however, structured to expand the number of people who can compete on the basis of merit.

## Opponents of the Equal Opportunity Act of 1995

There are those opposed to the Equal Opportunity Act. Among those leading the opposition are Patrick (Assistant Attorney General for Civil Rights) and Lee (U.S. Rep. from Texas). They presented their viewpoints regarding the Act before the House Judiciary Subcommittee. Patrick begins his argument stating the Equal Opportunity Act would eliminate remedies Congress has tried to implement in an effect to compensate for discrimination. Patrick (1996) discusses the contention that complete prohibition of lawful and flexible affirmative action programs rejects several decades of Supreme Court precedents and places unreasonable limits on affirmative action. He contends that the legislation attacks remedies that have evolved as modest, helpful responses to deep institutional practices perceiving African Americans as less deserving of jobs, business opportunities and places in universities. Patrick's view takes into consideration that the measures of social well-being for African Americans lag far behind those of white males. He alludes to studies that reveal enforcement of anti-discrimination laws alone have not successfully leveled the playing field between dominant white males and other citizens. It logically follows that affirmative action represents a sensible mechanism to assist society in its goal of integration. Patrick implies that opposition to affirmative action arises because too many have a very restrictive view of affirmative action and often perceive it as a singular construct. However, affirmative action encompasses a wide range of remedies. At one end of the spectrum are efforts to reach out to traditionally excluded individuals and to recruit talent from all American communities. At the other end of the spectrum, affirmative action is perceived as masquerading behind quotas, which specifically reserve a set number of positions for certain groups regardless of qualifications (Patrick, 1996). It is understood that just about every one opposes quotas. Federal Courts and federal laws have both demonstrated that quotas are unconstitutional.

Patrick recommends during his testimony that in order to assess affirmative action, one must fully understand what is implied by "affirmative consideration." In affirmative consideration, race and ethnicity become only one factor that is analyzed in evaluating qualified candidates (Patrick, 1996). It must be understood that this form of consideration does not guarantee success predicated on race. This form of affirmative action was supported by the early proponents of affirmative action, but is being opposed by those advocating such legislation as the Equal Opportunity Act of 1995 (Patrick, 1996).

Hence, Patrick suggests to the House Judiciary Subcommittee that the legislation is such an extreme measure that implementation would produce substantial harm. He contends that the Act is inconsistent with principles that have been developed over decades by the Supreme Court and would eliminate a substantial amount of federal statutes and executive orders which would curtail the battle against racial discrimination. Patrick suggests that these effects would occur without a deliberate and intensive examination of affirmative action programs.

In opposition to the Equal Opportunity Act of 1995, Lee (Rep. Tx.) argued strongly before the House Judiciary Subcommittee that the Equal Opportunity Act of 1995 would roll back the clock on civil rights in the United States. Lee contends that under the guise of returning to the "original intent" of civil rights laws, this legislation would forbid the use of race in governmental decision making and curtail proven, accepted remedies for present and past discrimination. Representative Lee stresses that there is still a need for affirmative action programs and that anti-discrimination laws are not sufficient to rectify the structural racial discrimination that persists in our society (Lee, 1995).

Lee points out that Dole, sponsor of the Equal Opportunity Act of 1995, claim's the legislation will put the federal government's own house in order by prohibiting the federal government from granting preferences predicated on race or national origin in federal procurement, federal employment, and the administration of federally conducted programs. The legislation defines granting a preference "as any preferential treatment that includes but is not limited to any use of a quota set-aside, numerical goal, timetable, or other numerical objective" (Lee, 1995).

Lee indicated in her testimony before the House Judiciary Subcommittee that federal affirmative action programs focus on giving everyone an equal opportunity to compete for good jobs, educational opportunities and government contracts. Goals are yardsticks to measure equal opportunity, not guarantee results. When fashioned properly, goals have legally and fairly provided equal opportunity for all Americans. They provide respect for both merit and hard work, while ensuring that everyone has an opportunity to participate (Lee, 1995). In her testifying, Lee strongly suggests to the Subcommittee that without affirmative action, numerous talented students would never have attended college, and many gifted teachers and researchers would not have been hired. Affirmative action policies are still critically needed to bring about equal opportunity in education and employment. Representative Lee further suggests that while the nation is in the midst of competitive global and technological markets, this is not the time to roll back affirmative action.

However, after extensive Judiciary Committee Constitutional Subcommittee Hearings in both houses, the plan to scale back the federal government's affirmative action programs got only as far as the subcommittee hearing stage of both houses (*Congressional Quarterly Almanac*, 1996). Republicans were uneasy regarding the Dole-Canady proposal because of its timing which paralleled the November, 1995 elections (*Congressional Quarterly Almanac*, 1996). As a result, the proposed legislation to end affirmative action on the federal government level was viewed as being too hot to handle (*Congressional Quarterly Almanac*, 1995). Therefore, congressional opponents of affirmative action were not able to translate their momentum received from federal court action into legislative success in 1995. House Republicans expressed the view that they wanted to take their time drafting a bill to replace affirmative action.   The Majority Whip Delay, R-Texas, emphasized the leadership's desire not merely to abolish existing programs but to replace them with something aimed at enhancing opportunities for the disadvantaged (*Congressional Quarterly Almanac*, 1995).  It was Delay's opinion that the Republican leadership was in no hurry.  In support of this perspective, Speaker Gingrich, R-Georgia, also indicated that when a new plan was introduced, it would contain initiatives to increase economic opportunities for the disadvantaged before moving broad legislation to end all federal affirmative action programs (*Congressional Quarterly Almanac*, 1995).

First, it is important to note that the proposed legislative plan of Dole-Canady came one month after the Supreme Court ruling of *Adarand Constructors Inc. v. Pena* 115 S. Ct. 2097 (1995). (See Chapter V). Second, the fact that after extensive hearings and expert testimony, Congress abandoned the push to end affirmative action with the Equal Opportunity Act of 1995, which gives a strong indication of how difficult and complex issues like affirmative action (including racial and gender-based preferences) are in this society.  The discussion here indicates that the proposal was dropped after substantive testimony in subcommittee hearings and the impact of such legislation as a strong election campaign issue (*Congressional Quarterly Almanac*, 1996).

## The Concept of a Color-Blind Society

The concept of "color-blindness" originated with Justice Harlan, a Supreme Court judge who employed the term with great normative effect in his powerful dissent in *Plessy v. Ferguson* 163 U.S. 537 (1896), which sanctioned the "separate but equal" doctrine and racial subjugation at the highest court level.  Justice Harlan's words were: "Our Constitution is color-blind, and neither knows nor tolerates classes among citizens.  In respect to civil rights, all citizens are equal before the law."  There are several key factors to note about Justice Harlan's dissenting opinion. Harlan's opinion never cast doubt on the validity of legislation and policy designed to benefit, as opposed to harm, the African American population.   Harlan (1896) had no difficulty in recognizing that the Constitution was "race-conscious" in its efforts to protect the rights of African Americans from discrimination, violence and tyranny by whites in power.  The question then arises as to Mr. Harlan's interpretation of the

Constitution in relation to African Americans' substantive rights of an economic and social livelihood exhibited through productive work.

In assessing Harlan's notion of a color-blind society, it can be inferred that the legal principle of color-blindness was inconsistent with the institution and perception of white supremacy. It could be argued that only a rhetorical perspective of color-blindness allows the perception that whites would maintain total dominance in society, government, and economy in the absence of legal apartheid. An important and yet interesting fact for consideration is that Justice Harlan's color-blind argument was incorporated in a dissenting opinion.

Critics of affirmative action attempt to promote the belief that we live in a color- blind society in which the last vestige of racial discrimination is affirmative action itself (Raskin, 1996). However, this view of American society could not equalize in the past, and cannot equalize now, differences in life chances, earnings, wealth, power, and a host of other factors between whites and African Americans.

Patrick (1996) believes that opponents of affirmative action decry the propriety of any race-conscious remedy. They question how long such remedies must last and the appropriateness of ever departing from the so-called color idea (Patrick, 1996). Some Americans feel that they are being forced to pay for other's past sins, and that affirmative action unfairly gives special preferences to African Americans. Hence, the argument goes, we should simply declare a color-blind society in which neither whites nor African Americans receive benefits or burdens predicated on race (Patrick, 1996). Patrick states that many of those who now advocate a color-blind society are the same people who for years fought any attempts to advance civil rights. He further suggests that many opponents refuse to acknowledge any differences between affirmative action which is lawful, and quotas, which are illegal, regardless of Supreme Court decisions. However, Patrick, does concede that supporters of affirmative action are suspicious that color-blindness is just a high sounding concept intended to block society's progress toward equal opportunity. Patrick argues that affirmative action is not dead, and if it dies, it will be because the American people forgot who they were. Many affirmative action opponents paint with a broad brush, arguing that all race conscious efforts to level the playing field and open up opportunities are unfair "quotas" or "preferences" and should be jettisoned in favor of color-blindness (Jones, 1996). To move toward a consensus, Kahlenberg (1995) argues that affirmative action should focus on nonracial criteria so as to unify those within the disparate groups and provide a proper mechanism for battling racism. Thus, Kahlenberg stresses that affirmative action based on race violates the precepts of the civil rights movement.

## The California Civil Rights Initiative

The State of California provided the testing ground for the life of affirmative action in that State. The California Civil Rights Initiative, which later became known as "Proposition 209," was originally introduced in 1993. As proposed, it would provide for a constitutional amendment to eliminate public affirmative action in California with the exception of court-ordered programs or those required to maintain federal funding (California Senate Office of Research, 1995). Proposition 209 would prevent state courts from ordering public entities to engage in future affirmative action, but it would not prevent federal courts from doing so. Governor Pete Wilson publicly announced his opposition to the concept of affirmative action and expressed his support for the proposed amendment. California voters recently approved this controversial amendment in 1996 which effectively eliminates all preferential treatment in hiring, promotion and education. Not only did this action provide a testing ground for California, it would become the barometer for the rest of the country.

The text of the California Civil Rights Initiative contains the following provisions, as added to Article I of the California Constitution (Section 31. [Civil Rights.]):

a) "Neither the State of California nor any of its political subdivisions or agents shall use race, sex, color ethnicity or national origin as a criterion for either discriminating against, or granting preferential treatment to, any individual or group in the operation of the State's system of public employment, public education or public contracting;

b) This section shall apply only to state action taken after the effective date of this section;

c) Allowable remedies for violations of this section shall include normal and customary attorney's fees;

d) Nothing in this section shall be interpreted as prohibiting classifications based on sex which are reasonably necessary to the normal operations of the State's system of public employment or public education;

e) Nothing in this section shall be interpreted as invalidating any court order or consent decree which is in force as of the effective date of this section;

f) Nothing in this section shall be interpreted as prohibiting state action which is necessary to establish or maintain eligibility for any federal program, where ineligibility would result in a loss of federal funds to the State;

g) If any part or parts of this section are found to be in conflict with federal law or the United States Constitution, the section shall be implemented to the maximum extent that federal law and the United States Constitution permit. Any provision held invalid shall be severable from the remaining portions of this section" (California Senate Office of Research, 1995).

Proposition 209 presents an interesting attack on affirmative action. It can be reasoned that if California, a state with extensive ethnic diversity, disallows affirmative action, other states will follow. It can be argued that this gives credence to the issue that affirmative action as viewed by conservatives has gone far enough. In November, 1997 the citizens of Houston, Texas were confronted with a city initiative designed to remove affirmative action practices from the city. Providing support for the argument that other states as well as cities may follow the lead of California in regards to affirmative action and its continued existence. It is interesting to note that the Houston initiative did not pass. But this presents another situation pertaining to the legality of affirmative action. The state of Texas is the sight of another test case for the legality of race-conscious admission requirements in the case of *Hopwood v. State of Texas* (78 F.3d 932, 1996). The impact of this case will be discussed in Chapter V. It remains, however, to be seen how much, if any, impact California's Proposition 209 will have on other states and cities regarding the attempt to disallow affirmative action programs and policies.

## The Voting Rights Act of 1965

The Voting Rights Act of 1965 (VRA) 42 U.S.C. 1971 et seq. was both an affirmation of the principles embodied in the Civil Rights Acts of 1957, 1960, and 1964, along with a statement of objectives regarding the elimination and prohibition of abhorrent practices of racial discrimination in voting in the United States (Ball et. al., 1982). According to Ball et. al., with the passage of the VRA, it became the policy of the United States government to eliminate the use of those devices that had traditionally been employed to prevent African American citizens from registering and voting in the states of the deep South, and to prohibit those states from introducing new processes or devices that would dilute or abridge the voting rights of African American citizens (Ball et. al., 1982). It has been suggested that the formulation and passage of the 1965 VRA was probably the most radical piece of civil rights legislation since Reconstruction (Ball et. al., 1982). Ball posits that the VRA of 1965 was the continuation of a haphazard civil rights policy developed by the mid-twentieth-century Congress in response to violent events that were taking place in the South in the 1960s as a result of white segregationists' responses to African American boycotts, sit-ins, voter registration drives, litigation, freedom rides and freedom summers, and Supreme Court decisions (Bell et. al., 1982). The VRA could be summarized as both an affirmation of principles and a statement of objectives regarding abhorrent practices of racial discrimination in voting in America.

While the 1964 CRA is considered the origin of affirmative action, the 1965 VRA 42 U.S.C. 1971 et seq. can be treated as an intervening variable. According to Kull (1992), with the passage of the 1964 Civil Rights Act and the Voting Rights Act of 1965, the Civil Rights Movement celebrated the formal achievement of its objective: a legal regime from which racial classifications had been largely expunged, and under which the most salient forms of private discrimination (in public accommodations and employment) were finally prohibited. The Voting Rights Act (42 U.S.C. Section 1971) was enacted on August 7, 1965 (U.S. Commission on Civil Rights, 1981) and has been amended three times: in 1970, 1975, and in 1982. It is important to understand that the VRA as amended was enacted to ensure that the rights of citizens to vote would not be denied or impaired because of racial or language discrimination. The original Act was intended to be a temporary measure but had to be extended on more than one occasion because of intransigence on the part of those who would deny the right to vote to African Americans, women, and other protected groups.

The VRA (42 U.S.C. 1971 et seq.) is composed of three titles. Title I is referred to as the Voting Rights Provision and Title II contains the Supplemental Provisions. Title III contains those regulations regarding the right of eighteen years old to vote as a result of passage of the Twenty-Sixth Amendment (U.S. Commission on Civil Rights, 1981). Davidson and Grofman (1994) point out that until the 1980s the key components of the original VRA were the temporary provisions contained in sections 4 through 9 of Title I, which were renewed and amended in 1970, 1975, and 1982. These particular sections will require congressional consideration in 2007. The language mandate of section 203 was extended to 1992 and now will require congressional consideration in 2007 as well (Davidson and Grofman, 1994).

The Act contains both general and special provisions. The general provisions, as amended in 1970 and 1975, are applicable to the entire nation. Special provisions of the 1970 Amendments were imposed on those jurisdictions that failed to comply with the 1965 Act. The general provisions of the Voting Rights Act protect the voting rights of Americans in several important ways. They prohibit voting qualifications or procedures that would deny or abridge a person's right to vote predicated on race, color, or inclusion in a minority group. These provisions also make it a crime for a public official to refuse to allow a qualified person to vote or for any person to use threats or intimidation to prevent an individual from voting or assisting another in voting (42 U.S.C. Sections 1973 I (a) and (b) 1976). The general provision allows for increased enforcement of voting guarantees by private parties. Section 3 of Title I of the VRA permits private parties, as well as the U.S. Attorney General, to file suit pertaining to the enforcement of voting rights guaranteed in the Fourteenth and Fifteenth Amendments to the United States Constitution (Section 1973a(c)). As a remedy for this provision, the Court may appoint federal examiners and observers or may require pre-clearance in any jurisdiction in the United States. Another permanent provision with nationwide application is the prohibition of test or devices as a prerequisite for voting (U.S. Commission on Civil Rights, 1981).

The amended (1975) Voting Rights Act provides certain criteria to determine if a region is subject to its provisions. A jurisdiction is "covered" if it meets one of the following tests or trigger mechanisms: 1) The jurisdiction maintained on November 1, 1964, any test or device as a precondition for voter registration, and less than fifty-percent of the total voting age population were registered on November 1, 1964, or voted in the Presidential election of 1964; 2) The jurisdiction maintained on November 1, 1968, a test or device as a precondition for voter registration, or less than fifty-percent of the total voting age population were registered on November 11, 1968, or voted in the Presidential election of 1968; 3) The jurisdiction maintained on November 1, 1972 any test or device as a prerequisite to voting or voter registration, and less than fifty-percent of its voting population were registered on November 1, 1972, or voted in the Presidential election of 1972; 4) and more than five percent of the citizens of voting age in the jurisdiction were members of a single language minority group and the illiteracy rate of such persons as a group is higher than the national illiteracy rate (42 U.S.C. Section 1973 b (b) (1976)). Those jurisdictions covered by the first and second triggers are subject to the special provisions of the original 1965 VRA, while jurisdictions covered by the third trigger are subject to both the special provisions and the minority language provisions. States under the auspices of the fourth trigger are subject only to the minority provision (Ball et. al., 1982).

The special provisions of the VRA applied to the following areas: the entire states of Alaska, Alabama, Arizona, Georgia, Louisiana, Mississippi, South Carolina, Texas, and Virginia. The provisions included counties or towns in Connecticut, California, Colorado, Florida, Hawaii, Idaho, Massachusetts, Michigan, New Hampshire, New York, North Carolina, South Dakota, and Wyoming (U.S. Commission on Civil Rights, 1981). The special provisions of the VRA are temporary inasmuch as all four triggers have "bail out" features. A jurisdiction may bail out by proving in a suit in the United States District Court for the District of Columbia that its voting practices or procedures were not used in a discriminatory manner for a prior period (17 years in the case of the first two triggers and ten years under the third). All jurisdictions covered by the special provisions of the original VRA were able to bail out in 1982 if they had refrained from using a discriminatory test or device since 1965, while those covered under the 1975 amendments were eligible to bail out after 1985 (Ball et. al., 1982). According to Sections 4 and 6 of the VRA, examiners from the Department of Justice and observers from the Office of Personnel Management were to be sent into the covered jurisdictions for the purpose of guaranteeing that African American citizens would be duly registered and permitted to vote (U.S. Commission on Civil Rights, 1981).

A key provision of the VRA is Section 5 of Title I. This section is referred to as the "preclearance" provision. Ball et. al. (1982) indicate that Section 5 was included in the VRA because of the "acknowledged and anticipated inability of the Justice Department to investigate independently all changes with respect to voting enacted by states and subdivisions covered by the Act." Section 5 shifted the burden from the victim of racially discriminatory voting practices to the perpetrator of these practices and brought adjudication of these issues to Washington, D.C. Ball et. al. (1982) theorizes that this stipulation effectively isolated from contact with the operation of the law those Southern District Court Judges in whom the Congress had apparently lost faith.

Section 5 of the VRA requires covered jurisdictions to obtain preclearance before any changes in voting qualifications or prerequisites for voting, or standards, practices, or procedures with respect to voting that are different from those in effect on November 1, 1964, can be enforced (U.S. Commission on Civil Rights, 1981). The submissions were to be examined to determine if they had either the purpose or effect of denying or abridging the right to vote on account of race or color (U.S. Commission on Civil Rights, 1981). It has been noted that Section 5 was included primarily to prevent the substitution of new discriminatory practices for old ones that violated the guidelines of the VRA (Ball et. al., 1982). It is important to understand that Section 5 is automatic in that all vote changes in the covered jurisdictions must be submitted for review to the federal government. The Attorney General must act on a submission within sixty days. A failure to do so would result in preclearance even though the submitted change might be discriminatory (U.S. Commission on Civil Rights, 1981). Ball et. al. (1982) suggests that Section 5 was included in the VRA based on two assumptions. First, those local jurisdictions determined to prevent African Americans from voting, as they have in the past, could become ingenious and devise some new device to replace the existing one. Second, the limited funds of the Justice Department would make it virtually impossible to conduct independent investigations (Ball et. al., 1982). As observed by Davidson and Grofman (1994) Section 5 in essence froze into place all voting statutes pending federal approval of the proposed changes. Preclearance decisions are not subject to judicial review. Today, those states in which elections remain covered by Section 5 include: Alabama, Alaska, Arizona, Louisiana, Georgia, Mississippi, South Carolina, Texas, and Virginia. States whose elections are covered in only certain counties today include California, Florida, Michigan, New Hampshire, New York, North Carolina and South Dakota (Davidson and Grofman, 1994).

It is important to note that the coverage formula is not limited to one geographic region, but includes jurisdictions throughout the nation. It is of further importance to note that four of the seven states in this study - - Mississippi, South Carolina, Georgia, and North Carolina - - are included within the coverage formula. The special provisions of the Voting Rights Act were enacted to provide protection against pervasive racial discrimination in registering, voting, and running for office. Prior to the enactment of these provisions, states and local officials were empowered to effectively exclude African Americans from political participation in numerous areas.

Understandably, the VRA is one of the most important civil rights statutes in American history, and represents a part of a struggle for African American enfranchisement transcending centuries. The VRA has evolved beyond its original primary purpose of securing for African Americans the right to vote. As a result of the VRA Congress and the federal courts have gradually developed a strategy of voting rights that are inclusive of protections against vote dilution. As argued by Davison and Grofman (1994), the attainment of the protections given to African American voters is a long and complicated story that cannot accurately capture in statistics volumes of essays.

Discussion of the VRA will continue in the data analysis. The discussion will link increase in African American elected officials with the VRA and the impact this might have on affirmative action and employment increases as the result of increased Blacks political influence.

# CHAPTER III

# THE HISTORY OF INEQUALITY

## The Struggle for Equal Employment

Public policy related to affirmative action is a natural extension of the long struggle for equal rights and equal employment opportunities for African Americans. Beginning with the origin of the United States Constitution, African Americans have fought for their rightful place as citizens in this country (Amaker, 1988). Policies in the past with regard to the African American have not been consistent in the areas of racial justice, freedom, and equality (Amaker, 1988).

In an historical analysis Fleming et. al. (1978) argues that African Americans in this country have experienced nearly two hundred fifty years of slavery and another one hundred years of officially sanctioned segregation. Both factors have contributed to the continued subjugation of the African American in society. Affirmative action, therefore, is one strategy for making the transition to a fair and equitable society. This country has experienced the difficulties of enforcing civil rights policies from the era of Reconstruction to the present without the advent of affirmative action programs (Amaker, 1988).

## The Constitution and Inequality

The original Constitution of the United States contained no provisions for civil rights for the African American. Inequality for African Americans existed within the legal framework of the Constitution as exemplified by the "Three-fifths Compromise" found in Article I, Section

II. This provision, in which African Americans are not considered human, was included for the purpose of apportioning congressional representation. Other sections also illustrate the lack of protection for African Americans. Article I, Section 9 prohibited Congress from ending the slave trade until 1808. The Constitution also included a provision for allowing ships to have no obligations to enter ports for inspection, thus allowing for the uninterrupted transportation of slaves. Article IV of the original United States Constitution contains a provision supporting harsh treatment for runaway slaves or reious slaves, and the return of fugitive slaves. This articles states that "No person held to service or labor in one state, under the laws thereof, escaping into another, shall, in consequence of any law or regulation therein, be discharged from such Service or Labor, but shall be delivered up on claim of the Party to whom such Service or Labor may be due" (Berry et. al., 1993).

A key case regarding the issue of the Constitution and racial inequality presented to the United States Supreme Court for adjudication was that of *Scott v. Sanford* (19 Howard 393, 1857). This case presents a prime historical example of judicial power exercised in the interest of racial subordination. Scott was a Missouri slave owned by an army medical officer name John Emerson, who took him to live at a military post in Illinois, in a federal territory where slavery had been prohibited by the Missouri Compromise. In 1846, Scott brought suit against Emerson's widow claiming that he had been emancipated by his residence on free soil. After two trials, Scott had won his freedom. However, in 1852, the Illinois State Supreme Court reversed the decision and declared that the state would no longer enforce anti-slavery laws of other jurisdictions against Missouri's own citizens. Thus, Scott remained a slave (19 Howard 393).

The principle issue in the *Scott* case was whether residence on free soil affected the legal status of a slave. It should be noted that early on, southern courts joined in upholding the rule that a slave domicile in a free state became free forever. However, beginning in the 1830s, as a result of anti-slavery pressure, this view began to dissolve. The northern states still maintained that any slave except a fugitive slave was free the moment their feet were set on free soil (19 Howard 393).

The case would come before the Supreme Court as a result of writ of error. The membership of the Supreme Court at this time consisted of five southern Democrats, two northern Democrats, one northern Whig and one Republican. The opinion of the Court was delivered by Chief Justice

Roger B. Taney. Justice Taney presented the argument that blacks-not just slaves but all blacks- were incapable of obtaining citizenship, because they were not members of "the People of the United States" identified in the Constitution's Preamble (Karst, 1986). Taney would argue that blacks had been excluded from membership in the national community because they (blacks) were considered as a subordinate and inferior class of beings, who had been subjugated by the dominant race, and whether emancipated or not, remained subject to their authority (19 Howard 393). Taney in this opinion disallowed any state legislation that was contrary to the Court's view. Taney's conclusion was that Scott could not become a citizen because he was black, and, therefore, he could not become a citizen because he was a slave (19 Howard 393).

The opinion given by Taney devoted about forty-four percent to the issue of citizenship for blacks, thirty-eight percent related to the territorial question; sixteen percent to various technical issues and only two percent to the original question of whether residence on free soil had the legal effect of emancipating a slave (19 Howard 393). Understandably, the legal issue regarding citizenship affected free blacks only. The lasting impact of the *Dred Scott* decision was that blacks had no rights which the white man was bound to respect (19 Howard 393). The ruling also declared the Missouri Compromise unconstitutional. During this era, the Court would not provide legal protection for African Americans in the area of equality. · The opinion in *Dred Scott*, as given by Taney, committed the judicial power of the United States totally to the defense of slavery.

As the struggle for racial equality continued in 1865-1866 during Reconstruction, former slave states enacted statutes that collectively were called "Black Codes" (Wilson, 1965). The purpose of Black Codes were to enumerate the legal rights essential to the status of freedom of blacks and to provide a special criminal code for blacks. The overall objective of Black Codes was one of race control and labor discipline (Wilson, 1965). This was due, in part to the view of southern whites that emancipation did not of its own force, create civil status or capacity for freedmen (Wilson, 1965). The Black Codes reenacted elements of the laws of slavery. They provided detailed lists of civil disabilities by recreating the race-control features of slave codes. For example, Black Codes included: "defining racial status, forbidding blacks from certain occupations or professions, owning firearms, it required proof of residence, the prohibition of congregating groups of blacks, restricted

living areas for blacks and a specified etiquette of deference to whites"
(Wilson, 1965). The Black Codes also incorporated prohibition against
racial intermarriage and invoked the death penalty for blacks raping white
women. Black Codes would not allow blacks to serve on juries, hold
public office or participate in voting (Wilson, 1965). In some cases,
Black Codes required racial segregation in public transportation and
schools.

The statutory Black Codes provided a basis for extending well into the
twentieth century provisions that contained legal and paralegal structures
compelling blacks to work, restricting occupational mobility, and
providing harsh systems of forced labor sometimes bordering on peonage.
According to Wilson (1965), Black Codes became offensive to
northerners and their view of equality before the law. As a result, Black
Codes were repealed or left enforced by northerners during the
congressional phase of Reconstruction. This action would lead to re-
enactment of Jim Crow provisions and labor contract statutes to provide
the statutory component of the twilight zone of semi-freedom
characterizing the legal status of blacks through World War I (Wilson,
1965).

Responding to the Black Codes, Congress passed it first civil rights bill
designed to enforce the Thirteenth Amendment and the Fourteenth
Amendment to the United States Constitution called the Civil Rights Act
of 1866. It is important to note that this Act's definition of national
citizenship superseded the decision in *Scott v. Sanford* (1857), which
excluded blacks. The Civil Rights Act of 1866 provided that all citizens
were to enjoy full and equal protection of all laws and procedures for the
protection of persons and property, and would be subject to like
punishments without regard to former slave status (14 Statute 27). It was
hoped that the Civil Rights Act of 1866 would dismantle Black Codes and
bring into existence a serious civil rights law.

Section 1 of the Act granted all persons the same rights as white
persons to make and enforce contracts, sue, be parties, give evidence,
inherit, purchase, lease, sell, hold, convey real and personal property, and
the full and equal benefit of all laws and proceedings for the security of
person and property. It should be pointed out that these provisions are
included today under Sections 1981 and 1982 of Title 42, United States
Code (Hyman, 1982). This section, along with Section 3, are pointed out
because each was utilized by the legal system in the continued quest for
equality. Section 3 set forth the guidelines for vindicating rights protected

by Section 1. They are now a part of Section 1988 of Title 42 United States Code (Hyman, 1982).

As Hyman points out, after 1870s, Section 1 would diminish in importance. Those state laws mandating racial discrimination in areas within Section 1 were attacked easier under the Fourteenth Amendment to the United States Constitution. This made Section 1 applicable only to private discrimination (Hyman, 1982). Hyman indicates that the primary significance of Section 3 was determination of whether a Section 1 violation should be handled in federal court or a state court. He reports that in a series of civil rights cases, the Court held that Section 3 expressly mandated a removal of racial distinctions that prevented blacks from receiving equal justice, and also stated that the removal was not necessary when the same results was achieved through other formal state statutory commands (Hyman, 1982).

The Civil Rights Act of 1866 was vetoed by then President Andrew Johnson. However, Congress was successful in overriding the presidential veto. To supplement the Act, Congress would pass the Fourteenth Amendment. However, the Fourteenth Amendment would constrain- only state action. This view would be augmented by the Courts beginning with the *Slaughter House Cases* (1873).

On March 1, 1875, the Forty-Third Congress passed the Civil Rights Act of 1875 (18 Statute 335). This Act would become the last Reconstruction measure and the last civil rights act until 1957. The Civil Rights Act of 1875 would be perceived as the most important congressional enactment in the field of public accommodations until the Civil Rights Act of 1964. The Act affirmed the equality of all persons in the enjoyment of transportation facilities, in hotels and inns, and in theaters and places of public amusement (18 Statute 335). Even though these were privately owned businesses, it was inferred that they were exercising public functions for the benefit of the public and were therefore subject to public regulations. The penalty for violating the Civil Rights Act of 1875 was civil liability in the amount of $500 damages and upon conviction in a federal court a fine of not more than $1,000 or imprisonment of not more than one year (18 Statute 335). The effect of this Act were short-lived because in 1883, the Supreme Court declared the Civil Rights Act of 1875 unconstitutional in what became known as the Civil Rights Cases.

An interesting development took place before the Supreme Court in 1873 that would make states rights the basis for primary citizenship and national rights (specifically the Fourteenth Amendment) secondary citizenship. This historical Court decision came between the Civil Rights Acts of 1866 and 1875. This decision became known as the *Slaughter House Cases* (83 U.S. 36, 1873). In this case the Court was confronted by the claim of a group of New Orleans butchers that a Louisiana statute of 1869, granted a monopoly of the slaughter of livestock in New Orleans. It was argued that the 1869 statute deprived the butchers of federally protected rights under the Fourteenth Amendment because they were unable to pursue their livelihood, as butchers involving the slaughter of animals (83 U.S. 36, 1873). The majority of the Court rejected this argument. Justice Miller, speaking for the Court, reasoned that the purpose of the Fourteenth Amendment was to insure the equal legal rights of black people. According to Miller, the Amendment was not created as a broad category of new individual rights against state government and it did not provide an equal protection clause forbidding states from formulating discriminatory practices among their citizens on grounds other than race (83 U.S. 36). It was argued by Justice Field and Bradley that the Fourteenth Amendment should be viewed as having certain broad general rights, inherent in all persons, defensible against the states (83 U.S. 36).

The constitutionality of the Civil Rights Act of 1875 was decided in what became known as the Civil Rights Cases (109 U.S. 3, 1883). The Civil Rights Act of 1875 provided equal accommodations for all people (18 Statute 335). The litigation in these cases was comprised of five cases decided together. The Act of 1875 had been enforced against innkeepers, theater owners, and a railroad company. In each of the five cases, an African American citizen had been denied the same accommodations, guaranteed by the statute, as white citizens enjoyed (109 U.S. 3). In an 8-1 decision, the Supreme Court ruled that Congress had no constitutional authority under the Thirteenth or Fourteenth Amendment to pass the Civil Rights Act of 1875 (109 U.S. 3). In the majority opinion given by Justice Bradley, it was the Court's view that the Fourteenth Amendment provided a prohibition against state action (109 U.S. 3). Bradley argued that individual invasion of individual rights is not the subject matter of the Fourteenth Amendment (109 U.S. 3).

It was Bradley's view that the legislative power given Congress by the Fourteenth Amendment did not authorize enactments on subjects which are within the domain of state legislatures. He advocated that only when the states act adversely to the rights of citizenship could Congress pass remedial legislation (109 U.S. 3). The Court, according to Bradley, suggested that the wrongful act of an individual, unsupported by any such authority, is simply a private wrong that Congress cannot reach (109 U.S. 3). The Court reasoned that the Thirteenth and Fourteenth Amendment did not validate the Civil Rights Act of 1875 (109 U.S. 3).

In this historic decision, Justice Harlan provided the lone dissent. Harlan argued that citizenship necessarily imports equality of civil rights among citizens of every race in the same state. Congress therefore could guard and enforce rights, including the rights of citizenship deriving from the Constitution itself (109 U.S. 3). Harlan stressed that the Court had generously construed the Constitution to support congressional enactments on behalf of slave holders (109 U.S. 3). According to Harlan, Congress had not promiscuously sought to regulate the entire body of civil rights nor had it entered the domain of states by generally controlling public conveyances, inns, or places of public amusement. Rather, Congress had simply declared that in a nation of universal freedom, private parties exercising public authority could not discriminate on the basis of race (109 U.S. 3). In assessing the case, Karst cites Levy's view stating "that the opinion had the effect of reinforcing racist attitudes and practices, while emasculating a heroic effort by Congress to prevent the growth of a Jim Crow society." Karst also quoted Levy as arguing "that the Court also emasculated the Fourteenth Amendment's enforcement clause and the Court made the Constitution legitimize public immorality on the basis of specious reasoning" (Karst, 1986).

A major test of equality for African Americans predicated on the Constitution was the famous case of *Plessy v. Ferguson* (163 U.S. 537, 1896). This case would become the legal linchpin for the structure of Jim Crow in America. The case of *Plessy* established the separate-but-equal doctrine in which blacks were not denied the equal protection of the laws safeguarded by the Fourteenth Amendment when afforded facilities substantially equal to those available to white persons (163 U.S. 537). The case arose from a Louisiana law requiring railroad companies carrying passengers in the state to have equal but separate accommodations for white and colored persons by designating coaches racially or by partitioning them (163 U.S. 537). Thus, Plessy, the plaintiff, became the test case for challenging separate transportation facilities. The chief issue was whether the state law violated the Fourteenth Amendment's Equal Protection Clause (163 U.S. 537).

The majority opinion was given by Justice Brown. In an 8-1 decision, the Court held that the state act did not infringe upon the Thirteenth Amendment. The Act, according to Brown, implied merely a legal distinction between two races and had no tendency to destroy the legal equality of the two races, nor reestablish a state of involuntary servitude (163 U.S. 537). Brown insisted that state-imposed segregation did not necessarily imply inferiority of one race over another (163 U.S. 537). The majority Court decision would establish a precedent that provided legitimacy for Jim Crow laws and would require separate-but-equal facilities as a way of life until *Brown v. Board of Education* (1954).

The lone dissenter again was Justice Harlan. He argued that state action could have no regard with respect to the race of citizens when their civil rights was at issue (163 U.S. 537). It was Harlan's view that compulsory racial segregation violated the Thirteenth Amendment and imposed a badge of servitude on blacks (163 U.S. 537). Harlan argued that the Fourteenth Amendment meant that the law in the States shall be the same for blacks and whites. Therefore, Harlan argued that segregation was discriminatory per se (163 U.S. 537). He concludes by stating that the Constitution was color-blind and neither knows nor tolerates classes among citizens (163 U.S. 537).

In a commentary by Kluger (1973) regarding the *Plessy* decision, he asserts that one reading Brown's opinion will discover a sense of judicial feebleness. It is Kluger's contention that the object of the Fourteenth Amendment was undoubtably to enforce the absolute equality of the two races before the law (Kluger, 1973). According to Karst (1986), *Plessy* makes sense only if one understands that the Court believed that racial segregation was not discriminatory. Karst sets forth the argument that prejudice cannot be legislated away, and suggests that the Courts had overlooked the extent to which prejudice had been legislated into existence amid continued Jim Crow statutes (Karst, 1986). It was Karst belief that Plessy cleared the constitutional way for legislation that forced the separation of races in all places of public accommodation (Karst, 1986). Thus, in *Plessy*, the Court did not invent Jim Crow but instead adapted the Constitution to it. When the Constitution granted citizenship and the right to vote to African Americans, the southern states passed "Jim Crow Laws" in response to newly granted freedoms for African Americans. The struggle for racial and political equality for African Americans was hindered by the passage of Jim Crow laws designed to replace the institution of slavery with what could be considered "legal apartheid." Hence, "*de jure*" segregation, or segregation required by law became the norm in the South. Jim Crow laws imposed not only social segregation, but also provided for barriers to voting rights and economic opportunity. The intent of Jim Crow laws was to keep African Americans segregated, politically powerless, and economically subservient. In support of Jim Crow laws, the Supreme Court upheld the "separate but equal" doctrine in *Plessy v. Ferguson* 163 U.S. 537 (1896). This decision gave virtual *carte blanche* to Jim Crow regimes in the southern states. The struggle to overcome *de jure* segregation proved to be the catalyst for African American citizens to seek social and economic parity in the Civil Rights Movement.

The quest for racial equality continued in the right to vote. It can be argued that a citizen without the right to vote lacks true citizenship. The promise of national citizenship for African Americans made in the Reconstruction Amendments was all but dead at the dawn of the new century and it appeared as if none of the organs of government seemed interested in rectifying the situation (Farber et. al., 1993). There were several mechanisms implemented by Southern states to circumvent the legal requirements of the Fifteenth Amendment and to disenfranchise African Americans. Such practices included: the Grandfather Clause, the White Primary, the literacy tests, and the payment of a poll tax. Beginning in 1915, the Supreme Court started a long, slow process of responding to civil rights litigation by invalidating a few of the more odious disfranchisement provisions (Bell, 1993). Accordingly, the Grandfather Clause was the first such provision to fall. The practice of the Grandfather Clause was challenged by the National Association for the Advancement of Colored People (NAACP), in its first brief amicus curiae (friends of the court) in the case of *Guinn v. United States*, 238 U.S. 347 (1915). The practice challenged by the NAACP regarded a provision that gave all those who had the franchise (right to vote) before a certain date and their descendants the right to register permanently before a certain time had lapsed without complying with the educational qualifications required of all other voters (238 U.S. 347). The date affixed to the Grandfather Clause was 1866, thereby establishing a date fixed at a time when African Americans were not permitted to vote. This allowed all illiterate whites to vote while disenfranchising ignorant African Americans, resulting in circumvention of the Fifteenth Amendment (238 U.S. 347). The case of *Guinn v. United States* centered on such practices in Oklahoma. The State of Oklahoma required a literacy test for everyone except those proving the right to vote before

1866 (238 U.S. 347). The date of 1866 was significant because that was the year Congress gave former slaves the right to vote in Southern states (Farber et. al., 1993). In *Guinn v. United States* (238 U.S. 347), the Supreme Court for the first time used the Fifteenth Amendment to invalidate a discriminatory voting practice. Thereby declaring the utilization of the grandfather clause unconstitutional. The effort of the NAACP was successful in demonstrating to the Court the invidious racial effect of the Oklahoma law. As noted by Bell (1992), by the time the Supreme Court declared the grandfather clause unconstitutional, the time limit had begun to expire in those states having adopted this practice.

The two key points of attack for civil rights lawyers after 1915 were the white primary and the poll tax. According to Bell, for almost thirty years, the NAACP and other civil rights groups labored in the courts to strike down the white primary (Bell, 1992). The white primary was an ingenious device that took advantage of the one-party politics that prevailed in the South and effectively frustrated the desire to vote by blacks in the primary election (Bell, 1992). It must be understood that winner of the primary election was tantamount to winning the general election since only one party, the Democrats, dominated southern politics.

In *Smith v. Allwright* (321 U.S. 649, 1944), the Court reopened the question of whether discrimination effected by a state convention, which denied African Americans the right to participate in primaries, was a private or state action when, in conducting the primary, the party was fulfilling duties delegated to it by a statutory electoral scheme. This case resulted from such a practice being enacted in Texas, used by the Democratic party in that state (321 U.S. 649). After reviewing the importance of the primary to the election process, the Court concluded in 1944 that, "We think this statutory system for the selection of party nominees for inclusion on the general election ballot makes the party which is required to follow these legislative directions an agency of the state in so far as it determines the participants in a primary election" (321 U.S. 649). The Court also explained that the constitutional right to be free from racial discrimination in voting was not to be nullified by a state through casting its electoral process in a form which permits a private organization to practice racial discrimination in the election (321 U.S. 649). The Court declared the practice of the white primary a violation of the Fourteenth and Fifteenth Amendments rights under the Constitution.

The next focal point was the issue of the poll tax. The tax served more as a financial deterrent to prospective African American voters than as a grant of administrative discretion to register African Americans, who used the device in a myriad of ways, all designed to bar the ballot to African Americans (Bell, 1992). The Supreme Court in 1937 found that the poll tax did not violate any rights protected by the Constitution in *Breedlove v. Shuttles* (302 U.S. 277). The issue of a national poll tax requirement was resolved with the ratification of the Twenty-Fourth Amendment in 1964. The Amendment declared the payment of a poll tax in any primary or other election for President, Vice-President, Senator, or Representative in Congress as a means of abridging ones right to vote unconstitutional (Berry et. al., 1993). Nevertheless, in *Harman v. Forssenius* (380 U.S. 528, 1965), Virginia, in an effort to circumvent the Twenty-Fourth Amendment, enacted a provision enabling citizens either to pay the tax or file a notarized or witnessed certificate of residence six months before the election. However, the Court ruled that the Virginia measure requiring a certificate of residency created an obstacle to voting more onerous than the poll tax (380 U.S. 528).

In 1966, the Court overruled *Breedlove v. Shuttles* (302 U.S. 277, 1937) and declared that the extent that it required payment as a condition for voting, Virginia's poll tax provision violated the Fourteenth Amendment's Equal Protection Clause. In *Harper v. Virginia Board of Elections* (383 U.S. 663, 1966), the Court declared the payment of a state poll tax unconstitutional. The Court reasoned that the right to vote in federal elections is conferred by Article I, Section 2 of the United States Constitution. The Court conceded that the right to vote in state elections is nowhere expressly mentioned. However, according to the Court, once the franchise is granted, the Equal Protection Clause of the Fourteenth Amendment prohibits the states from drawing artificial and discriminatory lines among voters (383 U.S. 663). The Court concluded that a State violates the Equal Protection Clause of the Fourteenth Amendment whenever it makes the affluence of the voter or payment of any fee an electoral standard (383 U.S. 666). It was the Court's reasoning that even though states have the authority to determine voter eligibility, the state may not draw arbitrary lines of affluence or the payment of the poll tax which has no reasonable criteria for establishing voter eligibility (Bell, 1992). As noted by Bell (1992) several states attempted blatant as well as *prima facie* neutral schemes in efforts to dilute the effect of increased voting by African Americans in the period prior to enactment of the Voting Rights Act of 1965 (Bell, 1992). He emphasizes that with both the white primary and poll taxes cases, the affirmative response of the judicial branch to petitioners for relief did more for the morale of African

Americans rather than increase the actual amount of African American voters.

Another phase in the struggle for racial equality was the issue of a segregated educational system in America. The legality of separate or segregated educational facilities had been established in *Plessy v. Ferguson* (163 U.S. 537, 1896). It can be argued that the legal struggle for racial equality would become the cornerstone for the establishment of affirmative action, predicated eventually on Title VI and VII of the Civil Rights Act of 1964. The key objective of the NAACP strategy was to bridge the gap between what was plausible under separate-but-equal and what, in fact, was experienced by African Americans as they attempted to balance their entitlement equity on scales the state had pre-set to favor separateness (Bell, 1992). The result was a series of decisions, generally referred to as the "graduate school desegregation cases" (Bell, 1992).

The test for racial equality in graduate school education began with the system as structured in Missouri fashioned by the separate-but-equal doctrine in *Plessy*. It was the practice of Missouri to find African American applicant's a legal education at an out-of-state school admitting African Americans. This procedure was challenged by the NAACP in 1938, in the case of *Missouri ex rel. Gaines v. Canada* (305 U.S. 337). Missouri had denied Lloyd Gaines (an African American) admission to the state law school because of his race. The state however, argued that Gaines could attend an out-of-state school and Missouri would provide him financial aid (305 U.S. 337). It was argued by the NAACP that this was on its face an unequal provision of state education to both white and African American citizens. It was the legal theory of the NAACP that considerations of what method other states applied was not important, the pertinent issue was that the system operated by Missouri furnished opportunities for whites while denying African Americans the same opportunities simply because of race (305 U.S. 337). Thus, the denial of the equality of the legal right to enjoyment of privileges enacted by the State violated the separate-but-equal criteria (305 U.S. 337). Consequently, in *Missouri ex rel. Gaines v. Canada* (305 U.S. 337), the Court held that the refusal to admit an African American to the Missouri State University Law School when no separate facility for African American law students existed was a violation of the Equal Protection Clause. The state's willingness to fund the African American applicant's legal education at an out-of-state school did not cure the constitutionality issue (305 U.S. 337). As a result, Missouri created a segregated law school for African Americans at Lincoln University to comply with the separate-but-equal doctrine.

The next test regarding the separate-but-equal doctrine was in the State of Texas. The case in point was *Sweatt v. Painter* (339 U.S. 629, 1950). According to Bell, this was perhaps the most important graduate school desegregation case and the one from which the demise of *Plessy* could be predicated (Bell, 1992). This case is distinguishable from *Gaines* (1938) because the Court would have occasion to find law school facilities provided by the state inadequate both in tangible terms, and more importantly, in the intangible aspects of a legal education, which was a vital assessment in the minds of the Court (Bell, 1992).

The case resulted from Sweatt (an African American) who had applied for admission to the University of Texas Law School in 1945. Sweatt was denied admission because of his race (339 U.S. 629). Sweatt filed suit in state court seeking admission. The state district court did not order Sweatt's admission immediately but warned that the state must either open a law school at the state-run African American university at Prairie View located in Houston, Texas, or admit Sweatt to the white school at Austin (339 U.S. 629). As a result, the state hired two African American lawyers to teach law courses in some rented rooms in a Houston motel and called it a law school (339 U.S. 629). The NAACP argued that racial classifications were per se unreasonable and that the law school established by Texas was inherently unequal to the University of Texas Law School. In this case, the Court ordered the University of Texas to admit Sweatt (339 U.S. 629). The Court also recognized the significance of intangible differences between the two schools. The Court theorized that the University of Texas Law School possessed to a far greater degree those qualities which are incapable of objective measurement but which make for greatness in a law school. Hence, the hastily assembled alternative could not hope to be an equal facility (339 U.S. 629). The Court, therefore, ruled the law school format in Texas in violation of the separate-but-equal doctrine.

In a rather interesting and unique situation, the struggle for racial equality in graduate education focused on the State of Oklahoma. The federal court had invalidated an Oklahoma statute prohibiting desegregated schools (339 U.S. 637, 1950). This ruling opened the way for the admission of McLaurin, a sixty-eight year-old African American student, to the University of Oklahoma's doctoral program in education. McLaurin was admitted, but on a segregated system forcing him to sit in segregated areas in the classroom, cafeteria, and library (339 U.S. 637).

The Supreme Court found that McLaurin's subsequent isolation in the classroom, library, and cafeteria handicapped his pursuit of an effective graduate education and violated his right to equal protection (339 U.S. 637).

Now having attained victories in both *Sweatt and McLaurin*, the NAACP had won two battles but not the war. The issue of how the Court could be forced to confront the legality of segregation itself still remained unsolved (Bell, 1992). However, the ultimate goal of the total dismantling of the *Plessy* precedent remained. As indicated by Farber et. al., (1993) by 1951 both the NAACP and the Justice Department were committed to ending *de jure* segregation (segregation by law) whose existence seemed increasingly bizarre as well as immoral. Farber et. al. (1993) also postulate that the Supreme Court at this time period was starting to lean toward removing *de jure* segregation.

Heretofore, the issue before the Supreme Court was the constitutionality of segregation at the college and graduate school level. The Court had not dealt with the issue whether racial segregation itself was unconstitutional (*Sweatt v. Painter*, 339 U.S. 629, 1950; and *McLaurin v. Oklahoma State Regents*, 339 U.S. 637, 1950). The Court was now confronted with adjudicating the legality of segregation per se.

The legal attack was presented in the case of *Brown v. Board of Education* (347 U.S. 483, 1954). The Brown case was actually four school desegregation cases (Kansas, South Carolina, Virginia, and Delaware) consolidated (347 U.S. 483). The facts and local conditions were different, but all presented a common legal query; whether public schools could be operated on a racially segregated basis without violating the Equal Protection Clause (347 U.S. 483). It would be argued by the plaintiff that segregated public schools were not equal, could not be made equal, and therefore denied equal protection of the laws (347 U.S. 483).

The focal person in this case was Linda Brown (an African American) who had been denied access to the white school because of her race. The case contained an interesting factor in that schools in Kansas were separate-but-equal (347 U.S. 483). Thus, the legal challenge was that separate-but-equal violated the Equal Protection Clause of the Fourteenth Amendment. It should be noted also that this was the first test of the constitutionality of separate-but-equal in public school education.

In an amazing 9-0 decision, the United States Supreme Court in *Brown* overturned the separate-but-equal precedent established in *Plessy* (1896), declaring separate-but-equal unconstitutional (347 U.S. 483). The Warren

Court decided that it could not turn the clock back to 1868 when the Fourteenth Amendment was adopted, nor to 1896 when *Plessy v. Ferguson* was written. But, instead, public education had to be considered "in light of its whole development and its current place in American life throughout the Nation." Then only could a determination be made regarding whether segregation in public schools deprive one of equal protection of the laws (347 U.S. 492-493). Justice Warren, speaking for the Court, argued that it was doubtful that any child may reasonably be expected to succeed in life if denied the opportunity of an education (347 U.S. 493). In resolving the major issue, the Court ruled affirmatively that segregation of children in public schools solely on the basis of race, even though the physical facilities and other tangible factors may be equal, does deprive African Americans of equal educational opportunities (347 U.S. 493). The Court held that in the field of public education, the doctrine of separate-but-equal has no place. Separate educational facilities are inherently unequal. Therefore, separate-but-equal violated the Equal Protection Clause (347 U.S. 483). It should be pointed out that the mechanism for implementing *Brown* (1954) came in *Brown II* (1955). The Court required that schools were to desegregate "with all deliberate speed" (349 U.S. 294, 1955).

In a commentary regarding the impact of *Brown* (1954), Bell surmises the Court decision fathered a social upheaval that was unmeasurable (Bell, 1992). Bell further theorizes that the desegregation order sparked a movement leading to the elimination of Jim Crow provisions in public facilities across a wide spectrum (Bell, 1992). He posits that the *Brown* decision altered the status of African Americans who were no longer supplicants, seeking, pleading, begging to be treated as full-fledged members of the human race. But it could be inferred that African Americans were entitled to equal treatment as a right under the Constitution (Bell, 1992).

It could be argued that *Brown I and II* completely altered the style, spirit, and stance of race relations in this society. Yet, concession must be give to the fact that some existing patterns of white superiority and African American subordination remained unchanged. It can also be advocated that with the *Brown* rulings, major strides were made in the quest for racial equality since the implementation of the original Constitution.

Needless to say, the struggle continued in the area of voting. There was the existence of concerted efforts designed to disenfranchise African Americans. As a result, Congress enacted the Civil Rights Act of 1957,

43 U.S.C. Section 1971 et seq., 1975(d) (1964). This was the first modern legislation designed to enforce the rights granted by the Fifteenth Amendment to African Americans. The 1957 Civil Rights Act contained five major sections: (1) a special three-judge federal district court could be convened and they were given jurisdiction to hear civil rights cases taken out of state courts; (2) federal judges were empowered to hold persons in civil and criminal contempt, if court orders involving voting rights were not carried out by defendants; (3) the Act authorized the appointment of an Assistant Attorney General for Civil Rights; (4) the Attorney General was empowered to file suits in federal district court seeking injunctive relief against violations of the Fifteenth Amendment; and (5) the United States Commission on Civil Rights was created to monitor voting activities in the nation, especially in the South, and compile an annual report on the conditions of civil rights in America (Ball et. al., 1982). Under the 1957 Civil Rights Act, the United States Attorney was authorized to institute civil actions on behalf of named individuals for injunctive relief against proscribed deprivations of the right to vote in federal elections (42 U.S.C. Section 1971(c)-(d) (1964)). Penalties were provided for interference with federal voting rights (42 U.S.C. Section 1971(b) (1964), and criminal contempt cases arising under the act could be tried without a jury where the sentence was less than a $300 fine or 45 days imprisonment (42 U.S.C. Section 1995(c) (1964)). Finally, a six-member bipartisan Civil Rights Commission was created to investigate deprivations of voting rights on account of race, religion, or national origin (42 U.S.C. Section 1975(c) (1964)).

In order to strengthen the privilege granted under the Fifteenth Amendment and to reduce disenfranchisement, Congress enacted the 1960 Civil Rights Act, 42 U.S.C. Section 1971 (c), (e), 1974(e), 1975(h) (1964). The Act provided that if injunctive relief were granted in a suit brought by the United States Attorney General under the provisions of the 1957 Act, to which the state could be now made a party defendant, the Attorney General could ask the court to find a pattern or practice of discrimination (42 U.S.C. Section 1971(c) (1964)). Upon such a finding, any individual within the jurisdiction of the defendant could apply to the court for an order that he was qualified to vote in any election. The Act required the applicant to prove qualifications to vote under state election laws, and that they had been denied the opportunity to register or vote by persons acting under the color of law subsequent to the Court's finding of a pattern or practice. The Court was authorized to appoint referees to hear the evidence on such applications *ex parte* (42 U.S.C. Section 1971(e) (1964)). The Civil Rights Act of 1960 also contained provisions for the preservation, production, and inspection of voting records (42 U.S.C. Sections 1974-1974(e) (1964)).

The attacks against affording African Americans full voting rights would continue even with the passage of the Civil Rights Acts of 1957 and 1960. It could be argued that the delay tactics and ploys of intimidation that had discouraged African Americans in the 1960s became the catalyst to enhance their determination to vote. It now becomes apparent that exclusionary policies heretofore condoned by the courts during the early segment of the twentieth century were now viewed not only as a denial of African American rights but as a challenge to judicial authority (Bell, 1992). Thus, as noted by Bell, the inadequacies of the 1957, 1960 and 1964 Acts became more apparent, and the often violent response to peaceful voting rights marches and protests first embarrassed, then alarmed, the nation, resulting in increased political pressure for what would later become the Voting Rights Act of 1965.

The struggle for equality evident in the early history of this country continues today with affirmative action. Affirmative action is quintessentially a question of race, rights and justice in a nation long and deeply divided by color prejudice (Hudson, 1995). Hudson asserts that one cannot comprehend affirmative action within the framework shaped by and saturated with the racial inaccuracies present in American history. This mythology terms racism and inequality "right" and affirmative action, an alternative vision for American society, as "wrong" (Hudson, 1995). Hudson suggests that accounts of this nation's history are replete with the idea that since this country was won by right of conquest and settled by whites of mainly Anglo-Saxon ancestry, the bounty of this nation should primarily benefit elite whites. This ideology perpetuates the belief that persons of color are genetically and culturally inferior to whites by continued efforts of keeping African Americans in subservient positions. This viewpoint is often times the focal point of the argument that affirmative action promotes the unqualified over the qualified. This mythology represents a throwback to the perception's of the founders and earliest settlers of America regarding African Americans. As Hudson suggests, this historic precept has been translated into modern times by implying that African Americans are dysfunctional people and thereby incapable of meeting the demands of life in contemporary society. It is thus concluded that African Americans are reflective of "pathological families, teenage mothers, welfare queens, criminals, drug addicts and teenage gang bangers" (Hudson, 1995).

The underlying rationale for this argument legitimizes for conservatives the assumption that the policy of affirmative action unfairly penalizes whites of this historical era for the wrongs perpetuated by their ancestors during slavery and subsequent periods of segregation. This view point concurs with that of Sowell (1983), who suggests that if the real objective of affirmative action is to compensate for past injustices, then those most deserving of reparations are long dead.

Conversely, West (1996), in a constitutional and historical retrospective analysis, states that the fundamental aim of affirmative action was to significantly dent tightly controlled networks of privileged white male citizens who had monopolized the economic and political arenas in American society. West also suggests that neo-conservative opposition designed to weaken affirmative action succeeded in defining it as a program to benefit the unqualified. He further states that the opponents next move was to give affirmative action the appearance of being "un-American," in that it provided a quota system for groups rather than individual merit. West proposes that if affirmative action disappears from American society, African Americans will still excel and succeed. However, the removal of affirmative action would suggest that white supremacy exists and African Americans have legitimate reason to lose trust in the promise of American democracy (West, 1996).

Williams (1996), in her assessment of historical inequalities as exemplified by the constitution presenting, a discussion of economic inequality notes three factors that have created the economic basis for the hostility to affirmative action. First, as a result of foreign competition and cheap labor markets abroad global economic change has produced job loss, especially in the relatively high wage manufacturing sector. The existence of fewer and fewer decent employment opportunities help transform the image of affirmative action from distributive policy to a re-distributive one. This concept implies that affirmative action has moved from a concern with equality of opportunity to that of equality of outcome, thereby striving to enhance the economic equality as well as opportunity for African Americans. The second key factor, that of automation, has produced a formidable and perhaps intractable problem and hastened the growth of re-distributive anxieties. The concern is that supposedly the exciting new world of high-tech automated production will replace human beings with intelligent machines in countless tasks, forcing millions of blue- and white-collar workers into unemployment lines or for many, breadlines (Williams, 1996). The third key factor producing a negative attitude regarding affirmative action was the economic policies of the Reagan-Bush era. This era saw the reduction of taxes for the rich, budgetary policies that amounted to shrinking domestic spending while increasing defense spending, deregulation, and monetary policies that benefitted the top fifth of the population at the expense of everybody else (Williams, 1996). These economic policies were detrimental to African Americans.

A historical view of Supreme Court decisions, constitutional amendments and congressional acts reveals that the problem of employment discrimination may still be very serious, even forty-two years after the policy of racial neutrality stated in *Brown v. Board of Education* ( 349 U.S. 294 1955) and thirty-three years after the passage of Title VII of the Civil Rights Act. As pointed out by Mandelbaum (1983), practices that have been in existence for 200 years do not disappear easily. Some research reveals that an African American male with the average job qualifications of a white male would have received much less income than typical whites because of racial difference in pay rates (Mandelbaum, 1983). Racial differences appear to account for as much as fifty percent of the total differences in earnings between whites and African Americans. Sadly, to say, the gap appears to be on the increase. Even though African Americans are making progress, the movement for African Americans from low paying service worker and labor jobs to mid-level management is lethargic at best.

# CHAPTER IV

# THE SUPREME COURT AND AFFIRMATIVE ACTION: 1971-1988

### The Role of the United States Supreme Court

African Americans, in pursuit of equal representation, equal employment and equal opportunity, frequently have had to rely on the federal court system as a mechanism for relief. The United States Supreme Court in *Brown v. Board of Education* (1954) overturned the "Separate But Equal Doctrine" of *Plessy v. Ferguson* (1896). The *Brown v. Board of Education* case, with a series of other cases including *Missouri ex rel Gaines v. Canada*, *McLaurin v. Oklahoma*, and *Sweatt v. Painter*, set the stage for the U.S. Supreme Court to embark on a new road as the protector of the rights of African Americans.

However, with the appointments of conservative justices Rehnquist, O'Connor, Kennedy, Scalia, and Thomas, the Supreme Court is now considered hostile to affirmative action and unsympathetic toward the rights and concerns of African Americans by others. Understandably, the change in Court personnel is important, since the political and legal philosophy of the Court changes, the manner in which the Constitution is interpreted changes as well. The Supreme Court utilizes the legal concept of "judicial review" to justify its role in decision making.

However, in the American political system, the United States Supreme Court does not retain ultimate political authority. The political system is an interlocking system of checks and balances and combined interpretation. Constitutional interpretation is not and was never intended to be solely within the auspices of the Court. It is certain that decisions by the Court are final "only so long as the other branches of government and the political process permit its last word to stand" (Agresto, 1984).

Agresto (1984), however argues that there is both philosophical and historic support for the idea that the Court is not the final arbiter, in affording the Supreme Court that authority provides a restraint on judicial autonomy. According to Agresto (1984), the Supreme Court has attained the level of an imperial judiciary not because it is active, but because the Court essentially remains unchecked. Agresto argues that the Court operates outside the boundaries of institutional checks and balances or democratic elections.

Affirmative action cases decided by the United States Supreme Court since 1978 reveal that the changes in legal and political philosophy has resulted in decisions that have restricted affirmative action programs. The examination of these cases suggests that the use of affirmative action will be limited in the future.

## The United States Supreme Court and Affirmative Action

*Griggs v. Duke Power Company* 401 U.S. 424, (1971) set a number of precedents that would affect subsequent rulings in affirmative action cases during the 1970s, 1980s, and 1990s. Consequently, the *Griggs* case will be discussed first because of the guidelines it established regarding affirmative action.

### Griggs v. Duke Power Company 401 U.S. 424, (1971)

The proceedings of this case were brought by a group of African American employees against Duke Power Company in North Carolina. The African Americans were employed at the company's Dan River Steam Station, a power-generating facility located at Draper, North Carolina. When this action was instituted, Duke Power Company had ninety-five employees at the Dan River Station; fourteen were African Americans and thirteen became involved in the case (401 U.S. 424,426, 1971).

The Dan River plant was organized into five departments: (1) Labor, (2) Coal Handling, (3) Operations, (4) Maintenance, and (5) Laboratory and Test. African Americans were employed exclusively in the Labor Department, where the highest paying jobs paid less than the lowest paying jobs in the other four departments. Promotions were generally made from within departments and were based on job seniority. Those seeking a transfer into another department were required to begin at the bottom of the hierarchy (401 U.S. 424,427, 1971).

"In 1955, the company instituted a policy requiring a high school education for initial assignment to any department except Labor, and for a transfer from the Coal Handling to any inside department (Operations, Maintenance, or Laboratory). After the company's abandonment of its policy restricting African Americans to the Labor Department in 1965, completion of high school became a prerequisite for transferring from Labor to any other department" (401 U.S. 424,427, 1971). It is important to note that from the time of implementation of a policy requiring the completion of high school, white workers maintained satisfactory work performance and continued to experience promotions (401 U.S. 424,427, 1971). This served as an indication that white employees were not disadvantaged by the implementation of the new policy.

On July 2, 1965 (when Title VII became effective), the company instituted an additional requirement for new employees. Applicants now were required to obtain a passing score for two professional aptitude tests (401 U.S. 424,427-428, 1971). However, the standard requirement of high school completion proved sufficient for those employees hired prior to implementation of the new standards to have the criteria for transferring to the other departments (401 U.S. 424,428, 1971). As of "September 1965, the company permitted incumbent employees lacking a high school education to qualify for a transfer from Labor or Coal Handling to an inside job by passing either the Wonderlin Performance Test (general intelligence test) or the Bennett Mechanical Comprehensive Test. Neither test was designed to measure ability to perform a particular job or job category" (401 U.S. 424,428, 1971).

In response to these actions African American employees brought action against Duke Power pursuant to Title VII of the Civil Rights Act of 1964. The plaintiffs challenged the legality of implementing the standard requiring passage of either a high school diploma or passage of the intelligence test as a prerequisite for employment or a job transfer. This alleged complaint filed by the African American employees suggested that the new requirements demonstrated no relationship between job performance and job category. Therefore, these requirements were in violation of Title VII of the Civil Rights Act of 1964, 42 U.S.C. Section 2000e-2 (401 U.S. 424, 1971).

The Act in question provides that it shall be an unlawful employment practice for an employer to: (1) limit, segregate, or classify employees in any way which would deprive or tend to deprive any individual of employment opportunity or otherwise adversely affect his status as an employee, based on race, color, religion, sex, or national origin; (2) notwithstanding any other provision of this title, it is not an unlawful employment practice for an employer to give and act upon the results of any professionally developed ability test provided that such a test, its administration, or action taken upon such results is not designed, intended or used to discriminate because of race, color, religion, sex, or national origin (42 U.S.C. Section 2000e-2).

It should be noted that the "litigation focused on whether, the requirements of a high school education or passage of a standardized general intelligence test as a condition of employment in or transfer to jobs was constitutional when: (1) neither standard is shown to significantly relate to successful job performance; (2) both requirements operate to disqualify African Americans at a substantially higher rate than white applicants; and (3) the jobs in question formerly had been filled only by white employees as part of a longstanding practice of preferential treatment for whites" (401 U.S. 424, 426, 1971).

The Federal District Court noted that previous racial discrimination practices exhibited by Duke Power Company had ceased. The district court held that Title VII was designed as a "prospective" measure, therefore, any previous demonstrations of inequality were beyond the scope of Title VII (401 U.S. 424, 428, 1971).

The Court of Appeals reversed the decision of the district court, indicating that "residual discriminatory practices" were protected from remedial action. The Court of Appeals ruled that "African Americans employed in the Labor Department at a time when there was no high school or test requirement for entrance into the higher paying departments could not now be made subject to those requirements, since whites hired contemporaneously into those departments were never subject to them" (401 U.S. 424, 429, 1971). The Court of Appeals also noted that seniority in regards to African Americans should be based on a plant-wide criterion. Nevertheless, the Court of Appeals did not grant relief to African American workers hired prior to the implementation of the educational prerequisite in the Labor Department (401 U.S. 424, 429, 1971). The Court of Appeals held "that in view of a failure to demonstrate employment discrimination, the educational requirement met the criteria of Title VII" (401 U.S. 424, 429, 1971).

The United States Supreme Court overturned the decision of the Court of Appeals. The opinion of the Supreme Court was delivered by Chief Justice Burger with all members joining except Brennan. Justice Brennan took no part in the consideration or decision of the case (401 U.S. 424,425, 1971). The Supreme Court focused on the objective and legislative intent in the enactment of Title VII of the Civil Rights Act of 1964 (401 U.S. 424,429, 1971). The Court, through Justice Burger, suggested, that "the purpose of Title VII was to achieve equality of employment opportunities and remove barriers that have operated in the past to favor an identifiable group of white employees over other employees" (401 U.S. 424,430, 1971). The Court further stated, that "under Title VII, practices, procedures, or tests neutral on their face, and even neutral in terms of intent, cannot be maintained if they operate to freeze the status quo of prior discriminatory employment practices" (401 U.S. 424,430, 1971).

Justice Burger also indicated that Title VII, was not designed to guarantee an individual employment absent the required qualifications. In essence, according to Burger, "the Act does not command that any person be hired simply because he was formerly the subject of discrimination, or because of membership in a minority group" (401 U.S. 424,431, 1971). Burger further stated, that "Congress intended the removal of artificial, arbitrary, and unnecessary barriers to employment when the barriers operate invidiously to discriminate on the basis of racial or other impermissible classifications" (401 U.S. 424,431, 1971).

The Court then defined the essential element of Title VII. The Court stated, that "the touchstone of employment tests is the factor of business necessity" (401 U.S. 424, 431, 1971). According to the Court, Title VII covered employment practices that ranged from overt discrimination to those constituting actual discriminatory practices (401, U.S. 424,431, 1971). The element of business necessity, therefore, requires "that if an employment practice operates to exclude African Americans and it cannot be shown to be related to job performance, the practice is prohibited" (401 U.S. 424,431, 1971).

In further explaining the business necessity principle, Burger wrote that there existed no relationship between the high school completion requirement and the general intelligence test leading to successful work habits (401 U.S. 424,431, 1971). Burger argued that both practices were enacted without any meaningful study of their relationship to job performance ability. He also provided the Court's perspective regarding employer intent in the establishment of employment requirements. Justice

Burger postulated, that "good intent or absence of discriminatory intent did not redeem employment procedures or testing mechanisms that operate as 'built-in headwinds' for minority groups and were unrelated to measuring job capability" (401 U.S. 424,432, 1971). Burger elaborated, that "Congress placed on the employer the burden of showing that any given requirement must have a manifest relationship to the employment in question" (401 U.S. 424,432, 1971). According to Burger, *Griggs* presented the issue of the legality of degree requirements as a means for determining satisfactory work performance (401 U.S. 424,432-433, 1971).

Burger wrote that Title VII was designed to established employment promotions predicated on qualifications rather than ethnicity (401 U.S. 424,434, 1971). He also wrote that Title VII did not forbid the utilization of meaningful employee testing. Congressional intent for Title VII prevented the utilization of "control factors" that had no bearing on job performance. It was not the intent of Congress that an insufficiently qualified individual receive preference simply because of ethnic status rather than qualifications. In fact, qualifications became the controlling factor rather than race, religion, nationality, and sex. Consequently, any employment test must measure job qualifications of the individual and the individual in the abstract (401 U.S. 424,436, 1971).

The case of *Griggs v. Duke Power Company* (401 U.S. 424, 1971) set the precedent for determining if the tests in question constituted business necessity. The case defined business necessity in fairly precise terms and related it to the employee and work. *Griggs* also addressed the concept of disparate impact, which meant that even though a certain practice appeared benign, if it's effects or impact was adverse to a particular constitutionally protected group, it was illegal. Finally, *Griggs* put the burden of proof on the employer to show that they are not discriminating against the employee or employees.

The remainder of this chapter focuses on legal cases addressing affirmative action from 1974, beginning with *DeFunis*, through 1988. Key cases pertaining to affirmative action are presented with in-depth discussion of legal issues, the Court's reasoning, and majority and minority opinions. This method allows for a detailed analysis of each case as it relates to affirmative action.

There are two key legal issues involved in the principle of affirmative action that this chapter addresses. The first issue is whether affirmative action constitutes "reverse discrimination," and therefore violates the

Equal Protection Clause of the Fourteenth Amendment. The second issue is whether affirmative action violates the Civil Rights Act of 1964, particularly Title VI. The initial and preliminary test regarding these two legal issues was presented in *DeFunis v. Odegaard*, 416 U.S. 312 (1974).

## DeFunis v. Odegaard, 416 U.S. 312 (1974)

Marco DeFunis, a white male, filed suit claiming, that "the admission policy of the University of Washington Law School was racially discriminatory in violation of the Equal Protection Clause of the Fourteenth Amendment" (416 U.S. 312, 1974). DeFunis argued that the admission's policy of the Law School invidiously discriminated against him solely on account of his race.

The trial court agreed with DeFunis' claim and granted the requested relief.   Consequently, he entered Law School in the fall of 1971. However, the Washington Supreme Court, on appeal, reversed the trial court decision and ruled that the admission's policy was not in violation of the Constitution.   At the time of this judgment DeFunis was in his second year (416 U.S. 312,315, 1974).   DeFunis petitioned the United States Supreme Court for a *writ of certiorari*, which was granted by Justice Douglas.   As a result of the stay, he remained in law school and was now in the final year of law school when the case was considered by the Supreme Court.

Since DeFunis was in the final year of law school, the Supreme Court considered another legal issue as priority over the issue of violation of the Fourteenth Amendment.   Instead, the Court began by focusing on the legal issue of "mootness," and required both litigants to discuss the issue (416 U.S. 312,315, 1974). During this litigation process, the Law School had consented to an agreement that DeFunis' registration would not be canceled unilaterally by the university.

On *certiorari*, the United States Supreme Court vacated the Washington Supreme Court's judgment and remanded the case for such proceedings as the latter court might deem appropriate.   In a *per curiam* opinion, expressing the views of the majority members, the court order was explained.   Predicated on the legal doctrine found in Article III of the United States Constitution, the Court established that the case was moot. Regardless of the ultimate resolution on the merits of the case by the Supreme Court, DeFunis would be entitled to complete the quarter and receive his degree if he fulfilled all requirements.    Furthermore, the Court pointed out that DeFunis had not sought a class action suit, therefore, once admitted to the law school there no longer existed a controversy establishing an "adverse legal" relationship (416 U.S. 312,316-320, 1974).

A dissenting opinion in the *DeFunis* case was presented by Justice Douglas. Justice Douglas argued that the case was not moot and that the merits of the case should have been addressed by the Court (416 U.S. 312,331, 1974). Douglas stated that "the Equal Protection Clause did not require that law schools employ an admissions formula based solely upon testing results and undergraduate grades, nor did it proscribe evaluation of an applicant's prior achievement in light of the barriers that he had to overcome" (416 U.S. 312,331, 1974). The key was that each application must be considered on its individual merits in a racially neutral manner (416 U.S. 312,331, 1974).

Justice Douglas explained that a university's admission policy employing racial classifications to favor certain minority groups was subject to strict scrutiny under the Equal Protection Clause of the Fourteenth Amendment (416 U.S. 312,333, 1974). It was his position that in view of the differences in cultural backgrounds and the inadequacies of testing procedures for determining qualifications for admission to school, the law school in the instant action had acted properly in processing students applications by students of color separately from other applications. He concluded that the case should be remanded for a new trial to consider whether the plaintiff had been invidiously discriminated against based on his race.

Justices Douglas, Brennan, White and Marshall wrote an additional dissent together. Their argument focused on the fact that this case presented an important constitutional question and could not be dismissed as moot. In support of their argument, the justices set forth an interesting query: "what would have happened if DeFunis had experienced an unexpected event - - such as illness, economic necessity, or academic failure - - that prevented him from graduating at the end of the current school term" (416 U.S. 312,348, 1974). In such a case, he would once again have to apply to the law school under the allegedly unlawful admissions policy (416 U.S. 312,348, 1974).

At this juncture the Supreme Court did not address the issue of alleged reverse discrimination. Rather, it ruled on the mootness of the case, leaving in place the issue of special admissions programs for colleges and universities. The legal question of whether special admissions policies violated the Equal Protection Clause of the Fourteenth Amendment would not be resolved during the 1974 term of the Court. The issue of whether affirmative action constitutes reverse discrimination, and therefore violates the Equal Protection Clause of the Fourteenth Amendment, and whether affirmative action violates the Civil Rights Act of 1964, particularly Title VI, would confront the Court four years later. These two legal issues constitute the foundation of *Regents of the University of California at Davis v. Bakke,* 438 U.S. 265 *(1978).*

## Regents of the University of California v. Bakke, 438 U.S. 265 (1978)

Not since *Brown v. Board of Education of Topeka, Kansas,* 347 U.S. 483 (1954) has a case raised civil rights issues of such profound importance as the *Bakke* case. The magnitude of the *Bakke* case was such that more that one hundred persons and organizations filed *amici curiae* briefs, thirty-two in support of Bakke, and eighty-four in support of the University of California (*Chronicle of Higher Education,* September 26, 1977). The focal point of the case the denial of admission of Alan Bakke, a white male to the Medical School of the University of California at Davis, because of the University's "special admission program."

The prevailing question in the *Bakke* case was whether the Equal Protection Clause of the Fourteenth Amendment permitted schools to consider the racial or ethnic background of applicants as a criteria in the selection of students (438 U.S. 265,266, 1978). In other words, can a state university, which was forced by limited resources to select a relatively small number of students from a much larger number of well qualified applicants freely, and voluntarily, take race into account in order to increase the number of minority groups trained in the profession. The question was whether the University's special admission program, which took race into account to correct past discrimination, violated the Equal Protection Clause of the Fourteenth Amendment.

According to Fleming et. al. (1978), the legal challenge of *Bakke* raised three constitutional issues. First, are racial classifications constitutional? Second, can racial classifications withstand the strict scrutiny and compelling state interest test which is applied when classifications are based upon suspect classifications such as race? The third issue was whether, in some special situations, race-conscious classifications need only meet the rational basis test.

In resolving related legal inquiries, the courts have traditionally utilized two approaches. The first approach is that if there is state economic and social welfare programs involvement, the state classification has been sustained if it bears some reasonable relationship to a legitimate state objective. The second approach focuses on whether a state accords disparate treatment through a classification based on race, sex, or ethnic background. If so, the court terms the classification "suspect" and it is subject to closer scrutiny. If a classification is suspect, disparate treatment has been allowed only if there is a "compelling" state interest to sustain it (Fisher, 1978).

In assessing the issue of "suspect classifications" the Court noted that in *Rodriquez v. San Antonio Independent School District*, 411 U.S. 1 (1973), the U.S. Supreme Court held that elementary and secondary education were of great importance, but were not a fundamental interest for the purpose of equal protection analysis. Based on this precedent, proponents of *Bakke* argued that the concept of a compelling state interest was not synonymous with the recognition of an important social objective. Moreover, it was proposed that the special admissions program was based upon a "racial quota" (438 U.S. 265,278, 1978). The university, on the other hand, argued, as "a compelling interest the educational value of a diverse student body, and the benefits of professionals of color as role models for other races of color" (438 U.S. 265,278, 1978).

*Bakke* presented a dilemma for the nation as attempts were undertaken to equalize opportunities for all citizens by correcting injustices caused by past discrimination without violating the rights of others. In *Regents of the University of California v. Bakke*, 438 U.S. 265 (1978), there were two 5-4 decisions. Four justices (Burger, Stevens, Stewart, and Rehnquist) wrote opinions stating that the constitutionality of affirmative action or quotas was not involved in *Bakke*. Accordingly, Title VI of the 1964 Civil Rights Act required absolute color-blindness. Consequently, Bakke was discriminated against. Powell represented the fifth and swing vote but used somewhat different reasoning. In their dissent, Justices Marshall, White, Brennan, and Blackmun wrote that the statute and its regulations required affirmative action plans where people of color had been absent from a program in the past. It was their opinion that not only could race be constitutionally used as a factor, but that the Davis Medical School practice of considering race as a controlling factor was not unconstitutional (438 U.S. 265,328, 1978). The Supreme Court affirmed the lower court's decision that Allan Bakke should be admitted to the Medical School of the University of California and invalidated its special admissions program. The Court also reversed the judgment that prohibited race from being used as a factor in university admissions. In the *Bakke* decision, the Court stated that under certain circumstances a carefully constructed admissions program that included race as one criterion was legally permissible (438 U.S. 265,267, 1978).

Justice William Powell wrote the opinion for the Court that included Burger, Stevens, Stewart, and Rehnquist. He reasoned that the guarantee of equal protection of the law was designed to protect all citizens and not some groups more than others (438 U.S. 265,267, 1978). Powell argued that a "benign preference toward one group would be reflective of racial politics, and therefore reinforce stereotypes that depicted certain groups as unable to achieve success without special protection" (438 U.S. 265,294, 1978). It was unfair to require innocent persons like Bakke to bear the burdens of redressing wrongs not of his making. Justice Powell further reasoned that the Court had never approved a classification system that aided persons in a perceived protected class at the expense of innocent individuals. Consequently, he rejected the Davis Medical School plan because it excluded non-minority applicants from a specific number of seats in the entering class. Since the decision in not accepting Bakke was based on an invalid policy, he was therefore entitled to admission to medical school. In short, the Court ruling invalidated quotas.

The Brennan four (Brennan, Marshall, White and Blackmun), however, concluded that Davis' "purpose of remedying the effects of past societal discrimination is sufficiently important to justify the use of race-conscious admission programs where there is a sound basis for concluding that minority under-representation is substantial and chronic, and that the handicap of prior discrimination is impeding access of minorities to the Medical School" (438 U.S. 265,362, 1978). Brennan devised a three-pronged test to gauge the validity of race-conscious admissions programs under the provisions of Title VI and the Equal Protection Clause of the Fourteenth Amendment. The first prong was that "a state government may adopt race-conscious programs if the purpose of such programs is to remove the disparate racial impact its actions might otherwise have had and if there is reason to believe that the disparate impact is itself the product of past discrimination, whether its own or that of society at large" (438 U.S. 265,369, 1978). The second prong was that "race as an admission criterion must be reasonably used in light of the program's objectives" (438 U.S. 265,373-374, 1978). The third prong was that "race-conscious programs cannot be used in a way that operates to stigmatize or single out any discrete and insular, or even identifiable, non-minority group" (438 U.S. 265,374, 1978).

Those endorsing the opinion of Justice Stevens questioned whether race could be used as a factor in admissions, suggesting it was not an issue in the case. For them, the merits of this case was based on a singular question: Was Allan Bakke entitled to be admitted to medical school? The Stevens bloc reasoned that by excluding Bakke because of his race, the Davis special admissions program violated Title VI of the Civil Rights Act of 1964. It was their argument that regardless of the fact that Bakke was white, he was entitled to admission to law school (438 U.S. 265,421, 1978).

### Thurgood Marshall and the Bakke Case

The *Bakke* decision evoked harsh criticism from the Court's only African American justice. Justice Marshall began his denunciation by stating, "I agree with the judgment of the Court only insofar as it permits a university to consider the race of an applicant in making admission decisions" (438 U.S. 265,387, 1978). He did not agree, however, that the special admissions program violated the Constitution. Marshall reminded the Court, that "for 200 years the Constitution, as interpreted by the Supreme Court, did not prohibit the most oppressive and pervasive forms of discrimination against African Americans" (438 U.S. 265,388, 1978). When the concept of "unalienable rights" was set forth, it became evident that those rights applied only to white men (438 U.S. 265,388, 1978). It was interpreted in a manner that was void of equality and legitimated the denial of human rights. Marshall was incensed that when an effort was exerted by a State to rectify past discrimination, the Constitution would become a barrier for such a remedy.

The thrust of Marshall's argument centered around the history of this country and its treatment of people of color. He reminded the Court, that "African Americans had been dragged to this country in chains and sold into slavery, and had since endured centuries of unequal treatment" (438 U.S. 265,388, 1978). Justice Marshall's discourse put this decision in perspective with the history of African Americans from the Civil War Amendments *to Plessy v. Ferguson* 163 U.S. 537 (1896), through *Brown v. Board of Education* 347 U.S. 483 (1954).

Marshall pointed out that the quest for equality for African Americans appeared as an unattainable dream. He wrote that "African Americans, based on the 1970 Census, at this time represented 11.5% of the population, but accounted for only 1.2% of the lawyers and judges, 2% of the physicians, 2.3% of the dentists, 1.1% of the engineers and 2.6% of the college and university professors" (438 U.S. 265,396, 1978). Justice Marshall emphasized that the correlation between these figures and the historical unequal treatment of African Americans could not be denied. He advocated that "in light of the sorry history of discrimination and its devastating impact on the lives of African Americans, bringing African Americans into the mainstream of American life should be a state of interest of the highest order" (438 U.S. 265,396, 1978). It was Marshall's belief that failure to attain this objective was a guarantee that America would forever remain a divided society (438 U.S. 265,396, 1978). Justice Marshall contended that the Fourteenth Amendment did not require acceptance of this fate. He wrote, "neither history nor past Supreme Court cases gave any support to the conclusion that a university could not remedy the cumulative effects of society's discrimination by giving consideration to race in an effort to increase the number and percentage of African American doctors" (438 U.S. 265,396, 1978).

Justice Marshall's arguments pointed out inconsistencies in *Bakke* compared to decisions of the previous term. In *United Jewish Organization v. Carey*, 430 U.S. 144 (1977), Marshall noted that "the Court upheld a New York reapportionment plan that was deliberately drawn on the basis of race to enhance the electoral powers of African Americans and Puerto Ricans" (438 U.S. 265,399, 1978). The plan incorporated diluting the electoral strength of the Hasidic Jewish community. In this case, Marshall stated, "the Court was willing to sanction the remedial use of a racial classification, even though it disadvantaged otherwise innocent individuals" (438 U.S. 265,399,1978). In *California v. Goldfarb*, 430 U.S. 199 (1977), Marshall noted that "the Court recognized the permissibility of remedying past societal discrimination through the use of otherwise disfavored classifications" (438 U.S. 265,399, 1978). Based on established precedent, there was nothing to suggest that a university could not adopt the action in question to remedy past discrimination (438 U.S. 265,399, 1978).

In a stunning conclusion, Justice Marshall advocated, "that it was ironic that after several hundred years of class-based discrimination against African Americans, the Court was unwilling to hold a class-based remedy for discrimination" (438 U.S. 265,400, 1978). He stated, "in refusing to uphold that policy, the Court was ignoring the fact that for several hundred years, African Americans have been discriminated against, not just as individuals, but solely on the basis of skin color" (438 U.S. 265,400, 1978). It was Justice Marshall's contention that in view of the historical mistreatment of African Americans, the Court should allow "societal institutions" the opportunity to review race when determining the positions of "influence, affluence, and prestige in America" (438 U.S. 265,401, 1978). He emphasized that "for far too long, the doors have been shut for African Americans to these positions and there now must be a willingness to take steps to open those doors" (438 U.S. 265,401, 1978).

Marshall expressed a fear that the Court had come full circle. After the Civil War, the U.S. Government started several "affirmative action programs" (438 U.S. 265,402, 1978). The United States Supreme Court, in the Civil Rights Cases and *Plessy v. Ferguson*, both of which were cited earlier, destroyed the movement toward complete equality. Marshall pointed out, "that for almost a century no action was taken, and this non-action was with the tacit approval of the Courts" (438 U.S. 265,402, 1978). The Court was then confronted with the legal issues in *Brown v. Board of Education* and the Civil Rights Acts of Congress, followed by numerous affirmative action programs. Now, he argued, "the Court has again stepped in to stop affirmative action programs of the type used by the University of California" ( 438 U.S. 265,387-402, 1978).

**Legal Implications of Bakke**

According to Powell's opinion, the message is clear: whether it is called a goal or quota, reserving a specific number of class spaces for people of color is prohibited. The use of race in a flexible admission policy designed to enhance student diversity, however, is permissible (Fisher, 1979). The Court, according to Fisher (1979), never indicated that race not be given consideration. It did, however, specify certain criteria which had to be met. The goals of a special admissions program must be well thought out, clearly stated, and defined. The goals must serve a valid educational purpose. A race-conscious admissions plan must be related, with some degree of precision, to the objectives sought by the enactment of the plan (Fisher, 1979).

There were several aspects of the *Bakke* decision that had an adverse effects on the graduate education and professional development of African Americans (Spratlen, 1979). The first effect was that the *Bakke* decision validated the notion of reverse discrimination and placed in jeopardy all compensatory efforts to correct past discrimination. As a result, establishing a target objective, goal or otherwise specifying a remedy for past exclusions and restrictions were now suspect and possibly subjected to being interpreted as a quota. A possible repercussion of that interpretation was that admission personnel would be discouraged from using numbers to attain goals and provide a basis for redefining or maintaining standards of diversity in student enrollments.

The second adverse effect was that the *Bakke* decision severely limits affirmative action programs, guidelines and procedures. It now appeared that benign or benevolent quotas had been invalidated. The end result was that "*Bakke*-decision thinking" justified actions that, in effect, deny opportunities to African Americans (Spratlen, 1979).

The third effect argued by Spratlen was that the *Bakke* decision produced a chilling effect on all affirmative action efforts. Anti-affirmative action forces now have a legitimate precedent to follow. This decision reinforced the rising tide of racial conservatism and retrenchment from affirmative action.

According to Spratlen (1979), the fourth effect of the *Bakke* decision added loopholes in administrative and judicial as well as regulatory proceedings regarding affirmative action. The vagueness of the *Bakke* decision meant trouble for African Americans. In answering the query of what it meant to consider race as a plus, Spratlen (1979) responded that it essentially meant whatever individual decisions makers and committees interpreted it to mean, short of specifying quotas. The by-product of this type application could very well result in an unfavorable future for African American educational and professional opportunities based on affirmative action and selective admissions. Spratlen also indicated that the *Bakke* decision deliberately confused language by equating quotas with goals and timetables. He suggested that opponents of affirmative action, when it suited their purposes, erroneously defined goals and the timetables for realizing them as quotas.

The National Association for the Advancement of Colored People (NAACP) argued in support of the special admissions program at Davis. The NAACP was disappointed by the decision of the Court, but did not view the decision as a defeat (*Crisis*, 1979). The NAACP's viewpoint was that the most serious harm created by *Bakke* was the problem of public misconception. The NAACP advocated that those who had never approved of affirmative action to integrate society will attempt to dismantle existing affirmative action plans predicated on *Bakke* (*Crisis*, 1979). The *Bakke* case was perceived as more of a symbolic victory than an actual one. In spite of *Bakke*, the NAACP continued to encourage all educational institutions to renew their commitment to affirmative action and to indicate their commitment through public announcements, and by the enhancement of efforts to increase the representation of African Americans in their student body, faculties, and administration (*Crisis*, 1979).

Binion (1987) set forth the argument that many parties with an interest were not represented in *Bakke*. African American medical students and those aspiring to become medical students were not involved. The NAACP was barred from participation in the actual litigation process. The informational and argumentative basis of the decision suffered immensely from the lack of inclusion of interested parties seeking to defend the medical school's affirmative action program.

Binion further stated that the Courts that judged the legality of the Davis program were not informed of the school's other affirmative action program. She pointed out that the "other" affirmative action program referred to a policy at Davis allowing five places in the entering class to be filled at the discretion of the Dean. These were normally used to admit the children of politicians along with other influential citizens. The existence of the "Dean's places" were relevant in defining the context of disparate. It must be considered whether the special "privilege" for the privileged embodied in the Dean's places was simply "balanced," in part, by the special admissions policy. Binion is of the opinion that the Dean's places did not meet the requirements of the Equal Protection Clause and Title VI of the 1964 Civil Rights Act. Binion presented an interesting query as to whether or not the Dean's places prevented Bakke from admission (Binion, 1987).

Binion also implied that Bakke's age could have been a key factor in the denial of admission. Almost all medical schools openly acknowledge that applicants over the age of thirty "must be unusually highly qualified" (Binion, 1987). There is no reason to assume that Bakke overcame this obstacle, especially given the refusal of the admissions committee to place him on the waiting list.

A year later (1979), the Supreme Court would review the effect of a voluntary affirmative action plan designed to eradicate past historical discrimination in employment. The case would also involve the issue of set-asides in the implementation of the affirmative action plan. The Court would now be asked to address congressional intent in passing Title VII of the 1964 Civil Rights Act, 42 U.S.C. 2000e et seq. It is important to note that the affirmative action plan was implemented by a private corporation.

## United Steelworkers of American, AFL-CIO-CLC v. Weber, 443 U.S. 193 (1979)

In 1974, "United Steelworkers of America (USWA) and Kaiser Aluminum and Chemical Corporation (Kaiser) entered into a master collective-bargaining agreement covering terms and conditions of employment at fifteen Kaiser plants" (443 U.S. 193, 1979). The agreement was established in hopes of providing a mechanism for the purpose of removing "racial imbalance found in Kaiser's almost exclusively white craftwork forces" (443 U.S. 193, 1979). The plan established hiring goals for African Americans at each Kaiser plant so that it would reflect the percentage of African Americans in the respective local labor forces (443 U.S. 193,198, 1979). In order to enable plants to attain the criteria outlined in the affirmative action plan, on-the-job training programs were established to teach unskilled production workers (African American and white) necessary skills to become a craftworker. The collective-bargaining agreement set forth for African American employees "fifty percent of the openings in the newly created in-plant training programs" (443 U.S. 193,198, 1979).

The challenges of this case arose from the implementation of the affirmative action plan at Kaiser's plant in Gramercy, Louisiana. Prior to 1974, Kaiser hired only craftworkers with previous experience. With few exceptions, African Americans were excluded due to a lack of previous experience. Therefore, pursuant to an established "national agreement," Kaiser amended its hiring practice in the Gramercy plant (443 U.S. 193,199, 1979). Consequently, Kaiser established a training program for the purpose of yielding "trained craftworkers" (443 U.S. 193,199, 1979). The training program provided that "selection of craft trainees was made on the basis of seniority with a provisional measure that at least fifty percent of the new trainees would be African American until the percentage of trainees approximated the percentage of African Americans in the local labor force" (443 U.S. 193,199, 1979).

The facts of the case revealed that "during the inception of the affirmative action plan, thirteen craft trainees were selected from the Gramercy workforce (six white and seven African American). However, the most senior African American had less seniority than several white employees whose bids for admission were rejected" (443 U.S. 193, 199,

1979). As a result, Weber (a white production worker) instituted a class action suit in the U.S. District Court for the Eastern District of Louisiana.

Weber's complaint charged that the filling of craft trainees positions at the Gramercy plant pursuant to the affirmative action plan resulted in junior African American employees attaining training preference over senior white employees. Weber maintained that the implementation of the affirmative action program violated Title VII, 42 U.S.C. 2000e-2(d) of the 1964 Civil Rights Act. This section provides that; "it shall be an unlawful employment practice for an employer, labor organization, or joint labor-management committee controlling apprenticeship or other training or retraining, including on-the-job training programs to discriminate against any individual because of his race, color, religion, sex, or national origin in admission to, or employment in, any program established to provide apprenticeship or other training" (42 U.S.C. 2000e-2(d)). The District Court held that the plan violated Title VII and granted a permanent injunction against predicating admission to the training program on race. The Court of Appeals of the Fifth Circuit ruled, "that all employment preferences based on race, inclusive of those preferences incidental to *bona fide* affirmative action plans, violated Title VII's prohibition against racial discrimination in employment" (443 U.S. 193,200, 1979). The Supreme Court granted *certiorari*.

The majority of the Court (Brennan, Stewart, White, Marshall, and Blackmun) established a 5-2 decision reversing the findings of the two lower courts (443 U.S. 193, 200, 1979). The dissenting opinion was written by Chief Justice Burger and Rehnquist. Justice Powell and Stevens took no part in the consideration or decision of the case (443 U.S. 193,195, 1979 ).

The majority opinion given by Brennan began by emphasizing the Kaiser-USWA plan did not violate state action. Brennan stated that "no allegation of a violation of the Equal Protection Clause of the Fourteenth Amendment existed" (443 U.S. 193,200, 1979). The Court instead discussed the fact that the Kaiser-USWA plan was a voluntary adopted plan by which private parties were seeking to eradicate historical racial segregation (443 U.S. 193,201, 1979). Therefore, it was the Court's contention that the prohibition against racial discrimination in Title VII must be reviewed with consideration for the legislative history as well as the context pertaining to the origin of the Act.

The Court suggested, "from a historical perspective, Congress' primary concern in enacting the prohibition against racial discrimination in Title

VII was with regard to the economic plight of African Americans" (443, U.S. 193,194, 1979). The focal point addressed in the prohibition against racial discrimination in employment was the predicament of having an insufficient number of job openings for African Americans that had traditionally been closed to them (443 U.S. 193,194, 1979). Reviewing the legislative history, the Court reasoned, that "the wording of the statute provided the catalyst to cause employers and unions to self-examine and self-evaluate their employment practices and thus endeavor to eliminate so far as possible the last vestiges of an unfortunately and ignominious page in the history of this country" (443 U.S. 193, 194, 1979). In accordance with this viewpoint, the Court proposed that it was clear to Congress that the essence of the problem was to open employment opportunities for African Americans in occupations heretofore denied. It was this issue, according to the Court, that Title VII was drafted to address (443 U.S. 193,203, 1979).

The Court supported their analysis with an in-depth examination of the language and legislative history of Title VII. It was the Court's interpretation, that "had Congress meant to prohibit all race-conscious affirmative action efforts, it easily could have answered any objections by providing such language" ( 443 U.S. 193,205, 1978). Hence, "Congress would have specifically stated that Title VII would not require or permit racially preferential integration efforts" (443 U.S. 193,205, 1979). The Court stressed that Congress did not choose that course of action (443 U.S. 193,205, 1979). Thus, the Court held, that "Title VII's prohibition against racial discrimination does not condemn all private, voluntary, race-conscious affirmative action plans" (443 U.S. 193,208, 1979).

In his conclusion, Brennan reasoned that the Kaiser-USWA plan was within the guidelines of permissibility. Brennan further argued, that "the purpose of the plan mirrored those of the statute, in that it was designed to break down old patterns of racial segregation and hierarchy" (443 U.S. 193,208, 1979). Brennan further stated that the focal point of Title VII was to increase employment opportunities traditionally closed to African Americans. The Kaiser plan, according to Brennan, "does not unnecessarily trammel the interest of white employees, neither does it require the discharge of white workers and their replacement with new African American employees" (443 U.S. 193, 208, 1979). According to Brennan, "the plan created an absolute bar to the advancement of white employees since half of those trained in the program would be white" (443 U.S. 193,208-209, 1979). Brennan stated, "the plan was a temporary measure not intended to maintain racial balance, but simply to eliminate a manifest racial imbalance" (443 U.S. 193,208, 1979).

In support of the majority, Justice Blackmun stated, "in assessing a *prima facie* case of Title VII liability, the composition of the employer's workforce is compared to the composition of the pool of workers who meet the valid job qualifications" (443 U.S. 193,208, 1979). Blackmun wrote that Title VII was designed to provide "guaranteed equal opportunity" for all citizens. Therefore, it should not be implied that Title VII negated private affirmative action plans from providing a remedy (443 U.S. 193, 214, 1979). Blackmun concluded by reiterating the opinion given by the majority, that "the Kaiser plan operated as a temporary tool for remedying past discrimination without attempting to maintain a previously achieved balance" (443 U.S. 193, 216, 1979).

The dissenting opinion was delivered by Chief Justice Burger. Burger began by explaining, "the view of the majority on the Court was contrary to the explicit language of Title VII, and was arrived at by a means totally incompatible with long established principles of separation of powers" (443 U.S. 193,216, 1979). Burger noted that under the guise of statutory "construction," the Court, "effectively rewrites Title VII to achieve what it regards as a desirable result" (443 U.S. 193,216, 1979). By amending the statute, through interpretation, Burger stated that this action allowed the statute to take on an undesired meaning for both parties (443 U.S. 193,216, 1979). Burger stated, "the quota embodied in the collective-bargaining agreement between Kaiser and Steelworkers unquestionably discriminates on the basis of race against individual employees seeking admission to on-the-job training programs" (443 U.S. 193,217, 1979). He reasoned, that "Congress may not have gone far enough in correcting the effects of past discrimination when it enacted Title VII" (443 U.S. 193,218, 1979). Burger emphasized a failure to understand how "voluntary compliance with the no-discrimination principle of Title VII" as currently written will be achieved by permitting employers to discriminate against some individuals and at the same time create preferential treatment (443 U.S. 193,218, 1979). Burger concluded his argument with the proposition that if affirmative action programs such as the Kaiser plan are permissible, it is a congressional issue and not judicial one (443 U.S. 193,218, 1979). Burger stated, that "the majority justice's exceeded the scope of their authority and rewrote a crucial part of Title VII to reach their desired result" (443 U.S. 193,218, 1979).

Justice Rehnquist joined in the dissent and wrote, that "the operative sections of Title VII prohibited racial discrimination in employment" (443 U.S. 193,220 1979). Specifically, Rehnquist stated "the language of Title VII prohibits a covered employer from considering race when making an employment decision" (443 U.S. 193,220, 1979). Rehnquist suggested, "the Court heretofore had never wavered in its understanding of Title VII in that it prohibited all racial discrimination in employment" (443 U.S. 193,220, 1979). Fashioning the majority justices as "escape artists," he indicated that the Court eluded clear statutory language and formulated a language permitting considerations of race in making employment decisions (443 U.S. 193,222, 1979). Rehnquist noted, that "Kaiser's racially discriminatory admission quota was flatly prohibited by the plain language of Title VII" (443 U.S. 193,228, 1979).

Rehnquist's legislative and historical interpretation of Title VII acknowledged that the issue of discrimination against African Americans was the primary impetus for passage. Nevertheless, he reasoned, "Congress did not intend to leave employers free to discriminate against white people" (443 U.S. 193, 229, 1979). He strongly suggested only a concise examination of Title VII would accurately define congressional intent. This conclusion was supported in his presentation of an in depth re-examination of the congressional debate on Title VII (443 U.S. 193,231-254, 1979). Rehnquist concluded his argument purporting that there was no device more destructive to the concept of equality than a quota. Whether described as "benign discrimination" or "affirmative action," a racial quota was nonetheless "a creator of a caste with preferential treatment" (443 U.S. 193,254, 1979). "Title VII outlawed all racial discrimination, recognizing that no discrimination based on race was benign and no action disadvantaging a person because of their color was affirmative" (443 U.S. 193,254, 1979).

This case represented the Court's first decision regarding a private voluntary affirmative action program designed to eradicate historical racial discrimination in employment. The Court's opinion established the legal precedent that Title VII, 42 U.S.C. 2000e, allowed preferential treatment. The Court established the guidelines for future affirmative action programs. The Court, in *Weber*, set forth the principle that an affirmative action program may not unnecessarily trammel the interests of white employees and the plan must be a temporary measure. It may be inferred that the concluding statement in Rehnquist's dissenting opinion provides insight into the longevity of this decision. Rehnquist postulated, that "by going not merely beyond, but directly against Title VII's language and legislative history, the Court has sown all reasoning to the wind" (443 U.S. 193,255, 1979). Later courts, according to Rehnquist, "will face the impossible task of reaping the whirlwind" (443 U.S. 193,255, 1979).

During the 1980's, the issue of set-asides based on race and ethnicity would confront the justices. The Court now adjudicated whether or not set-aside contracts designed to enhance African American businesses along with other people of color were permissible under Title VII and the Equal Protection Clause of the Fourteenth Amendment. In future cases, the question of Due Process in the Fifth Amendment would be included as a factor in determining the legality of affirmative action cases.

According to Amaker (1983), the Reagan administration had an impact on the Court and it's adjudication of affirmative action cases. The Reagan administration was elected with the perception that there should be a mandate for the reduction of affirmative action programs and the advancement of civil rights legislation (Amaker, 1983). The political philosophy of Reagan was seen in the judicial philosophy of the justices appointed by him (i.e., Rehnquist, Scalia, O'Connor, and Kennedy). The political philosophy of Reagan combined with that of the Court beginning in the 1980s was viewed as creating a trend leading to the reversal of existing policies and programs in the area of affirmative action and civil rights (Amaker, 1983).

## Fullilove v. Klutznick, Secretary of Commerce, 448 U.S. 448 (1980)

The court reviewed the issue of set-asides in *Fullilove*. In May of 1977, Congress enacted the Public Works Employment Act of 1977, Public Law 95-28, 91 Stat. 116. The 1977 amendment "authorized an additional $4 billion for federal grants by the Secretary of Commerce on behalf of the Economic Development Administration (EDA) to state and local governmental entities for use in local public works projects" (448 U.S. 448,453, 1980). Included within the amendment was the provision of Section 103(f)(2) referred to as the "minority business enterprise" or the MBE provision. The MBE provision outlined the following measures:

Except to the extent that the Secretary determines otherwise, no grant shall be made under this Act for any local public works project unless the applicant gives satisfactory assurance to the Secretary that at least 10 per centum of the amount of each grant shall be expended for minority business enterprise. For the purpose of this paragraph, the term minority business enterprise means a business with at least 50 per centum of which is owned by minority group members or, in case of a publicly owned business, at least 51 per centum of the stock of which is owned by minority group members. For the purpose of the preceding sentence, minority group members are citizens of the United States who are Negroes, Spanish-speaking, Orientals, Indians, Eskimos, and Aleuts (91 Statute 116, 42 U.S.C. Section 7605(f)(2); 448 U.S. 448,454, 1980).

This amendment provided the impetus for *Fullilove v. Klutznick* (448 U.S. 448, 1980).

In view of impending regulations, grantees and private contractors were required, as much as feasible, to attain the 10% MBE requirement. "The plan included seeking all available, qualified, *bona fide* MBE's and soliciting assistance from the Office of Minority Business Enterprise, the Small Business Administration, or other sources to assist MBE's in obtaining required work capital, as well as giving guidance through the intricacies of the bidding process" (448 U.S. 448,454, 1980). It should be noted that administrative programs allowed an administration waiver of the "10% MBE requirement on a case-by-case basis if it could be demonstrated that, despite affirmative efforts, such a level of participation could not be achieved without departing from the program's objectives" (448 U.S. 448,456-462, 1980). The program also provided a mechanism to ensure that only *bona fide* MBE's were encompassed in the program. The objective was to prevent minority firms from participating that heretofore had not been "impaired by past discrimination" (448 U.S. 448,462-463, 1980).

As a result of the amendment to the Public Works Employment Act of 1977, "on November 30, 1977, petitioners filed a complaint in the U.S. District Court for the Southern District of New York seeking declaratory and injunctive relief to enjoin enforcement of the MBE provision" (448 U.S. 448,455, 1980). "The petitioners included several associations of construction contractors and subcontractors, and a firm engaged in heating, ventilation, and air conditioning work" (448 U.S. 448,455, 1980). "The complaint alleged that they had sustained economic injury due to the enforcement of the 10% MBE requirement and the MBE provision, on its face violated the Equal Protection Clause of the Fourteenth Amendment, the equal protection component of the Due Process Clause of the Fifth

Amendment, and various statutory anti-discrimination provisions" (448 U.S. 448,455, 1980).

In a hearing, "held the day the complaint was filed, the District Court denied a requested temporary restraining order" (448 U.S. 448,455, 1980). On December 19, 1977, the District Court issued a memorandum opinion upholding the validity of the MBE program and denying the injunctive relief sought" (448 U.S. 448,455, 1980).

The United States Court of Appeals for the Second Circuit affirmed the lower Court's decision, stating that "even under the most exacting standard of review, the MBE provision passes constitutional muster" (448 U.S. 448,455, 1980). In consideration of the context of many years of governmental efforts to remedy past racial and ethnic discrimination, the Court of Appeals held, that "it was difficult to imagine any purpose for the MBE program other than the remediation of past discrimination" (448 U.S. 448, 456, 1980). The Court of Appeals maintained that a number of pertinent factors contributed to the legitimacy of the MBE provision. The most significant factor was, "the narrow focus and limited extent of the statutory and administrative program regarding size, impact, and duration" (448 U.S. 448,456, 1980). Thus, the Court of Appeals rejected the challenge, that "the 10% MBE requirement violated the equal protection guarantees of the Constitution" (448 U.S. 448,456, 1980). The case was then appealed by plaintiffs to the United States Supreme Court.

The 6-3 judgement of the Supreme Court was given by Chief Justice Burger, with White and Powell joining. Powell wrote a concurring opinion. Another concurring opinion was filed by Marshall, with Brennan and Blackmun joining. A dissenting opinion was filed by Stewart, with Rehnquist joining, and a separate dissent was given by Stevens (448 U.S. 448,452, 1980).

The judgement of the Court focused first on the legislative and administrative intent of the Employment Act of 1977. The Court found, that "the legislative and administrative background of the Act provided that grantees who participated would not employ procurement practices that Congress had decided would result in the perpetuation of prior discrimination, i.e., the impairing or foreclosing of access to public contracting opportunities by minority business" (448 U.S. 448,456-473, 1980). Burgers' opinion focused on the proper powers of Congress to implement this Act. He indicated, that "Congress could have implemented the Act under congressional spending power authorization, the Commerce Clause, or the Fourteenth Amendment to the Constitution"

(448 U.S. 448,473-478, 1980). Therefore, the MBE provision was within valid congressional jurisdiction.

The judgement of the Court as filed by Burger focused on whether Congress could use racial and ethnic criteria in a limited manner regarding conditions attached to a federal grant (448 U.S. 448,480, 1980). The Court responded by stating, that "the use of race and ethnicity was a valid means for accomplishing its constitutional objectives and the MBE provision, on its face, had not violated the equal protection component of the Due Process Clause of the Fifth Amendment" (448 U.S. 448,480-492, 1980). Burger reasoned, that "the MBE program's remedial context did not contain the requirement that Congress act in a color-blind fashion" (448 U.S. 448,482, 1980).

The Court's judgement stated, that "the MBE program was not unconstitutionally defective because it disappointed the expectation of access to a portion of government contracting opportunities of white firms that were innocent of any prior discriminatory actions" (448 U.S. 448,484, 1980). Furthermore, "when effectuating a limited and properly tailored remedy to cure the effects of prior discrimination, a sharing of the burden by innocent parties was permissible" (448 U.S. 448,484-485, 1980). "In discussing the merits of inclusiveness, i.e., whether the MBE program limited its benefit to special minority groups, rather than extending its remedial objectives to all businesses whose access to government contracting was impaired by disadvantage or discrimination, the Court raised the issue of legislative intent" (448 U.S. 448,450, 1980). The implication was, that "Congress had not sought to give select minority groups a preferred standing in the construction industry, but had instituted a remedial program to place them on a equitable footing with respect to public contracting opportunities" (448 U.S. 448,486, 1980). There had been no showing in *Fullilove* that "Congress inadvertently supported invidious discrimination by excluding from coverage an identifiable minority group that had been the victim of a degree of disadvantage and discrimination equal to or greater than that suffered by the groups encompassed by the MBE program" (448 U.S. 448,486, 1980). The Court also held, that "the MBE program was not over-inclusive in that it bestowed benefits on businesses identified by racial or ethnic criteria which could not be justified on the basis of competitive criteria or as a remedy for the present effects of identified prior discrimination" (448 U.S. 448,486, 1980). The Court stated, "the MBE provision, with due account for its administrative program, provided a reasonable assurance that application of racial or ethnic criteria would be narrowly limited to accomplishing the remedial objectives of Congress" (448 U.S. 448,486, 1980). Any misapplication of the program would be promptly and adequately remedied by utilizing administrative procedures (448 U.S. 448,486-487, 1980). In conclusion, Burger stated, that "when a program narrowly tailored by Congress to achieve its objective comes under judicial evaluation, it should be upheld if the courts are satisfied that the legislative intent, along with projected administration of the program, gave reasonable assurance that the program would function within constitutional limitations" (448 U.S. 448,491, 1980).

In a separate concurring opinion, Powell noted, that "the MBE provision of the Act was justified as a remedy that served the compelling governmental interest in eradicating the continuing effects of past discrimination identified by Congress" (448 U.S. 448,496, 1980). Accordingly, Congress had reasonably concluded that private and governmental discrimination had contributed to the negligible percentage of public contracts awarded minority contractors (448 U.S. 448,503, 1980). Justice Powell suggested, that "intentional discriminatory action denying minority contractors economic opportunities was covered under the provisions of Title VII of the Civil Rights Act of 1964, 42 U.S.C. Section 2000d et seq., as well as provisions outlined in the Fourteenth Amendment" (448 U.S. 448,506, 1980).

Powell also addressed the legality of set-asides. He contended that a race-conscious remedy should not be approved without consideration of the effect of set-asides on innocent parties (448 U.S. 448,514, 1980). In view of the facts of *Fullilove*, he concluded, that "the set-asides were permissible in that they created a reasonably necessary means of furthering the compelling governmental interest in redressing the discrimination affecting minority contractors" (448 U.S. 448,515, 1980).

Justice Marshall presented a concurring opinion, joined by Brennan and Blackmun. In his declaration, Marshall pointed out, that "the 10% minority set-aside provision in Public Works Employment Act of 1977 passed constitutional muster" (448 U.S. 448,517, 1980). As such, set-asides did not per se violate the Equal Protection Clause of the Fourteenth Amendment. The MBE (set-aside) provisions were constitutional in that they were "narrowly tailored and simultaneously avoided stigmatizing and penalizing those least able to protect themselves in the political process" (448 U.S. 448,521, 1980). Marshall concluded, that "the set-aside provisions of *Fullilove* were in direct correlation with his view in *Bakke-*

-they were designed to remedy the present effects of past racial discrimination" (448 U.S. 448,521, 1980).

A dissenting opinion was delivered by Justice Stewart with Rehnquist joining. Justice Stewart emphasized that "the Constitution is color-blind and neither knows nor tolerates classes among citizens. The law regards man as man and takes no account of his surroundings or color" (448 U.S. 448,523, 1980). He stated, that "the view established eighty-four years ago in *Plessy v. Ferguson*, 163 U.S. 537 (1896) was also applicable in *Fullilove*" (448 U.S. 448,523, 1980). The equal protection standard of the Constitution had a clear and central meaning, "the absolute prohibition of invidious discrimination by government" (448 U.S. 448,523, 1980).

In opposition to the Marshall camp, Stewart maintained that MBE provisions denied equal protection of the law (448 U.S. 448,527, 1980). Stewart stressed, that "preferential treatment for a group predicated on race or ethnicity was actual discrimination" (448 U.S. 448,529, 1980). Furthermore, "the decision reached by the Court forced statute books to invoke the odious practice of delineating qualities that defines one's racial identity" (448 U.S. 448,531, 1980). As a result, notions of racial entitlement would be fostered and private discrimination would be encouraged (448 U.S. 448,532, 1980).

Justice Stevens also dissented, but for different reasons. He emphasized "the issue of the unconstitutionality of set-asides predicated on race" (448 U.S. 448,532-536, 1980). Foremost in his argument was the premise, that "statutory preference was a perverse form of reparation for the members of the injured class" (448, U.S. 448,548, 1980). The random distribution to a favored few was a poor form of compensation for an injury shared by many. He did not share the conviction, that "the MBE provision contained an absolute prohibition against any statutory classification based on race" (448 U.S. 448,548, 1980). Instead, he advocated, that "the MBE provisions imposed special obligations to scrutinize any governmental decision-making process that draws nation-wide distinctions between citizens on the basis of their race and incidentally discriminated against a non-citizen in the preferred racial classes" (448 U.S. 448,548, 1980). Stevens concluded, that "the MBE provision of the Employment Act of 1977 was not narrowly tailored because it simply raised too many serious questions that Congress failed to answer or even address in a responsible manner" (448 U.S. 448,552, 1980).

The case *Fullilove*, is important in the realm of affirmative action because it allowed the Court to constitutionally impart set-aside programs.

The Court specifically was supportive of set-aside programs that are narrowly tailored and do not unnecessarily trammel the interest of others. Furthermore, this case was important because it meant that set-asides are constitutional if they are designed to eradicate the effects of past racial discrimination in the area of employment. At this juncture, the view of the Supreme Court was that set-aside for MBE's do, in fact, pass constitutional muster.

In the initial case of *Stotts* and later during the 1986 term, the United States Supreme Court reviewed the legality of the constitutionality of collective-bargaining agreements regarding lay-off practices and the issue of seniority. The Court was requested to determine the legality of a lay-off plan designed by an educational school board to compensate for historical discriminatory practices (*Wygant v. Jackson Board of Education*, 476 U.S. 267, 1986). The other legal issue brought before the Court involved the constitutionality of affirmative hiring policies. The challenged practice focused specifically on discriminatory employment against nonwhite workers in the area of recruitment, selection, training, and admissions to unions. At issue before the Court was also the legality of a Special Employment, Training, Education and Recruitment Fund (*Sheet Metal Workers v. EEOC*, 478 U.S. 421, 1986).

### Firefighters Local Union No. 1784 v. Stotts, 467 U.S. 561(1984)

In *Stotts* (1984) the legality of lay off plans and seniority systems were the focal issues. The issue in this case centered on a consent decree enacted by the Memphis, Tennessee, Fire Department. In 1977, Carl Stotts filed a complaint charging the Memphis Fire Department and certain city officials with engaging in a pattern or practice of implementing hiring and promotion decisions predicated on race in violation of Title VII of the Civil Rights Act of 1964 (42 U.S.C. Section 2000e et seq. and 42 U.S.C. Sections 1981 and 1983). The case was certified as a class action suit and consolidated with action filed by Fred Jones, claiming a denial of promotion based on race. An approved consent decree was entered by the Federal District Court, on April 25, 1980 (467 U.S. 561,565, 1984).

The purpose of the consent decree was "to remedy the hiring and promotional practices" of the fire department regarding the employment of African Americans. "The city of Memphis agreed to promote thirteen named individuals and provided back-pay to eighty-one employees of the fire department" (467 U.S. 561,565,1984). The department adopted the "long-term goal" of increasing the proportion of African American representation in each job classification reflective of African Americans in the labor force in Shelby County, Tennessee (467 U.S. 561,565, 1984). "The 1980 consent decree included provisions that established the interim hiring goal for filling on an annual basis fifty percent of the departmental vacancies with qualified African American applicants. The decree further provided for the awarding of twenty percent of the promotions in each category to African Americans" (467 U.S. 561,566, 1984).

Due to a projected budgetary deficit, the city of Memphis announced in early May of 1981, "the reduction of nonessential personnel throughout city government" (467 U.S. 561,566, 1984). The layoffs were based on the "last hired, first fired" rule under which city-wide seniority had been established (467 U.S. 561,566, 1984). Thus, seniority was determined based upon each employee's length of continuous service from the latest date of permanent employment. In essence, if a senior employee's position was eliminated, "the employee could bump down to a lower position rather than receive a layoff" (467 U.S. 561,566, 1984).

"On May 4, 1981, the Federal District Court entered a temporary restraining order forbidding the lay-off of any African American employee" (467 U.S. 561,566, 1984). The union was granted permission by the court to intervene, even though it was not an original party. During the preliminary injunction hearing, "it was revealed that fifty-five of the filled positions in the department at the time were designated for elimination, and thirty-nine of those positions were occupied by employees with bumping rights" (467 U.S. 561,567, 1984). At this time "forty of the least senior employees within the department were subjected to lay-offs" inclusive of twenty-five white and fifteen African American (467 U.S. 561,567, 1984). Consequently, it was discovered that "fifty-six percent of the employees hired since 1974 were African American (467 U.S. 561, 567, 1984).

The Federal District Court for the Western District of Tennessee, issued an injunction. The court ruled that the consent decree was in compliance with the city's seniority system and "was not adopted with intent to discriminate" (467 U.S. 561,567, 1984). The court realized that implementation of the layoff policy provided "a racially discriminating effect and the seniority system was not a *bona fide* plan" (467 U.S. 561, 567, 1984). The District Court ordered, that "the city not apply the seniority policy, since it resulted in the reduction of African Americans as lieutenants, drivers, inspectors and privates" (467 U.S. 561,567, 1984).

An approved modified layoff plan designed to protect African American employees was submitted. This layoff plan resulted in white employees with more seniority than African American employees receiving either layoffs or demotions in rank (467 U.S. 561,567, 1984).

On appeal, the Court of Appeals for the Sixth Circuit ruled that the District Court was wrong in finding that the seniority system of the city was not a *bona fide one* (467 U.S. 561,568, 1984). The Court of Appeals held that the District Court acted properly in preventing African Americans from being adversely affected by unanticipated layoffs. The rationale for the Court of Appeals was based on the fact that the District Court had authorization to "modify the consent decree because the new and unforseen events created a hardship on one of the parties to the consent decree" (467 U.S. 561,568, 1984). The Court of Appeals also held, that "the decree modification was not in violation of Title VII. It was argued that the claims set forth were moot, based on the fact that all of the white employees laid off were restored to their old positions one month after the layoff and demotion" (467 U.S. 561,569, 1984). Hence, the issue of mootness was presented as part of the litigation.

The majority of the Court (White, Burger, Powell, Rehnquist, O'Connor, and Stevens) split 6-3 in reversing the findings of the two lower courts (467 U.S. 561, 563, 1984). Justice Stevens filed an opinion concurring in the judgement. O'Connor filed a concurring opinion. The dissenting opinion was written by Blackmun, with Brennan and Marshall joining (467 U.S. 563).

Justice White wrote for the majority of the Court. The Court first ruled on the issue of mootness. It was noted, that "since all white employees laid off as a result of the injunction were restored to their duty, and the injunction was no longer effective, the case was now moot" (467 U.S. 561, 198). The Court, however, reasoned, that "the injunction was still in force and unless it was set aside, it required compliance regarding future layoffs" (467 U.S. 561,569, 1984). The issue was not whether the injunction was still in effect, but "whether the mandated modifications of the consent decree continued to have an impact on the involved parties" (467 U.S. 561,569, 1984). White wrote that the Court was not convinced that layoffs, if carried out in accordance with the seniority system, would violate the decree. Therefore, the Court stated that the case was not moot (467 U.S. 561,570, 1984). Even though the white employees who were laid off or demoted received restoration, "the employees had not been made whole again." Justice White stated, that "as long as the parties had a concrete interest in the outcome of the litigation, the case was not moot" (467 U.S. 561,571, 1984).

According to White, another key issue in the case was whether the Federal District Court exceeded its powers with the implementation of an injunction requiring the layoff of white employees with less seniority (467 U.S. 561,573, 1984). Regarding this issue, the Court's majority ruled that the Court of Appeals had erred. The Court stated, that "the city of Memphis had a general obligation to increase the proportion of African Americans in the fire department" (467 U.S. 561,575, 1984). According to the Court, "the decree's stated purpose was to remedy past hiring and promotion practices" (467 U.S. 561,575, 1984). White pointed out that the remedy of the consent decree was not inclusive of the displacement of white employees with seniority over African Americans (467 U.S. 561, 575, 1984). He stated, that "Title VII protected *bona fide* seniority systems and that it was inappropriate to deny an innocent employee the benefits of seniority in order to provide remedial relief" (467 U.S. 561, 575, 1984).

Justice O'Connor, in a separate concurring opinion, stated that the issue was not resolved by vacating the preliminary injunction. She stated, that "when collateral effects of a dispute remain and continue to affect the relationship of the litigants, the case was not moot" (467 U.S. 561,585, 1984). O'Connor further stated, that "Title VII affirmatively protected *bona fide* seniority systems which included those with discriminatory effects on people of color" (467 U.S. 561,587, 1984). O'Connor stated, that "a court may use remedial powers to modify a consent decree to prevent future violations and compensate identified victims of unlawful discrimination" (467 U.S. 561, 588, 1984).

In an additional concurring opinion, Justice Stevens wrote, that "the District Court's preliminary injunction remained reviewable because of the continued effects on the city's personnel policies" (467 U.S. 561,590, 1984). Stevens noted that the injunction implemented by the city would not be utilized in such a manner as to cause a decline in the percent of African Americans in the Memphis Fire Department. In the event of future lay-offs, the city could not use the seniority system (467 U.S. 561,590, 1984).

Stevens stated that the Court's discussion of Title VII was "wholly advisory." He suggested that the focal point of the case was the "administration of a consent decree" and not a legal issue relating to Title VII (467 U.S. 561,590, 1984). Consequently, Stevens noted, that "the governing factor was not Title VII but the consent decree" (467 U.S. 561, 591, 1984).

The dissenting opinion written by Blackmun, with Brennan and Marshall joining, began with a discussion of the Court's ignorance of the law. In discussing the issue of mootness, Blackmun wrote, that "the usual rule in federal cases was that an actual controversy must exist at stages of appellate process or *certiorari*, and not simply at the date the action was initiated" (467 U.S. 561,593, 1984). He further stated that a case becomes "moot" at that juncture when the "intervening acts" lead to the destruction, of the interest of those involved in the litigation. It was Blackmun's view, that "the controversy underlying the suit was whether the city of Memphis proposed a layoff plan that violated the 1980 consent decree" (467 U.S. 561,594, 1984). Blackmun implied that since implementation of the injunction, those laid off had been restored and the city had replaced everyone affected by the modified plan. Thus, "the preliminary injunction no longer restrained the city's conduct and the adverse relationship between the parties involved was negated" (467 U.S. 561,594, 1984). According to Blackmun, "the Court suggested that the back pay and seniority issues kept the case alive despite the absence of an adversarial party" (467 U.S. 561,597, 1984). Hence, it was Blackmun's view that the Court's decision was based on a theoretical defense that was never presented (467 U.S. 561,601, 1984).

*Stotts* (1984), presented the Court with the issue of deciding the legality of *bona fide* seniority systems. This case was important in the area of affirmative action, in that the Court held that a *bona fide* seniority system was protected under Title VII (467 U.S. 561,575, 1984). Justice O'Connor argued, that "Title VII affirmatively protected *bona fide* seniority systems which included those with discriminatory effects on people of color" (467 U.S. 561,587, 1984). Thus, in the instant case, O'Connor planted the seed that *bona fide* seniority systems were protected under Title VII, even when elements of discrimination were present.

### Wygant v. Jackson Board of Education, 476 U.S. 267 (1986)

In *Wygant v. Jackson Board of Education*, the case focused on the legality of school boards implementing preferential protection to individuals because of race or ethnicity as a protection against lay-offs The issue resulted from action taken in 1972 by the Jackson Board of Education (Michigan). Due to racial tensions permeating the community and subsequently extending to the schools, the Board of Education added a policy provision between the Board and the Jackson Education Association (Union) called the Collective-Bargaining Agreement (CBA) (476 U.S. 267,270, 1986). The CBA was designed to provide a "protective measure" for minority employees against lay-offs. Article XII of the CBA, provided that: "in the event that it becomes necessary to reduce the number of teachers through layoff from employment by the Board, teachers with the most seniority in the district shall be retained, except that at no time will there be a greater percentage of minority personnel laid off than the current percentage of minority personnel employed at the time of the layoff" (476 U.S. 267,270, 1986).

When it became apparent that lay-offs would be implemented, it was noted that adherence to the CBA would result in tenured white teachers receiving lay-offs. The CBA agreement caused the retention of probationary status for African American teachers. "The Board retained the tenured teachers and laid off probationary minority teachers, thereby failing to maintain the percentage of minority personnel that existed at the time of the lay-off" (476 U.S. 267,271, 1986). The Union and two African American teachers affected by the cut-back filed suit in federal court (476 U.S. 267,271, 1986). The claim was, that "the Board's failure to adhere to the lay-off provisions violated the Equal Protection Clause of the Fourteenth Amendment and Title VII of the Civil Rights Act of 1964" (476 U.S. 267,271, 1986). When reviewed by the Federal District Court, it held that "insufficient evidence" had been presented to support the alleged claim of discrimination (476 U.S. 267,271, 1986) The court also held there was a failure by the complainant to petition the Equal Employment Opportunity Commission (EEOC).

During the 1976-1977 and 1981-1982 school years, "non-minority teachers were laid off, while African American teachers with less seniority were retained" (476 U.S. 267,272, 1986). Consequently, the "non-minority teachers" brought litigation charging that their rights had been violated predicated on, "the Equal Protection Clause, Title VII, 42 U.S.C. Section 1983, along with other federal and state statues" (476 U.S. 267,272, 1986). The Federal District Court held, that "racial preferences were permissible under the Equal Protection Clause as an attempt to remedy societal discrimination by providing role models for African American schoolchildren and declared the lay-off provision constitutional" (476 U.S. 267,271, 1986). The Court of Appeals for the Sixth Circuit affirmed. The United States Supreme Court granted *certiorari* "to resolve the important issue of the constitutionality of race-based layoffs by public employers" (476 U.S. 267, 273, 1986).

In a 5-4 decision, "the Supreme Court declared the lay-off policy unconstitutional. The judgement of the Court was given by Justice Powell with Chief Justice Burger, and Justice Rehnquist joining. Justice O'Connor filed an opinion concurring in part with the opinion and concurring in the judgment, while Justice White concurred with the judgment. A dissenting opinion was filed by Marshall with Brennan and Blackmun joining. Justice Stevens filed a separate dissenting opinion" (476 U.S. 267,268, 1986).

Justice Powell began the opinion by focusing on the alleged violation of the Equal Protection Clause of the Fourteenth Amendment. Powell emphasized the Court's previous view regarding race-conscious mechanisms. He wrote, "the Court had consistently repudiated distinctions between citizens because of their ancestry as being odious to a free people whose institutions were founded upon the doctrine of equality" (476 U.S. 267,273, 1986). Powell pointed out that the utilization of "racial and ethnic" distinctions were subject to serious scrutiny as established by the legal precedents in *University of California Regents v. Bakke*, 438 U.S. 265, 291 (1978). The Court indicated that "the level of scrutiny did not change because the challenged classification operated against a group that had been historically subjected to governmental discrimination" (476 U.S. 267,273, 1986).

The reasoning of the Court centered on Article XII of the CBA, which created a classification based on race. The Court noted, that "any preference based on racial or ethnic criteria must necessarily receive a thorough examination to ensure that it does not conflict with constitutional guarantees" (476 U.S. 267,274, 1986). According to Powell, "the legal issues were whether a racial classification must be justified by a compelling government interest and whether the means selected by the state to effectuate its purpose must be narrowly tailored to the achievement of that goal" (476 U.S. 267,274, 1986). It was noted by Powell that "the Court has never held that societal discrimination alone is sufficient justification for racial classification" (476 U.S. 267,274, 1986). Rather, it has been the practice of the Court to have substantiated historical discrimination on behalf of the governmental unit in question in allowing racial classification as a desired remedy (476 U.S. 267,274, 1986).

Justice Powell suggested that the role model theory presented by the District Court lacked legal significance. According to this theory the Board had extended "discriminatory hiring and lay-off practices" beyond the allocated time frame required to establish a "legitimate remedial purpose" (476 U.S. 267,275, 1986). The role model theory, "does not necessarily bear a relationship to the harm caused by prior discriminatory hiring practices, but it actually was used to escape the obligation to remedy such practices by justifying the small percentage of African American teachers by reference to the small percentage of African American students" (476 U.S. 267,276, 1986). Powell wrote, that "the concept, if carried to its logical extreme, i.e., the idea that African American students are better off with African American teachers, could create the system the Court rejected in *Brown v. Board of Education*, 347 U.S. 483 (1954)" (476 U.S. 267,276, 1986). Powell indicated that evidence had fail to support a causal relation between "the disparity of African American students and the percentage of African American faculty" (476 U.S. 267,276, 1986).

In reference to public employers and lay-off policies, Powell stated, that "public employees, including public schools, also must act in accordance with a core purpose of the Fourteenth Amendment, which abolished governmental imposed race-based discrimination" (476 U.S. 267,277, 1986). The Court noted that in an affirmative action program, the employer in question must submit legal justification in supporting the desired legal remedy (476 U.S. 267,277, 1986).

Assessment of the race-conscious aspect of the lay-off plan was based on the application of strict scrutiny. Justice Powell indicated that under strict scrutiny, the method used to accomplish the State's purpose must be specifically and narrowly framed so as to accomplish the purpose. This view demonstrated the Court's consistency regarding preferential lay-off plans and imposition on innocent parties (476 U.S. 267, 282, 1986). Powell suggested that lay-offs disrupt lives in a manner of greater devastation than general hiring goals. It was contended that the lay-off plan was not sufficiently narrowly tailored. Powell reasoned, that "lay-offs impose the burden of achieving racial equality on particular individuals, often resulting in serious disruption of lives by creating an intrusive burden for others" (476 U.S. 267,282, 1986). Based on the protections provided by the Equal Protection Clause, the Board's lay-off measure was unconstitutional (476 U.S. 267,284, 1986).

The rationale for Justice O'Connor's opinion was based on the precept that the case required definitional application of the standards regarding the Equal Protection Clause, when a governmental agency agrees to give preference predicated on race or national origin in determining employee lay-offs (476 U.S. 267,284, 1986). Accordingly, "the specific question in this case was whether the Constitution prohibits a union and a local school board from developing a collective-bargaining agreement apportioning lay-offs between two racially determined groups in preserving the effects of affirmative action hiring policies" (476 U.S. 267,284, 1986). She reasoned, that "an agreed plan of race-consciousness need not be limited to the remedying of specific instances of identified discrimination for it to be ruled sufficiently narrowly tailored, or substantially related to the correction of prior discrimination by the state actor" (476 U.S. 267,287, 1986). O'Connor's explained that the Court based on established precedents held in favor of "affirmative action programs" that meet constitutional muster. It should be kept in mind, that Court approved affirmative action programs were those adhering to the established guidelines of "not imposing disproportionate harm on the interests, or unnecessarily trammel the rights of innocent individuals who are directly and adversely affected by a racial preference plan" (476 U.S. 267,287, 1986). O'Connor indicated, that "a governmental agency's interest in remedying societal discrimination that is, discrimination not traceable to its own actions cannot be viewed as sufficiently compelling in order to pass constitutional muster under the strict scrutiny principle" (476 U.S. 267,288, 1986).

Justice White concurred with the judgement. He asserted that "the School Board's policy required laying off non-minority teachers on the basis of race, including teachers with seniority, and retaining other teachers because of their race," even those with probationary status was in violation of the Equal Protection Clause (476 U.S. 267,294, 1986). White cited his personal belief, that it was unexplainable to integrate a workforce by discharging whites and hiring blacks to attain a diversified workforce (476 U.S. 267,295, 1986). He concluded the lay-off policy was unconstitutional. White indicated that the Court was not following its precedent.

Marshall's dissenting opinion was joined by Brennan and Blackmun. It was his belief, that "... a public employer, with the agreement of its employees, should be permitted to preserve the benefits of a legitimate and constitutional affirmative-action hiring plan even while reducing its workforce ..." (476 U.S. 267,296, 1986). In support of his view, Marshall reminded the Court that because of historical discriminatory practices by the Jackson School Board, the lay-off plan in question was a step in the "positive direction" (476 U.S. 267,297-298, 1986). Marshall stressed that Article XII, the focus of the litigation, was a compromise approved by both groups. "In 1982, white teachers claiming a right not to lose their jobs ahead of African American teachers with less seniority, petitioned the Court challenging Article XII as a violation of the Equal Protection Clause of the Fourteenth Amendment" (476 U.S. 267,299, 1986).

It was Marshall's view that the sole question present in this case was the constitutionality of the parties involved in establishing guidelines for implementation of a "affirmative hiring policies" (476 U.S. 267, 300, 1986). Based on the Court's rationale in *Bakke* (1978) and *Fullilove* (1980), Article XII passes constitutional muster, according to Marshall. His analysis of Article XII revealed, that "the provision was narrowly tailored because it allocated the impact of an unavoidable burden proportionately between two racial groups" (476 U.S. 267,309, 1986). The plan placed no absolute burden or benefit on one race; it also preserved the hierarchy of seniority in the selection of individuals for layoff" (476 U.S. 267,309, 1986). As such, Article XII did not use lay-offs as a means for increasing minority representation. Marshall wrote, that "Article XII was narrowly tailored and it did not interfere with the cherished American ethic of fairness in individual competition" (476 U.S. 267,309-310, 1986). The collective-bargaining process presented a legitimate mechanism for resolving the issue of discriminatory employment. Marshall stated, that "the best supporting evidence that Article XII was narrow could be found in the simple fact that the Article had been approved six times since its inception" (476 U.S. 267,312, 1986).

Justice Stevens, in a separate dissent, stated "the race-conscious lay-off policy met the criteria that the Court had previously established as permissible" (476 U.S. 267,318, 1986). Stevens suggested that the lay-offs were predicated on "economic conditions and special contractual protections intended to preserve the newly integrated character of the faculty in Jackson schools, and not on the basis of race" (476 U.S. 267,319, 1986).

In *Wygant v. Jackson Board of Education* (1986), the Supreme Court declared invalid the proposed lay-off provision, citing that it violated the Equal Protection Clause of the Fourteenth Amendment. This now meant that employers would have to strongly justify race-conscious mechanisms when considering laying-off employees. The Court again required that any race-based affirmative action policy and program must be narrowly tailored and it must be in response to a compelling state purpose to rectify past historical discriminatory practices. The plurality set forth the guidelines that societal discrimination alone was insufficient to justify racial classification. They clearly indicated that instead, there must exist substantive evidence of prior discrimination by the governmental unit in question. As a result of *Wygant v. Jackson Board of Education*, it became increasingly difficult to justify lay-off provisions that were race-based. The Court indicated, however, that the problem could have been resolved utilizing hiring goals. Interestingly, the Court declared that there was no correlation between the number of African American students and the number of African American faculty. This finding attacked the issue of having faculty diversity and student diversity as a rationale for protecting African Americans from being laid-off based upon race-based preferential treatment.

### Local 28 of the Sheet Metal Workers' International Association v. Equal Employment Opportunity Commission, 478 U.S. 421, 1986

"This case began as a result of action taken in 1975, when the Local 28 Sheet Metal Workers were found guilty of engaging in a continuous pattern and practice of employment discrimination against African Americans and Hispanic Americans in violation of Title VII of the Civil Rights Act of 1964, 42 U.S.C. Section 2000e et. seq." (478 U.S. 421,426, 1986). Local 28 was ordered to discontinue their discriminatory practices and admit a certain percentage of African Americans and Hispanic Americans to union membership by July, 1981. It should be noted that both in 1982 and 1983, Local 28 was charged with disobeying orders of the District Court (478 U.S. 421,426, 1986).

The case resulted from discriminatory practices engaged in by the Sheet Metal Workers, Local 28 regarding their admission of union members to the four year apprenticeship training program. This program was established to train sheet metal skills. It should be noted that in order for one to receive admission into the union, successful completion of the apprenticeship program was required. "In 1964, an investigation by the New York Commission for Human Rights revealed that Local 28 had excluded African Americans and Hispanic Americans from the union and the apprenticeship program, violating state law" ( 478 U.S. 421,427, 1986). The State Commission discovered, that "Local 28 had never allowed African Americans to become a part of the apprenticeship program and the admission into the program was predicated on nepotism" (478 U.S. 421, 427, 1986). As a result, Local 28 was ordered to cease and desist the racially discriminatory practices. The findings of the State Commission were upheld by the New York State Supreme Court (478 U.S. 421,427, 1986). However, the Court's orders proved ineffective, thereby causing the State Commission to institute legal proceedings against Local 28 (478 U.S. 421,428, 1986). It was revealed that Local 28 had failed to alter their discriminatory practices and were required by the State Commission to admit African Americans and Hispanic Americans into the apprenticeship program. Nevertheless, Local 28 continued defiance of the Court's mandate.

"In 1971, the United States instituted legal action against Local 28 based on Title VII of the Civil Rights Act of 1964 and Executive Order No. 11246" (478 U.S. 421,428, 1986). The legal action sought to enjoin Local 28 "from engaging in discriminatory patterns and practices against African Americans and Hispanic Americans" (478 U.S. 421,428, 1986). Prior to this legal action, New York City had adopted a plan requiring city contractors to employ a proportion of African and Hispanic Americans" (478 U.S. 421,429, 1986). The city assigned a total of six African American and Hispanic American trainees to the job site under the guidance of Local 28. Rather than comply, Local 28 stopped working in violation of its contractual obligations (478 U.S. 421,429, 1986).

"Following the trial in 1975, the Federal District Court held that Local 28 had violated both Title VII and the New York law" (478 U.S. 421,429, 1986). The District Court found that Local 28 had instituted standards of admission into the union that required an entrance examination and high school diploma, both of which had an adverse effect on African Americans and Hispanic Americans (478 U.S. 421,429, 1986). During this time, Local 28 implemented a "training fund" for the purpose of assisting "friends and relatives" in enrolling (478 U.S. 421,430, 1986). Accordingly, this procedure allowed Local 28 to deny union access to "people of color" (478 U.S. 421,430, 1986). Consequently, the District Court implemented a remedial racial goal requirement in conjunction with preference admissions designed to eradicate the effects of past discriminatory employment practices (478 U.S. 421,431-432, 1986). The District Court established the hiring goal of 29% membership "for people of color predicated on the percentage of people of color in the relevant labor pool in New York" (478 U.S. 421,432, 1986). In order to implement these requirements, the District Court, in conjunction with a court appointed administrator, adopted an affirmative action program.

The affirmative action program required that Local 28 adhere to the stipulations set forth by the court. The Court of Appeals for the Second Circuit affirmed, "the District Court's ruling that Local 28 had engaged in consistent egregious violation of Title VII" (478 U.S. 421,433, 1986). "The 29% membership goal for people of color was confirmed as constituting a temporary remedy justified by the long and persistent pattern of discriminatory employment practices exhibited by Local 28" (478 U.S. 421,433, 1986). As a result of this legal action, a revised affirmative plan was instituted and referred to as the "Revised Affirmative Action Program and Order" (RAAPO), (478 U.S. 421,433, 1986).

"In April 1982, the city and state brought charges against Local 28 alleging contempt for failure to adhere to the requirements of RAAPO in not attaining the 29% hiring goal" (478 U.S. 421,434, 1986). To remedy Local 28's contempt, "the court imposed a $150,000 fine to be placed in a fund designed to increase membership for African and Hispanic Americans" (478 U.S. 421,435, 1986). In 1983, the city brought a second contempt charge against Local 28, "alleging that it had failed in a timely manner to provide racial and ethnic data as required" (478 U.S. 421,436, 1986). The Court also increased the hiring goal from 29% to 29.23% based on the labor pool in the area covered by the union. Local 28 subsequently filed charges in Federal District Court appealing the required Fund order and adoption of the affirmative action requirement of including people of color in the union (478 U.S. 421,438, 1986). The Fund order, along with the hiring goal was affirmed by the District Court. The District Court held, that the hiring goal was legal because of the union's continued racial discrimination was of an egregious nature. Furthermore, "the plan did not unnecessarily trammel the rights of any readily ascertainable group of white individuals" (478 U.S. 421,439, 1986). The Fund order was substantiated because the court viewed it as a temporary measure (478 U.S. 421,439, 1986).

Local 28 appealed the decision on the basis that the District Court had "relied on incorrect statistical data" in establishing the hiring goal and that the contempt remedies were "criminal in nature and constituted denial of due process" (478 U.S. 421,439-440, 1986). Additionally, "the union charged that the Fund order and membership goals were unconstitutional" (478 U.S. 421,440, 1989). The rationale set forth by Local 28 focused on the fact that the legal remedies established by the District Court were a violation of Title VII. Specifically "race-conscious preferences" were extended to those not viewed as "victims" of the litigation (478 U.S. 421,440, 1986).

In a 6-3 decision, the Supreme Court (Brennan, Marshall, Blackmun, Powell, Stevens, O'Connor) affirmed the findings of the District Court (478 U.S. 421,424, 1986). The judgement was written by Justice Brennan. This decision held, that "the District Court did not use incorrect statistical evidence in evaluating Local 28's membership practices" (478 U.S. 421,440-442, 1986). According to Brennan, "the Fund order constituted a proper remedy for civil contempt since it was designed to coerce compliance with the District Court's order" (478 U.S. 421,442-444, 1986). The language of Title VII did not preclude the District Court from implementing race-conscious relief as a remedy for past discrimination. He explained, that "such relief was appropriate when an employer engaged in persistent or egregious discrimination" (478 U.S. 421,445, 1986). Title VII, as interpreted by the Court, was viewed as allowing relief for those who were "not actual victims" in litigation (478 U.S. 421, 447, 1986). He supported his position by citing previous cases that endorsed utilization of racial preferences to remedy past discrimination (*Fullilove v. Klutznick*, 448 U.S. 448, 1980 and *University of California Regents v. Bakke*, 438 U.S. 265, 1978).

According to Brennan, the membership goal and Fund order were legal remedies designed to eliminate "the lingering effects of past discrimination" (478 U.S. 421,477, 1986). It was the Court's view that the Fund was designed to provide assistance for African and Hispanic American workers as it had provided for whites. The membership goal was interpreted as a measurement mechanism to determine compliance by Local 28 "rather than a strict racial quota" (478 U.S. 421,471, 1986). The Court argued that these remedies were constitutional because they were "temporary measures," the Fund would "terminate" at the time Local 28 attained the legally required membership objective, thus satisfying the legal parameters established by the Court (478 U.S. 421,478-479, 1986). The Court ruled, that "neither the Fund nor the membership goal unnecessarily trammeled the interest of white employees" (478 U.S. 421,479, 1986). Brennan concluded by stating, that "the relief order in this case passed the most rigorous test, in that it was narrowly tailored to further the government's compelling interest in rectifying past discriminatory employment practices" (478 U.S. 421,480, 1986) .

Justice Powell in concurring, noted that the parameters of the case were not in violation of the protection given by "Title VII, nor the Equal Protection Clause of the Fourteenth Amendment and the Due Process of

Law under the Fifth Amendment" (478 U.S. 421,484 1986). Powell reasoned that the text of Title VII was written explicitly so that remedies could be extended to those who were "non-victims" at the time of the litigation (478 U.S. 421,483, 1986). He emphasized, that "in view of the egregious conduct exhibited by Local 28, the Court may impose race-based sanctions to eliminate present effects of past discrimination" (478 U.S. 421,484, 1986).

Powell stated that "the violations of Title VII by Local 28 established a compelling governmental interest sufficient to justify the imposition of a racial-based remedy" (478 U.S. 421,485, 1986). The legal remedy met constitutional muster and the  "Fund" was imposed as a result of "contempt" by Local 28 (478 U.S. 421,485, 1986). Powell noted that the plan imposed by the Court was structured in order to "vindicate the compelling government interest" (478 U.S. 421,485, 1986).

Justice O'Connor presented an opinion concurring in part and dissenting in part. She devoted the majority of her attention to explaining her rationale for dissenting.  Her primary argument, was that "the membership goal operated as a racial quota that could not have feasiblely been attained in good-faith by Local 28" (478 U.S. 421,489 1986). According to O'Connor, a majority of the justices were of the legal opinion that Title VII did not preclude non-victims from receiving protection in the form of racial preferences (478 U.S. 421,490, 1986). However, it was O'Connor's view that "this form of race-conscious affirmative relief was impermissible because it operated as racial quotas and not as a goal as implied by the majority Court" (478 U.S. 421,490, 1986).

In concluding her dissenting opinion, O'Connor stated that she did not question the past practices exhibited by Local 28, in that they were clearly egregious.  However, she pointed out that "the timetable set before Local 28 was unrealistic and could not have been met in good-faith" (478 U.S. 421,498, 1986). O'Connor reasoned that the required "membership goal" in practice created a "membership quota," and therefore violated Title VII (478 U.S. 421,498, 1986).

Justice White presented a dissenting opinion.  He stated, that "the general policy set forth by Title VII was to limit relief for racial discrimination in employment practice to actual victims of the discrimination" (478 U.S. 421,499, 1986).  White reasoned, "the cumulative effect of the revised affirmative action plan and the contempt judgments against Local 28 established not just a membership goal for people of color, but, in actuality created a strict racial quota, violating Title VII" (478 U.S. 421,499, 1986). White's contention was that the remedy supported by the Court was inequitable.

Justice Rehnquist also dissented with Chief Justice Burger joining. Rehnquist wrote, that "Title VII forbids a court to order racial preferences that effectively displace whites" (478 U.S. 421,500, 1986). Only individual people of color who have been the actual victims of a particular employer's racial discrimination could benefit. Rehnquist held the opinion that Title VII guidelines applied only to those that were actual victims, and the Court, therefore, could only issue remedies for those who were victims (478 U.S. 421,500, 1986).

This case had an important impact on affirmative action and human resource personnel because it addressed the issue of discriminatory hiring practices, with an emphasis on continued intentional discrimination. An important aspect of this case was whether Title VII benefits included those who were not actual victims. The Court agreed "that an order of preferential relief benefitting individuals who were not the actual victims of discrimination was permissible as a remedy for violation of Title VII" (478 U.S. 421,482, 1986). The Court also set forth the guidelines as to when a race-based goal was permissible as opposed to a racial quota. The Court held, that "when there was continuous egregious discriminatory employment practices, utilization of employment goals were permissible as a means of monitoring the progress of the alleged violator" (478 U.S. 421,478, 1986). The Court also allowed the implementation of a Fund order to aid African and Hispanic Americans, so long as it was a temporary measure. The Court once again applied the criteria of a race-based remedy aimed at rectifying present effects of historical discriminatory practices. The ruling in this case, it can be argued, constituted an important victory for affirmative action in the area of discriminatory employment practices.

Affirmative action programs and policies continued to provide the Court with litigation for adjudication. In the 1986 term, the Court was presented with deciding whether the consideration of race and sex as a factor in employment hiring practices violated Title VII of the Civil Rights Act of 1964. The Court also considered the implementation of a voluntary adopted affirmative action plan by a public agency.

## United States v. Paradise 480 U.S. 149 (1987)

"In 1972, the National Association for the Advancement of Colored People (NAACP) brought action challenging the Alabama Department of Public Safety's (here after referred to as Department) longstanding practice of excluding African Americans from employment. The United States was joined as a party plaintiff and Philip Paradise, Jr. intervened on behalf of a class of African American plaintiffs" (480 U.S. 149,154, 1987). The case was brought before Federal District Judge Johnson. Judge Johnson stated, that "the plaintiffs had shown without contradiction that the defendants had engaged in a blatant and continuous pattern and practice of hiring discrimination in the Alabama Department of Public Safety, in the areas of both troopers and supporting personnel" (480 U.S. 149,154, 1987). Johnson indicated that throughout the thirty-seven year history of the Department, there had "never been an African American State Trooper" (480 U.S. 149,154, 1987). Furthermore, the only African Americans employed by the Department were in non-merit positions (480 U.S. 149,154, 1987). The District Court ruled, that "the racial discrimination in the case permeated the Department's employment policies to the extent that both mandatory and prohibitive injunction relief was necessary to end the discriminatory practices and eliminate the effects of it" (480 U.S. 149,154, 1987).

Consequently, the District Court instituted a 1972 order mandating the Department "hire one African American trooper for each white trooper hired until African Americans constituted approximately twenty-five percent of the state trooper force" (480 U.S. 149,154-155, 1987). Judge Johnson "enjoined the Department from engaging in employment practices, including recruitment, examination, appointment, training, promotion, retention or any other personnel action for the purpose or effect of discriminating against any employee, or actual or potential applicant for employment on the basis of race or color" (480 U.S. 149,155, 1987). The Fifth Circuit Court of Appeals denied the defendant's appeal and upheld the requirement. The Fifth Circuit Court held, that "the use of quota relief in employment discrimination cases was based on the chancellor's duty to eradicate the continued effects of past unlawful practices" (480 U.S. 149,156, 1987). The Court of Appeals also held that the "one-for-one hiring order" did not deny "due process or equal protection" to the white applicants having higher qualifications than African Americans (480 U.S. 149,156, 1987).

In 1974, "shortly after the Court of Appeals decision," the plaintiffs decided to seek further relief from the Federal District Court. Judge Johnson held, that "the defendants had frustrated the relief for the plaintiffs and artificially restricted the size of the trooper force along with new hires" (480 U.S. 149,156-157, 1987). The court reaffirmed the 1972 hiring order. In "September 1977," the plaintiffs returned to the Federal District Court for supplemental "relief regarding the question of the department's promotion practices" (480 U.S. 149,157, 1987). After extensive discovery, the court implemented a decree in 1979. Based on the 1979 decree, "the department agreed to develop within one year a promotional procedure that was fair to all applicants and contained little adverse impact on African Americans seeking promotion to the rank of corporal" (480 U.S. 149,157, 1987). The 1979 decree contained guidelines for promoting those in the "upper ranks" (480 U.S. 149, 157, 1987).

Five days later, the defendants requested clarification of the hiring order established in 1972. The Department interpreted the 1972 order as applying "only to officers in entry-level positions and not the upper ranks" (480 U.S. 149,158, 1987). The District Court responded, stating "there was no ambiguity in the 1972 hiring order. The 1972 order required one-for-one hiring until approximately twenty-five percent of the state trooper force was African American" (480 U.S. 149,158, 1987). The District Court noted that the order contained no references that provided for distinction by rank (480 U.S. 149,158, 1987). The District Court again reminded the defendants that for "thirty-seven years there had never been an African American trooper at any rank" (480 U.S. 149, 159, 1987).

"In April 1981, more than a year after the deadline set in the 1979 decree, the Department proposed a selection procedure for promotion to corporal and sought approval from the District Court. This request led to the implementation of a 1981 decree. The 1981 decree reaffirmed the commitment set in 1979 implementing a promotional procedure with no adverse impact on African Americans" (480 U.S. 149, 159, 1987). Nevertheless, in April 1983, the plaintiffs returned to District Court and requested enforcement of the two consent decrees. The plaintiffs requested that the defendants meet the requirement of "promoting African Americans to corporal at the required one-for-one format" (480 U.S. 149,160, 1987). The United States was opposed to the hiring order, but nevertheless felt the decree should be enforced. The District Court noted that "the defendants had failed to offer a rationale as to why promotions had not been made" (480 U.S. 149,161, 1987). There was also no explanation as to why progress had stopped in regards to rectifying the effects of past discrimination (480 U.S. 149,161, 1987).

After the motion for enforcement, four white applicants argued that the 1979 and 1981 decrees were "unreasonable, illegal, and unconstitutional" (480 U.S. 149,161, 1987). The Department responded with the submission of a proposal that would promote "fifteen persons to the rank of corporal, with four designated as positions filled by African Americans" (480 U.S. 149,162, 1986). The white plaintiffs, in turn, alleged that the proposed promotional plan negated past injuries suffered and the new proposal did not prevent the development of "future delays" (480 U.S. 149,162, 1987). An assessment by the District Court revealed that "if there was to become in the future an orderly method for African American troopers entering the upper ranks, the court must address the Department's delay" (480 U.S. 149,163, 1987).

Thus, the District Court implemented the one-for-one hiring format. It was the District Court's conclusion that the effects of past discrimination in the Department would not end "without promotional quotas" designed to eliminate the effects of historical discrimination (480 U.S. 149,163, 1987). The decision was affirmed by the Eleventh Circuit Court of Appeals. The case was granted a *writ of certiorari* to the United States Supreme Court (480 U.S. 149,163, 1987).

In a 5-4 decision, the Court ruled for the first time that judges may order strict racial promotional quotas to overcome "long-term, open, and pervasive discrimination" (480 U.S. 149,171-177, 1987). The justices in the plurality consisted of Brennan, Marshall, Blackmun, Stevens, and Powell. The dissenting opinion was written by O'Connor with Rehnquist, White, and Scalia joining.

The judgement written by Brennan began by addressing the challenge set forth by the United States. The United States maintained, that "the race-conscious relief order violated the Equal Protection Clause of the Fourteenth Amendment" (480 U.S. 149 166, 1987). Based on the previous judgements established in *Sheet Metal Workers* (1986) and *Wygant* (1986), Brennan cites the rationale of O'Connor stating, "that in remedying past or present racial discrimination, it created a sufficient weight to warrant the remedial use of a carefully constructed affirmative action program" (480 U.S. 149,166, 1987). Brennan pointed out, that "the Court had consistently held that some elevated level of scrutiny was required when a racial or ethnic distinction was made for remedial purposes" (480 U.S. 149,166, 1987). Brennan noted that the relief meet constitutional muster (480 U.S. 149,167, 1987). He contended that "the egregious discriminatory conduct exhibited by the Department unquestionably violated the Fourteenth Amendment" (480 U.S. 149,167, 1987). Brennan stated that failure to allow African Americans entry into the Department served to create a "white dominated department" (480 U.S. 149,168, 1987). He included a reminder that in 1972, "it was revealed that not only was the Department found guilty of discrimination, but that the Court also found that in 37 years there had never been an African American trooper at any rank" (480 U.S. 149,168, 1987). Brennan pointed out that promotions came only after "implementation of the decree and not as the result of any voluntary departmental plan" (480 U.S. 149,169, 1987). The Court held, that "the race-conscious relief was justified by the compelling interest in remedying the discrimination that permeated entry-level hiring practices and the promotional process" (480 U.S. 149,170, 1987). The Court also addressed the issue of societal impact. Brennan agreed that the District Court's enforcement order was supported by the "societal interest in compliance with federal court judgements" (480 U.S. 149,170, 1987). In view of the "consistent history of resistence," the Court reasoned that consideration of "societal interest" was relevant (480 U.S. 149,170, 1987).

Brennan noted that the one-for-one requirement was temporary. "The plan was flexible in that it applied to all ranks. The requirement was waived if there was no available, qualified, African American candidates" (480 U.S. 149,177, 1987). He suggested, that "the terms of application for the one-for-one requirement depended on the conduct of the Department" (480 U.S. 149,178, 1987). Brennan pointed out that the requirement did not trammel upon the rights of white applicants. "The one-for-one requirement did not layoff nor discharge any white employees" (480 U.S. 149,182-183, 1987). Brennan concluded with a discussion of an affirmative action plan meeting the narrowly tailored requirement. He suggested that the remedy was "an effective, temporary, and flexible measure" (480 U.S. 149,185, 1987). Therefore, "the race-conscious relief imposed was justified and narrowly tailored to serve the legitimate purpose of the Federal District Court" (480 U.S. 149,185-186, 1987).

Justice Powell, in his concurring opinion, agreed that "the one-for-one promotion to corporal was appropriate" (480 U.S. 149,186 1987). He stated that five factors were important in determining if the affirmative action remedy was narrowly drawn. The factors included: (1) "efficiency of alternative remedies, (2) planned duration of the remedy, (3) the relationship between the percentage of African American workers to be employed and the percentage of African Americans in the relevant work force, (4) the availability of waiver able provisions if the hiring plan was not met, and (5) the effect of the remedy upon innocent third parties" (480 U.S. 149,187, 1987).

Stevens concurred in the judgement setting forth a historical overview of Alabama's employment practices. Stevens pointed out, that "the record disclosed an egregious violation of the Equal Protection Clause" (480 U.S. 149,190, 1987). Stevens wrote that based on historical discriminatory employment practices, the District Court was justified in establishing the hiring order (480 U.S. 149,190, 1987).

A dissenting opinion was written by Justice O'Connor, with Rehnquist and Scalia joining. O'Connor stated, that "the level of Fourteenth Amendment scrutiny did not change because the challenged classification operated against a group that historically had not been subjected to governmental discrimination" (480 U.S. 149,196, 1987). "In evaluating the constitutionality of the District Court's order," O'Connor suggested that "consideration be given to the compelling governmental interest along with the narrowly tailored requirement" (480 U.S. 149,196, 1987). O'Connor indicated, that "the rigid quota was impermissible because it adopted an unjustified conclusion regarding the extent to which past discrimination had ongoing effects" (480 U.S. 149,197, 1987). O'Connor stated that the District Court order "was not necessary to achieve compliance with the court's previous order" (480 U.S. 149,197, 1987). O'Connor wrote that in order to eliminate the effects of historical discrimination, the hiring order would have to become permanent (480 U.S. 149,198, 1987) She further stated that "the one-for-one quota" was not justified by the Department's delay (480 U.S. 149,198, 1987). It was O'Connor's contention, that "the one-for-one promotion quota exceeded the percentage of African Americans in the trooper force, and no evidence revealed that the extreme quota was necessary to eradicate the departmental delay" (480 U.S. 149,198, 1987). She further suggested, that "the promotional plan was not narrowly tailored, since it had no designated end point" (480 U.S. 149,199, 1987).

In her conclusion, O'Connor suggested that the Court could have employed alternative measures. She argued that a court-appointed trustee to develop promotional procedures was consistent with the decree. The implementation of fines was presented as another alternative by

O'Connor. In concluding, O'Connor argued that "the District Court imposed the promotional quota without consideration of any possible alternatives" (480 U.S. 149,200, 1987). In a brief dissenting opinion, Justice White stated that the District Court had exceeded its power in devising the promotional plan (480 U.S. 149,196, 1987).

*United States v. Paradise* (1987) was important in affirmative action, in that the Court set forth the guidelines that strict racial quotas in promotions met constitutional muster in the public sector. The Court held that the promotional quotas were designed to remedy past historical discriminatory employment practices. The Court stated, that "in view of the thirty-seven years of not having an African American State Trooper, this demonstrated a sufficient compelling state interest" (480 U.S. 149,168, 1987).

### Johnson v. Transportation Agency, Santa Clara County, California 480 U.S. 616 (1987)

The Supreme Court in the case of *Johnson v. Transportation Agency, Santa Clara County, California* 480 U.S. 616 (1987), now reviewed the legality of affirmative action and gender discrimination. This case resulted from action taken in December 1978 by the Santa Clara County Transit District Board of Supervisors (hereafter referred to as Agency). At this time, the Santa Clara County Transit District Board of Supervisors adopted an Affirmative Action Plan (AAP) for the County Transportation Agency. The adopted AAP stated, that "the mere prohibition of discriminatory practices was insufficient to remedy the effects of past practices and to permit attainment of an equitable representation of African Americans, women and handicapped persons" (480 U.S. 616,620, 1987). As a result, the AAP provided, that "in making promotions to positions within a traditionally segregated job classification in which women have been significantly under-represented, the Agency is authorized to consider as one factor the sex of the qualified applicant" (480 U.S. 616, 620-621, 1987).

When reviewing its "workforce," the Agency discovered that women were under-represented in actual numbers far less in proportion to the labor force in "five of the seven job categories" (480 U.S. 616,621, 1987). The Agency stated, "specifically that women were concentrated largely in EEOC job categories traditionally held by women" (480 U.S. 616,621, 1987). For example, "women composed 76% of the Office and Clerical Workers, but only 7.1% of Officials and Administrators, 8.6% of

Professionals, 9.7% of Technicians, and 22% of Service and Maintenance Workers" (480 U.S. 616,621, 1987). It was revealed, that "none of the 238 Skilled Craft Workers positions were held by women" (480 U.S. 616,621, 1987).

Consequently, the Agency implemented the AAP designed, "to achieve statistically measurable yearly improvement pertaining to the hiring and promoting of women throughout the Agency" (480 U.S. 616, 621, 1987). The AAP included, "a benchmark containing a long-term goal providing for the attainment of a workforce reflective of the portion of African Americans and women in the area labor pool" (480 U.S. 616,622, 1987). The AAP took into consideration the potential for this objective being unrealistic. Consideration was given to such factors as "the low turnover rates, jobs requiring heavy labor, the small number of positions within some job categories, and the limited number of entry positions along with the fact that limited numbers of African Americans and women qualified for positions requiring specialized training and experience" (480 U.S. 616,622, 1987). In order to compensate for those difficulties, the AAP included "a short-range goal providing for annual adjustments" implemented to provide attainable employment objectives. It is important to note, that "the AAP did not set aside a specific number of positions for African Americans or women, but it authorized the consideration of ethnicity or sex as a factor when evaluating qualified candidates for employment in which members of such groups were under-represented" (480 U.S. 616,622, 1987).

"On December 12, 1979, the Agency announced a vacancy for the promotional position of road dispatcher in the Roads Division" (480 U.S. 616,623, 1987). The job description required at least "four years" as either a dispatcher or road maintenance employee. This position was designated by EEOC classifications as a Skilled Craft Worker. There were a total of twelve applicants for the position, two (Johnson and Joyce) of whom were the integral parties in the litigation. Joyce's employment history with the County began in 1970 as an "account clerk." She had previously applied for a dispatcher's position in 1974, but due to lack of experience she was not accepted. However, in 1975, Joyce was transferred to road maintenance and became "the first woman to occupy the position" (480 U.S. 616, 623, 1987). Johnson's employment history began in 1967 with the position of road clerk. Johnson, like Joyce, had · applied for the dispatcher position in 1974 and was denied. Nevertheless, in 1977, Johnson transferred to the position of road maintenance worker.

It should be noted that during the tenure of Johnson and Joyce as a road maintenance worker, both occasionally worked as a road dispatcher (480 U.S. 616,632, 1987).

After subsequent testing and interviewing for the position, "it was determined that Johnson had compiled a score of 75 (making him second) and Joyce a score of 73 (making her third)" (480 U.S. 616,623, 1987). Following the second interview conducted by three agency supervisors, "it was agreed that Johnson would receive a recommendation for the promotion" (480 U.S. 616,623, 1987). However, prior to her second interview, "Joyce contacted the County's Affirmative Action Office because of her fear that her application would not receive just review" (480 U.S. 616,624, 1987). Consequently, the Affirmative Action Office contacted the Agency with a reminder of the need "to accomplish the objectives set forth in the AAP" (480 U.S. 616,624, 1987). In turn, the Coordinator for the Affirmative Action Office recommended Joyce to the Agency Director for promotion (480 U.S. 616,624, 1987). According to the Director, after reviewing Joyce's total application and considering gender as a factor, the promotion was given to Joyce.

Following the announcement of the promotion, "Johnson filed a complaint with the EEOC alleging denial of promotion based on his gender in violation of Title VII. After receiving a right-to-sue letter from the EEOC, Johnson filed suit in the United States District Court for the Northern District of California" (480 U.S. 616,625, 1987). The District Court ruled that Johnson was the most qualified and therefore should have received the promotion. The District Court cited that Joyce received the promotion predicated on consideration of gender, in violation of Title VII. The District Court, in applying the precedent established in *Steelworkers v. Weber*, 443 U.S. 193 (1979), "found that the Agency's AAP was invalidated because it was not temporary" ( 480 U.S. 616, 625, 1987). The Court of Appeals for the Ninth Circuit reversed the District Court decision, ruling "that absent an expressed termination date in the AAP and the fact that the AAP's objective was the attainment rather than the maintenance of a workforce reflecting the labor force in the County, the AAP was legal" (480 U.S. 616,625, 1987). The Court of Appeals also ruled, that "the AAP established no fixed percentage of positions for African Americans or women" (480 U.S. 616, 625, 1987). The Court held that the consideration of Joyce's gender was a factor and therefore, presented a legal consideration (480 U.S. 616,625-626, 1987).

In a 6-3 decision the majority of the Court (Brennan, Marshall, Blackmun, Powell, Stevens, and O'Connor) held that the AAP did not violate the requirements of Title VII (480 U.S. 616,618, 1987). The Court began its deliberation by considering the required "burden of proof" as established in *Wygant v. Jackson Board of Education*, 476 U.S. 267, 277-278 (1986). The Court affirmed, that "the ultimate burden remained with the employees to demonstrate the unconstitutionality of an affirmative action program" (480 U.S. 616,626, 1987). It was the Court's contention, that "once a plaintiff established a *prima facie* case that race or sex had been taken into consideration in an employer's employment decision, the burden shifted to the employer to articulate a nondiscriminatory rationale for its action" (480 U.S. 616,626, 1987). "If such a plan is articulated as the basis of the employer's decision, then according to the Court, the burden was shifted to the plaintiff to prove that the employer's justification was pretextual and the resulting plan is unconstitutional" (480 U.S. 616,626, 1987).

According to Brennan, the assessment of the AAP must be predicated on the guidelines established in *Weber* (1979). Brennan wrote that a key consideration was whether the issue of gender was the primary factor in considering the employment of Joyce. According to Brennan, this was important in view of the "under-representation of women" in a traditionally segregated job classification. In addressing this issue, he discussed the fact that "including consideration of race and sex was allowable under the parameters of Title VII, when seeking eradication of employment discrimination" (480 U.S. 616,632, 1987). Brennan stated, that "the purpose of Title VII also extended to the interest of those employees not benefitting from the plan and ensuring that their rights were not unduly infringed" (480 U.S. 616, 632, 1987). The Court stated, that "the decision to hire Joyce was made in accordance with the Agency AAP directing that sex or race be given consideration for the purpose of remedying under-represented of women and African Americans" (480 U.S. 616,634, 1987). The Court also noted, that "the AAP recognized that women were egregiously under-represented in the Skilled Craft Worker category, especially considering that of the 238 positions, none were occupied by women" (480 U.S. 616,636, 1987). The selection of Joyce, according to the Court, was in line with the attainment of the short-term goals proposed in the Plan. Brennan pointed out, that "the AAP simply calculated imbalances in all categories according to the proportion of women in the area labor pool, thus substantiating the legality of the AAP" (480 U.S. 616,636, 1987).

The Court stated, that "the AAP did not authorize blind hiring" (480 U.S. 616, 637, 1987). It was the Court's view that the hiring of Joyce was not based on a "statistical preference for gender" (480 U.S. 616,637, 1987). The Court observed that given "the gender imbalance" in the category of the Skilled Craft category, there was a legal rationale to allow "gender consideration" as a factor in the hiring decision (480 U.S. 616, 637, 1987). Therefore, the procedure utilized in promoting Joyce met the criteria established in *Weber* (1979). It was designed to "eliminate an imbalance in traditionally segregated job categories" (490 U.S. 616,637, 1987).

The next issue before the Court was whether the AAP unnecessarily trammeled the rights of male employees or created an absolute bar to their advancement. The Court explained that it did not because the AAP set aside no positions for women. It expressly stated, that "the goal established should not be viewed as a quota that had to be met" (480 U.S. 616,638, 1987). The AAP required no gender distinction when competing for employment. According to Brennan, "there were no automatically excluded applicants and that all applicant's qualifications were weighed equally" (480 U.S. 616, 638, 1987). Brennan explained that Johnson had no "absolute entitlement" to the road dispatcher position (480 U.S. 616,638, 1987). After all, there were seven applicants qualified and Johnson had no legitimate reason to presume the job was his (480 U.S. 616,638, 1987).

Brennan concluded by indicating that "the AAP was designed to attain a balanced workforce, not to maintain one" (480 U.S. 616,639, 1987). In assessing the overall objective of the AAP, the Court reasoned, "that substantial evidence demonstrated that the Agency had sought to implement an incremental approach to eliminate the imbalance in its workforce" (480 U.S. 616,640, 1987). The incremental AAP established "realistic guidelines that presented minimal intrusion on the legitimate expectation of other employees" (480 U.S. 616,640, 1987). The AAP was made pursuant to an affirmative action goal designed to attain a workforce reflective of the qualified workforce and the AAP was consistent with the criteria of Title VII. Thus, it was declared constitutional (480 U.S. 616,642, 1987).

Justice Stevens wrote a separate concurring opinion for the purpose of explaining the issue of anti-discrimination law and to discuss the implications of the limits established by the Court in this decision (480 U.S. 616,642, 1987). He implied that the Court properly ruled that the shield of Title VII allowed the Agency to take Joyce's gender into consideration as a factor in reaching the hiring decision. The decision was consistent with "the Court's earlier view that Title VII permitted voluntary adoption of special programs to benefit members of groups of color for whose protection the statute was enacted" (480 U.S. 616, 642, 1987). Stevens stated, that "Title VII was intended to protect historically disadvantaged groups against discrimination and the AAP was consistent with that purpose" (480 U.S. 616,646, 1987).

Justice O'Connor also consented with the judgement (480 U.S. 616,648, 1987). She wrote, that "the question presented in this case was whether a public employer violated Title VII by promoting a qualified woman rather than a marginally better qualified man when there was statistical imbalance sufficient to support the claim of a pattern or practice of discrimination against women under Title VII" (480 U.S. 616,648, 1987). She concurred that the Court had ruled correctly in answering that legal issue.

However, O'Connor wrote a separate opinion, "because it was her view that the Court had chosen to follow an expansive and ill-defined approach to voluntary affirmative action by public employers, despite the limitations of the Constitution and Title VII" (480 U.S. 616,648, 1987). It should be noted that O'Connor believed she should follow *Weber* because it was a controlling precedent. Thus, from her perspective, "the mechanism for evaluating the legality of an affirmative action plan by a public employer was no different than that required of a private employer" (480 U.S. 616,649, 1987). Title VII was designed to take into account sex or race for the purpose of "eliminating the effects of employment discrimination" (480 U.S. 616,650, 1987). According to O'Connor, "the legal issue was the statistical imbalance between the percentage of women in the workforce and the percentage of women in the particular specialized job classification" (480 U.S. 616,652, 1987).

O'Connor noted that "the Court today had given little guidance for what degree of statistical imbalance is sufficient to support an affirmative action plan" (480 U.S. 616,652, 1987). She stated that an "affirmative action plan" that promotes "marginally qualified" applicants based on race or gender violated Title VII (480 U.S. 616,656, 1987). However, the Court had agreed that sex was a factor and not the total essence of the promotion of Joyce (480 U.S. 616,656, 1987). Thus, the AAP in this case met the constitutional muster set forth in both *Weber* (1979) and *Wygant* (1986).

According to the dissenting opinion set forth by Scalia, the Court had essentially rewritten Title VII to guarantee "that race and sex would be the basis for determining employment" (480 U.S. 616,658, 1987). He argued that the AAP was not designed to "remedy prior sex discrimination" by the Agency because this was not an issue in the litigation (480 U.S. 616,659, 1987). Scalia augmented his position with the implication that it would be statistically impossible to match race and gender composition with every portion of the qualified workforce. Thus, "the AAP imposed racial and sexual tailoring that would be in defiance of normal expectations and along with the law of probability, provided each protected racial and sexual group a predetermined proportion for each job category" (480 U.S. 616,660, 1987). Scalia noted that the discrimination against Johnson (the man) was much clearer than any discrimination against Joyce (the woman) (480 U.S. 616, 662, 1987). The most significant proposition of law that was established by the Court's decision, according to Scalia, was that, "racial or sexual discrimination was permitted under Title VII when it was designed to overcome the effects of societal attitudes that had limited the entry of certain races or a particular sex into certain jobs" (480 U.S. 616,664, 1987). The decision reached by the Court modified the judgement in *Wygant v. Board of Education*, 476 U.S. 267 (1986) and now implied, that "societal discrimination can provide the rationale for remedial affirmative action plans, contrary to the guidelines of Title VII" (480 U.S. 616,664, 1987). Justice White also wrote a dissenting opinion. He simply stated that the interpretation given by the Court presented a new understanding of Title VII, thereby rewriting the meaning established in *Weber* (1979) (480 U.S. 616,657, 1987). Therefore, he would overrule *Weber*.

The case of *Johnson v. Transportation Agency, Santa Clara County, California*, it can be argued, provided a milestone for affirmative action. The Court in this case established the legal criteria that both sex and race may be utilized as a factor in the consideration of employment hiring and promotion decisions. The Court also upheld the constitutionality of an affirmative action plan voluntarily adopted by a public agency. The Court in Johnson set forth the requirement that an affirmative action plan was legal if it was designed to remedy historical discrimination. The Court, more importantly, allowed the utilization of statistical evidence if demonstrated that the statistics provide an attainment of the goal and not the maintenance of a quota.

## Summary of Supreme Court: 1971-1988

During the years from 1971-1988, the Supreme Court, it could be argued, was generally protective of the rights of the employee. At this juncture, the Court decisions provided judicial protection for those advocating affirmative hiring and promotional practices. The Court began with the legal criteria of business necessity as established in *Griggs v. Duke Power Company* (1971). The issue of reverse discrimination was avoided by the Court until the dramatic confrontation in *Bakke* (1978). In this case, the emergent division of judicial philosophies became apparent. The Court, in essence, established two legal principles in *Bakke* (1978). The Court held that it was unconstitutional to have special admissions criteria for protected groups and ruled that the utilization of race as the sole criteria for admissions was unconstitutional. In addition, the Court ruled that racial goals were constitutional.

The composition of the Court was important in how decisions were reached. The era of 1971-1988 revealed the existence of a clear liberal bloc in the early years. Justices Brennan, White, Marshall, and Blackmun constituted the liberal vote in each case pertaining to affirmative action. These justices continuously voted together in major decisions. The judicial philosophy of Brennan, White, Marshall, and Blackmun became known as those championing the rights of protected groups in affirmative action cases. The dissolution of influence of this liberal bloc resulted in many of the cases during the latter part of the 1971-1988 era going against affirmative action as a result of the changing composition in the Court. As noted by Justice Marshall, "the Supreme Court in the latter years began moving in the opposite direction in protecting the rights of its citizens" (438 U.S. 265,402, 1978).

The allegation of reverse discrimination may be viewed as the major nemesis for affirmative action. The Supreme Court did not adjudicate reverse discrimination in *DeFunis* (1974). However, due to the fact that DeFunis was entering the third and final year of law school, the Supreme Court avoided adjudication by ruling that the case was moot. Thus, the issue of reverse discrimination confronted the Court again in the *Bakke* case (1978).

It was a foregone conclusion that sooner or later the issue of reverse discrimination would appear before the Supreme Court, especially in view of what seemed to be the proscriptive intent of the Fourteenth Amendment with respect to race, along with the established judicial precedents pointing to color-blindness of the Constitution (Abraham and Perry, 1998). In *Bakke* (1978) the Court dealt with the issues of quotas, establishing goals, reverse discrimination and the utilization of strict scrutiny. A key player in the *Bakke* decision was the role of Justice Powell. Powell's judicial philosophy established him as the swing vote. The pivotal vote of Powell allowed the Supreme Court to rule that quotas were unconstitutional based on the Fourteenth Amendment to the United States Constitution. Yet, while the Court established that race cannot be the sole criteria for special admissions programs, it suggested that race may be one of the several factors in consideration for college admissions (Abraham and Perry, 1998). *Bakke* left intact the bulk of affirmative action programs that gave special consideration for constitutionally protected groups.

According to Abraham and Perry (1998), the Court also held that the use of race in any program benefitting from statutory-provided federal financial assistance was illegal. It also rejected the notion that any benign affirmative action use of race was constitutional. Nevertheless, *Bakke* did not with any degree of finality settle the issue of reverse discrimination.

*Weber* (1979) was decided one year after *Bakke*. The case was a triad of reverse discrimination cases that, in effect, provided a green light, or at least a green and yellow one, regarding the widespread implementation of affirmative action programs. The key legal issues in *Weber* (1979) included the utilization of a voluntary plan, the meaning of Title VII as interpreted by the Court, past discrimination and the use of quotas. The Court had already established that quotas were unconstitutional in the public sector. The Court ruled that Title VII did allow for preferential treatment, however, a private voluntary affirmative action plan designed to eradicate historical racial discrimination in employment was constitutional (443 U.S. 193,208, 1979). In *Weber* (1979), the Court allowed for the establishment of quotas, and granted constitutionality to race-conscious affirmative action programs in the private sector (443 U.S. 193,208, 1979).

The Court addressed the issue of setting aside contracts for MBE's in *Fullilove*. The case established the fact that in the area of affirmative action, the Court allowed set-aside programs. The Court supported set-aside programs that were "narrowly tailored and did not unnecessarily trammel the interests of others" (443 U.S. 193,208, 1979). The Court instituted guidelines for set-asides that were constitutional if they were designed to eradicate the effects of past racial discrimination in the area of employment (*Fullilove*, 1980). It was established, that set-asides for MBE's passed constitutional muster.

In *Firefighters v. Stotts* (1984) the Supreme Court was requested to adjudicate the constitutionality of a seniority system. The key issue was the proposed layoff plan that was designed to protect African Americans from discriminatory employment practices. The layoffs were based on the last-hired-first-fired precept of the seniority system. In *Stotts* (1984) the Court held, that "Title VII clearly protected *bona fide* seniority systems unless the system was intentionally discriminatory or African American workers could demonstrate individual victimization as a result of discriminatory employment practices" (467 U.S. 561,576, 1984). It should be noted that the majority opinion was written by Justice White, who was on the other side of the judicial fence in *Bakke*, *Weber* and *Fullilove*. In *Stotts* (1984) the Court held, that "a *bona fide* seniority system was protected under the guidelines of Title VII" (467 U.S. 561,575).

Two years later, following *Stotts*, in *Wygant v. Jackson Board of Education* (1986) the Supreme Court experienced continued confrontation with affirmative action and reverse discrimination cases. In *Wygant* (1986) the Court handed down a decision that seemed to say yes and no at the same time to racial preferences. The Court, in this case, "held unconstitutional as a violation of the Equal Protection Clause of the Fourteenth Amendment the school board's plan in Michigan for laying off teachers that gave preference to people of color" (476 U.S. 267,268, 1986). In *Wygant*, "the Court addressed the issue of role models. Justice Powell cautioned giving preference to teachers as role models for students of color to overcome discrimination in society, indicating that it was not a sufficiently compelling reason to lay off white employees" (476 U.S. 267,276, 1986). Powell concluded by suggestion that in previous cases, the Court had not ruled that society discrimination justified racial preference (476 U.S. 267, 274, 1986).

The legal issue of strict scrutiny also played a role in deciding *Wygant*. The Court applied the strict scrutiny test that heretofore had applied in *Bakke* (1978). According to Powell, "the level of scrutiny did not change because the challenged classification operated against a protective group" (476 U.S. 267,273, 1986). The Court indicated that the employer must present convincing evidence that the remedial action was essential (476 U.S. 267,277, 1986). The Court, however, gave an indication that "there may be times when it becomes necessary to take race into account, even if it meant that innocent persons may be required to bear some of the burdens required in the remedy" (476 U.S. 267,282, 1986). Finally, the Court reasoned, that "the plan presented by the school board was not narrowly tailored" (476 U.S. 267,284, 1986).

However, Justices Marshall, Brennan, and Blackmun agreed that the layoff plan, when judged according to *Bakke* (1978) and *Fullilove* (1980), met constitutional muster. The dissenting opinion argued that the plan was justified based on historical discriminatory practices (476 U.S. 267,303, 1986). In a separate dissent, Justice Stevens suggested, that "diversity was an important part of public education" (476 U.S. 267,315, 1986). The Court established the principle, nevertheless, that faculty diversity and student diversity were not legitimate rationales for protecting African Americans from layoffs.

In the case of *Sheet Metal Workers* (1986) the Court resolved the legal issue of egregious discrimination, willful contempt, and interpretation of the meaning of Title VII. The case centered around "the continued blatant discriminatory practices against African Americans and Hispanic Americans not in a union, which was a violation of Title VII" (478 U.S. 421,426, 1986). The contempt phase of the case resulted from Local 28's refusal to comply with Federal District Court orders in 1982 and again in 1983.

A majority of the Court (which included the liberal core of Brennan, Marshall, and Blackmun) held that when there was continued egregious discriminatory employment practices, utilization of an employment goal was permissible (478 U.S. 421,483, 1986). It should be noted that in this case, conservative Justice O'Connor voted with the liberal core on some parts of the judgement.

As a result of Local 28's willful contempt of the Federal District Court's order, "the Court ordered a relief fund designated for the enhancement of membership for African Americans and Hispanic Americans" (478 U.S. 421,439, 1986). The Court ruled, that "the fund was constitutional based on that fact that it was a temporary measure" (478 U.S. 421,439, 1986).

In *Sheet Metal Workers* (1986) the Court also discussed the congressional meaning of Title VII. Justice Brennan stated, that "the language of Title VII did not preclude the implementation of a race-conscious relief as a remedy for past historical discrimination" (478 U.S. 421,445, 1986). He suggested, that "the language of Title VII allowed relief for those who were not actual victims" (478 U.S. 421,447, 1986). Finally, Brennan stated, that "the scope of Title VII included the removal of barriers that had operated in the past to favor an identifiable group of white employees over employees of color" (478 U.S. 421,448, 1986). Thus, Title VII was created "to achieve equality of employment opportunities" (478 U.S. 421,448, 1986).

During the 1987 term of the Supreme Court, the Court addressed the legality of a court-ordered affirmative action plan in the *United States v. Paradise* (1987). The case resulted from the hiring practices of the Alabama State Troopers. An Alabama Federal District Judge had ordered in 1983 and 1984 the implementation of a one-for-one promotion scheme. The purpose of the hiring requirement "was to promote one African American state trooper for each white trooper until the state developed an acceptable promotion plan" (480 U.S. 149,160, 1987). A key fact in *Paradise* was that it focused on promotional practices rather than hiring practices as demonstrated in *Sheet Metal Workers*. Thus, the Court ruled for the first time, that "judges may order strict racial promotional quotas to overcome long-term, open, and pervasive discrimination" (480 U.S. 149, 1987).

The writers of the plurality judgement in *Paradise* (1987) included Brennan, Marshall, Blackmun, Stevens, and Powell. It should be noted that the vote of Powell in promoting quotas represented a departure from his view in *Bakke* nine years earlier (480 U.S. 149,186, 1987). Powell suggested that in *Paradise*, "the state of Alabama had engaged in the persistent violation of constitutional rights and had repeatedly failed to carry out the Federal District Court's order" (480 U.S. 149,167, 1987). The Court in *Paradise* (1987) established the guidelines "that strict racial quotas in promotions met constitutional muster in the public sector" (480 U.S. 149,167, 1987). The Court concluded that a race-specific, court-ordered affirmative action plan was narrowly tailored to serve a compelling governmental interest.

Four weeks after *Paradise* (480 U.S. 149, 1987) in *Johnson v. Transportation Agency, Santa Clara County* (480 U.S. 616, 1987) the Court decided the most significant affirmative action/reverse discrimination decision since *Bakke* (1978). The issues in *Johnson* (1987) included gender and affirmative action, temporary plans or goals, and the problem of occupational segregation. In *Johnson*, "the Agency had voluntarily adopted an affirmative action plan with a long term goal of attaining a workforce reflective of the proportion of women and people of color in the relevant labor market" (480 U.S. 616, 621-622, 1987). The plan encompassed "the short-term goal establishing an annual adjustment to provide guidelines for obtaining the desired long-term objective" (480 U.S. 616,622, 1987). It is important to note that the plan set no specific number of positions for women of color. But, instead, "authorized consideration of race and sex as a factor, but not the sole factor, in the evaluation of qualified applicants" (480 U.S. 616,622, 1987).

The majority of the Court (Brennan, Marshall, Blackmun, Powell, and Stevens) relied on the legal precedent established in *Weber* (1979) as the established criteria for analyzing affirmative action plans (480 U.S. 616,627-628, 1987). As noted in *Weber*, consideration must be given to determine if the affirmative action plan was designed to break down historical patterns of a discriminatory hierarchy. *Weber* also required that the plan must be temporary and not designed to maintain a sex or race-based balance in the workplace. The plan, according to *Weber*, must not "unnecessarily trammel the interest of white employees" (443 U.S. 193,208-209, 1979). The Court held that the plan established in Johnson (1987) met the judicial criteria of *Weber* (1979). The Court ruled, that "it was permissible to take gender and race into account as a factor in employment decisions" (480 U.S. 616,632, 1987). The Court also argued "that women and African Americans can receive preferential treatment" (480 U.S. 616,632, 1987). *Johnson* marked the first time that the Court ruled on an affirmative action plan that provided job preferences to women. The Court took into consideration the fact that women were "egregiously under-represented in the labor force" (480 U.S. 616,636, 1987).

The Court noted that the Agency's plan was consistent with the purpose of Title VII, "which entailed the elimination of the effects of employment discrimination" (480 U.S. 616,632 1987). It was the majority's viewpoint, that "the plan was designed to attain an organizational workforce reflective of the qualified workforce" (480 U.S. 616, 642, 1987).

In concurring with the judgement, Justice O'Connor indicated, that "the majority had expanded affirmative action too far" (480 U.S. 616, 649, 1987). Interestingly, Justice White (who voted in the majority in *Weber)* suggested overturning *Weber* and argued that *Johnson* "perverted the congressional intent of Title VII" (480 U.S. 616,657, 1987). Justice Scalia argued, that "*Johnson* (1987) had effectively required employers, public as well as private, to engage in intentional discrimination based on race or gender" (480 U.S. 616,658, 1987).

According to Belton (1988), the central concern in *Paradise* (1987) and *Johnson* (1987) for the majority, concurring, and dissenting opinions was whether race or sex-specific remedies harmed innocent victims; whether approval of affirmative action plans meant that unqualified African Americans and women benefitted at the expense of presumptively qualified innocent victims. He suggested that the establishment of affirmative action plans must be aligned with the parameters of national policies and laws against discrimination (Belton, 1988). He also suggested that *Johnson* presented an analytical approach for determining whether white males were actual victims of discrimination when an employer voluntarily adopted an affirmative action program. Belton (1998) stated that the dissenters in *Paradise* and *Johnson* offered no analytical framework for determining when white males are, in fact, actual victims of unlawful discrimination. In his conclusion, Belton (1988) implied that affirmative action brought to the forefront the fact that rarely was there an objective standard to determine the best qualified from a pool of otherwise qualified applicants.

Perhaps the cases during the time frame from 1971-1988 pertaining to affirmative action, reverse discrimination and the diverse issues of employment discrimination suggest that the "wrench" still turns on the quest for equality. It may be inferred that the Supreme Court continued to tighten the wrench , thereby clouding the distinction between judicial restraint and judicial activism as it applied to affirmative action. It can be argued that the Court has moved from the judicial role of "finding the law" to that of "hiding the law." The next section, Chapter V, reveals a sharp turn to the political right with regard to judicial restraint. This became more obvious as the political climate began to change and the composition of the Court continued to move in a judicially conservative direction.

# CHAPTER V

# THE SUPREME COURT AND AFFIRMATIVE ACTION: 1989-1996

### The Supreme Court and It's 1989 Decisions

The bulk of the Court's agenda during this term focused on two issues. The first was whether reverse discrimination violated the Equal Protection Clause of the Fourteenth Amendment. The second was whether affirmative action violated the Civil Rights Act of 1964, particularly Title VI. The Court was requested to address the principles related to set-asides, to establish guidelines for strict scrutiny, and disparate impact, and rule on consent decrees. Six cases related to affirmative action were ruled on in 1989. These were *Richmond v. Croson*, 488 U.S. 469; *Wards Cove Packing Company v. Atonio*, 490 U.S. 642; *Martin v. Wilks* 490 U.S. 755; *Price Waterhouse v. Hopkins*, 490 U.S. 288; *Lorance v. AT&T*, 490 U.S. 900; and *Patterson v. McLean Credit Union*, 491 U.S. 164. In these cases the Court handed down decisions of a tremendous impact pertaining to the longevity of affirmative action. The Court's decisions in each of the previously mentioned cases had a direct impact on personnel and the composition of the workforce in the public and private sector. Each case will be discussed and analyzed with regard to affirmative action and its implication for a diversified workforce.

## Richmond v. Croson 488 U.S. 469 (1989)

This case was a result of the legal precedent set by Congress which the Court upheld in *Fullilove* 488 U.S. 497. "In *Fullilove*, the Burger Court upheld a federal law under the Public Works Employment Act of 1977 which was designed to enhance the economic position of contractors in protected groups" (488 U.S. 469,497,1989). The Act required at least 10 percent of contracts awarded to be given to contractors of color. Pursuant to the decision in *Fullilove*, numerous state and local governments adopted their own set-aside programs. The City of Richmond, Virginia adopted a plan that provided compensation for manifest past discriminatory practices against contractors from protected groups. "The Richmond plan required 30 percent of future contracts awarded by the city set aside for contractors from protected groups" (488 U.S. 469,478, 1989).

The plan was established in April 1983, "by the Richmond City Council, (which consisted of five African Americans and four whites), and was adopted by a vote of 6-2 with one abstention" (488 U.S. 469,481, 1989). "The council-adopted protected group business plan required prime contractor's awarded city construction to subcontract at least 30 percent of a contract to one or more Minority Business Enterprise(s) (MBEs)" (488 U.S. 468,478, 1989). Any MBE meeting the city's criteria could employ a subcontractor from anywhere in the United States. The Richmond city plan "contained a waiver to set-aside only when it had been demonstrated that every feasible effort to comply was exhausted and that sufficient, relevant, qualified MBE's were unavailable or unwilling to participate in the contract" (488 U.S. 469,478, 1989).

The legal dispute arose after the J.A. Croson Company was awarded the contract "to install fixtures and plumbing at the city jail" upon submission of the lowest bid (488 U.S. 469,482, 1989). Initially, Croson made a reasonable effort to find an MBE to supply the necessary fixtures. However, the only MBE found submitted a bid quotation substantially higher than one given by a white business. In view of the MBE's unexpected high quote, "Croson asked the city to waive the set-aside requirement or approve raising the contract price" (488 U.S. 469,484, 1989). The city refused to comply and litigation arose with Croson claiming "the practice of set-asides violated the Equal Protection Clause of the Fourteenth Amendment" (488 U.S. 469, 484, 1989).

The issue before the Court centered on whether race-conscious classifications implemented to overcome the effects of past discrimination violated the equal protection guarantee. In a 6-3 vote (O'Connor, Rehnquist, White, Kennedy, Stevens and Scalia), with the opinion delivered by O'Connor, "the Supreme Court ruled the Richmond city ordinance requirement that 30 percent of the total dollar amount of city construction awarded to MBE's was unconstitutional" (488 U.S. 469, 470, 1989). The Court reasoned, that "the practice of set-asides violated the Equal Protection Clause of the Fourteenth Amendment" (488 U.S. 469,470, 1989).

In deciding the case, the Supreme Court utilized the strict-scrutiny standard of review for assessing state and municipal set-aside programs (488 U.S. 469,471-472, 1989). The strict-scrutiny standard was appropriate in *Croson* because of the political power wielded by African Americans in the City of Richmond. The Court based its decision on, "the fact that 50 percent of the population was African American and five of the nine city council members were African Americans" (488 U.S. 469,495, 1989). The Court was concerned with the "lack of evidence demonstrating prior discrimination by the City of Richmond" (488 U.S. 469,472, 1989).

The Court's view was that the Richmond set-aside plan suffered from generalized assertions of past discrimination in the construction industry. Reviewing the Richmond plan, the Court made the following assessment regarding past discriminatory practices: (1) "the 30% quota had no reasonable relation to injury suffered by anyone; (2) the comparison of the use of contractor's of color to the city's general population of color did not reflect the percentage of qualified contractor's of color in the population; (3) the city did not know how many MBE's in the relevant market were qualified to become prime contractors or subcontractors; (4) the city did not know the percentage of total construction dollars firms of color received as subcontractors; (5) the low number of people of color in the local contractor's association did not show a disparity between eligible MBE's and MBE membership; and (6) the city arbitrarily included other groups of color --Eskimos and Aleutes–that were not in the geographic region" (488 U.S. 469, 504-506, 1989).

The *Croson* decision simplified the process for whites, who sought to challenge non-federal set-aside provisions. In a commentary given by Rice (1991), the legal aftermath of *Croson* created the judicial dismantling of set-aside programs and the voluntary termination/suspension of other such programs. As a result of the Court's strict-scrutiny approach, a state or municipality had the following burdens: "(1) it must demonstrate a compelling state interest by establishing a *prima facie* case of past discrimination and/or discrimination by the legal construction industry; (2) it must demonstrate that other race-neutral alternatives were carefully considered, and the set-aside program adopted was narrowly tailored so as to rectify the effects of past discrimination" (488 U.S. 469,472-473, 1989).

Nevertheless, the Court failed to establish the exact formula for determining minority business capacity, for contractors of color, ethnic classifications and subgroups, and market discrimination. Consequently, defending set-aside programs involved preparing a "disparity study that statistically documented how minorities and minority-owned firms had been discriminated against in government contracting" (488 U.S. 469, 473, 1989).

The Court noted that when race and gender-neutral goals were compared to set-aside programs, "there were increases in the amount of money targeted to specified programs" (488 U.S. 469, 473, 1989). The Court allowed established precedents, "to maintain set-aside contracting levels that adopted higher percentage goals under a race and gender-neutral system" (488 U.S. 469,474, 1989). It can be inferred from the Court's decision, that "it only deterred local governments uncommitted to correcting pass societal ills" (488 U.S. 469,474, 1989). The decision did not discourage however, those committed to providing the necessary resources required to adopt permissible set-aside programs for people of color.

Justice Marshall expressed the views of the minority (Brennan, Blackmun, and Marshall). Marshall began his dissent by applauding the efforts of a former "Confederate" state for devising a plan "to confront the effects of racial discrimination" (488 U.S. 469,528, 1989). Marshall noted, that "the plan utilized by Richmond was patterned after a federal set-aside plan confirmed by the Supreme Court in *Fullilove v. Klutznick*, 448 U.S. 448 (1980)" (488 U.S. 469,529, 1989). He pointed out that Richmond, because of past decisions by both lower federal courts and the Supreme Court, had demonstrated historical racial discrimination (488 U.S. 469,529, 1989). According to Marshall, the Court took a deliberate and giant step backward in the area of affirmative action jurisprudence in *Richmond* (488 U.S. 469,529, 1989). He was fearful the majority Court's decision would inevitably prevent states as well as local governments from enacting programs "to rectify the scourge of past discrimination" (488 U.S. 469, 530, 1989).

Marshall pointed out that one of the problems with the current Court was "a failure to agree on a means for applying the Equal Protection Clause to an affirmative action program" (488 U.S. 469,535, 1989). The question was, "whether or not Richmond had proffered satisfactory proof of past discrimination to support its twin interests in remediation and governmental non-perpetuation" (488 U.S. 469,539, 1989). Marshall argued that the evidence supplied by Richmond provided a "strong, firm and unquestionably legitimate basis for the city to determine the effects of past discrimination warranting a remedial and prophylactic governmental response" (488 U.S. 469,540, 1989).

In documenting the inconsistencies of the Court, Marshall referenced a statement made by Justice O'Connor in *Johnson v. Transportation Agency, Santa Clara County,* 480 U.S. 616, 656-657 (1987). In that case, O'Connor stated that, "when alleged discrimination had prevented African Americans from obtaining experience necessary to qualify for a position, the relevant comparison was not the percentage of African Americans in the pool of qualified candidates, but the total percentage of African Americans in the labor force" (488 U.S. 469,542, 1989). Marshall argued that the Court's decision in Richmond was contradictory to *Johnson* and a reversal of the Court's position (488 U.S. 469, 542, 1989).

Marshall disagreed with the majority's dismissal of the congressional and executive branch findings cited in *Fullilove* (448 U.S. 448, 1980). He stated that "the majority decision in essence required cities seeking to eradicate the effects of past discrimination to impact the evidentiary wheel and engage in unnecessarily costly fact-finding endeavors" (488 U.S. 469,547, 1989). In Marshall's opinion, Richmond's set-aside plan satisfied the criteria of equal protection and it ensured "that municipal contract procurement had not perpetuated discrimination" (488 U.S. 469,548, 1989). The Richmond plan did not "interfere with any vested right of a contractor to a particular contract, but rather operated prospectively" (488 U.S. 469,549, 1989). Marshall concluded, stating that "the majority had gone beyond the facts of this case and announced a set of principles that unnecessarily restricted the power of governmental entities to take into consideration race-conscious measures when redressing the effects of prior discrimination" (488 U.S. 469,551, 1989).

Justice Blackmun, in a dissent  joined by Brennan, attacked the decision, stating that "the supposed bastion of inequality struck down

Richmond's efforts as though discrimination had never existed or was not demonstrated in the litigation" (488 U.S. 469,561, 1989). He indicated that this decision was a "regression" by the Court (488 U.S. 469,562, 1989). However, he remained hopeful that the Court would again, "fulfill the great promises of the Constitution's Preamble and of the guarantees embodied in the Bill of Rights" (488 U.S. 469,562, 1989).

*Richmond v. Croson*, 488 U.S. 469 (1989) presented an interesting legal dilemma for affirmative action. The plurality essentially took the position, that "set-aside programs designed to compensate for past historical discrimination were unconstitutional" because they violated the Equal Protection Clause of the Fourteenth Amendment (488 U.S. 469, 1989). The Court applied the legal standard of "strict scrutiny" (488 U.S. 469, 471-472, 1989). At this juncture, the Supreme Court held a narrow view of affirmative action programs. The pertinent issue of programs designed to negate past historical racial discrimination was circumvented by the majority opinion. As indicated by Justice Marshall, "the opinion drastically reversed" as well as reduced the effect of *Fullilove v. Klutznick*, 448 U.S. 448 (1980) and *Johnson v. Transportation Agency, Santa Clara County*, 480 U.S. 616 (1987). As suggested by Justice Blackmun, the decision in this case not only restricted affirmative action, "it presented a regression of the rights set forth in the Constitution's Preamble and Bill of Rights" (488 U.S. 469,562, 1989).

## Wards Cove Packing Company v. Antonio, 490 U.S. 642 (1989)

This case involved two companies operating salmon canneries in "remote and widely separate areas of Alaska" (490 U.S. 642, 1989). Employment at the canneries were of two general types: "cannery jobs which were unskilled positions and noncannery jobs classified as skilled positions" (490 U.S. 642,646, 1989). The hierarchical structure resulted in, "cannery positions occupied by people of color while noncannery positions resulted in the domination of white employees" (490 U.S. 642,646-647, 1989). The pay scale also reflected the hierarchical format. Employment required the implementation of separate housing and dining facilities based on race (490 U.S. 642,647, 1989).

The District Court rejected all claims of "disparate treatment" (490 U.S. 642, 648, 1989). Disparate impact occurred when there was substantial under-representation of protected-class members as a result of employment decisions that worked to their disadvantage. The District

Court rejected "the disparate impact challenges involving the subjective employment criteria used by petitioners to fill noncannery positions, on the grounds that the criteria was not subject to attack from a disparate impact theory" (490 U.S. 642,648, 1989). The Ninth Circuit Court of Appeals however, "held that the plaintiffs had presented a *prima facie* case of disparate impact in hiring for both skilled and unskilled noncannery positions" (490 U.S. 642,649, 1989). The Court of Appeals, relied "solely on statistical evidence presented by the plaintiffs which documented the existence of a high percentage of workers of color in the cannery status and a low percentage of workers of color in the noncannery category" (490 U.S. 642,650, 1989).

In a 5-4 decision, the conservative majority (Rehnquist, O'Connor, Scalia, White, and Kennedy) rejected the employees challenge of alleged discriminatory employment practices. The opinion of the Court was given by Justice White. The Court held, that "the Court of Appeals erred in ruling that a comparison of the percentage of cannery workers who were people of color and the percentage of noncannery workers who were people of color constituted a *prima facie* disparate impact case" (490 U.S. 642,650, 1989. However, "the proper comparison was between the racial composition of the at-issue jobs and the racial composition of the qualified population in the relevant labor market" (490 U.S. 642,650, 1989). White contended that "with respect to the skilled noncannery issue, the cannery workforce was in no way reflective of the pool of qualified job applicants or the qualified labor force population" (490 U.S. 642,651, 1989).

White stated that "the Court of Appeals erred with respect to the unskilled noncannery positions" (490 U.S. 642,653, 1989). It was noted, that "racial imbalance in one segment of an employer's workforce did not alone establish a *prima facie* case of disparate impact with respect to the selection of workers for the employer's other positions, even where workers for various positions might have had somewhat fungible skills" (490 U.S. 642,653, 1989). The Court continued with the statement, that "the isolation of cannery workers as a potential labor force for unskilled noncannery workers was both too broad and too narrow" (490 U.S. 642,653, 1989). White wrote that "it was too broad because the majority of cannery workers had not sought noncannery jobs" (490 U.S. 642,653, 1989). It was "too narrow because many qualified persons in the relevant labor market were not cannery workers" (490 U.S. 642,653-654, 1989). Analyzing the issue of disparate impact, White reasoned, that "a demonstration of statistical disparity in a complaint must be the result of one or more employment practices and must specifically show that each challenged practice constituted a significant disparate impact on employment opportunities for whites and people of color" (490 U.S. 642,657, 1989).

Justice White's conclusion pointed out that, if on remand, the plaintiffs established a *prima facie* disparate impact case regarding the defendants employment practice, the burden of proof was shifted to the defendants, however, the burden of persuasion remained with the plaintiff (490 U.S. 642,660, 1989). He noted, that "this rationale aligned with judicial rules for persuasion and production burdens in the area of disparate treatment cases" (490 U.S. 642,661, 1989).

A dissenting opinion was written by Justice Blackmun with Brennan and Marshall joining. Blackmun reported that the plurality of justices on the Court took "three major strides backwards in the battle against race discrimination" (490 U.S. 642,661, 1989). Blackmun delineated those steps as follows: (1) the Court overturned "the longstanding distribution of burdens of proof in Title VII disparate impact cases" (490 U.S. 642,661, 1989); (2) "it bars the use of internal workforce comparisons in the making of a *prima facie* case of discrimination, even where the structure of the industry in question renders any other statistical comparison meaningless" (490 U.S. 642,661-662, 1989); and (3) "it requires practice-by-practice statistical proof of causation, even where, as here, such proof would be impossible" (490 U.S. 642,662, 1989). Justice Blackmun asserted that the rationale of the Court "immunized these practices from attack under a Title VII disparate impact analysis" (490 U.S. 642,662, 1989). In his conclusion, Blackmun wrote, as to "whether the majority still believes that race discrimination- or more accurately, race discrimination against nonwhites is a problem in society, or even remembers that it ever was" (490 U.S. 642, 662, 1989).

An additional dissent was written by Justice Stevens with Brennan, Marshall and Blackmun joining. Stevens stated that "over eighteen years ago, the Supreme Court unanimously held that Title VII of the Civil Rights Act of 1964 prohibited employment practices that had discriminatory effects as well as those that are intended to discriminate" (490 U.S. 642,662, 1989). He asserted that the Court, decision negated *Griggs v. Duke Power Company*, 401 U.S. 424 (1971). Stevens noted, that "federal courts and federal agencies consistently have enforced the view of a national goal of eliminating barriers that defined economic opportunity not by aptitude or ability but by race, color, national origin and other traits that were easily identified but utterly irrelevant to one's qualification for a particular job" (490 U.S. 642,662-663, 1989). Stevens stated that "regrettably, the Court had decided to retreat from those objectives and instead based on an interlocutory judgment disregarded the particular facts of this lawsuits" (490 U.S. 642,663, 1989). He implied, quite frankly, that the essence of the Court's decision was tantamount to turning a "blind eye to the meaning and purpose of Title VII" (490 U.S. 642,663, 1989). The Court rejected "a longstanding rule of law as a result, and underestimated the probative value of evidence of a racially stratified workforce" (490 U.S. 642,663, 1989).

Stevens had trouble comprehending the Court's "redefinition of the employees' burden of proof in a disparate impact case" (490 U.S. 642,672, 1989). Stevens suggested that "the additional proof requirement was unwarranted" (490 U.S. 642,672, 1989). Justice Stevens stated that "the majority opinion began with the settled rule that a facially neutral employment practice may be deemed violative of Title VII without evidence of the employer's subjective intent to discriminate as required in a disparate treatment case" (490 U.S. 642,678, 1989). However, the opinion of the plurality, according to Stevens, "departed from the body of law engendered by disparate impact theory and reformulated the order of proof and the weight of the respective parties burden" (490 U.S. 642,678-679, 1989).

The Rehnquist Court in *Wards Cove* dealt a severe blow to affirmative action. The burden of proof now required created stringent guidelines necessary to win a disparate impact case. The essential factor was that the burden of proof became greater for the individual bringing the charges. The Court disavowed "statistical data for substantiating a disparate impact claim" (490 U.S. 642,650, 1989). The Court now required that "appropriate statistical comparisons must be formulated based on the racial percentage of jobs in question along with the racial composition of the local labor market" (490 U.S. 642, 1989). The Court retreated from earlier concessions granted in the area of affirmative action.

## Martin v. Wilks, 490 U.S. 755 (1989)

The *Martin v. Wilks*, 490 U.S. 755 (1989) decision followed *Wards Cove* (490 U.S. 642, 1989) one week later. The key issue in *Martin v. Wilks* (1989) was a consent decree. The litigants in this case were firefighters in Birmingham, Alabama who were not a party to the original judicial proceedings (490 U.S. 755, 1989).

"This case resulted from African American individuals, and the Ensley Branch of the National Association for the Advancement of Colored People (NAACP), who filed suit in Federal District Court against the City of Birmingham, Alabama, and the Jefferson County Personnel Board (hereafter referred to as Board)" (490 U.S. 755,759, 1989). It was alleged, that "the defendants had engaged in racially discriminatory hiring and promotional practices in violation of Title VII of the Civil Rights Act of 1964, 42 U.S.C. Section 2000e et seq., and other federal laws" (490 U.S. 755,759, 1989). As a result, two consent decrees were established, one between the African American individuals and the city; and a consent decree between the African American individuals and the Personnel Board. The proposed decrees, "set forth an extensive remedial scheme, including long-term and interim annual goals for the hiring of blacks as firefighters" (490 U.S. 755,759, 1989). Also the decrees provided promotional goals for African Americans.

After public notice of a fairness hearing reported in two local newspapers, seven white firefighters (members of the Birmingham Firefighters Association) filed a complaint against the city and the Board seeking injunctive relief. The seven firefighters argued, that "the decrees illegally discriminated against them, the District Court denied relief" (490 U.S. 755,759-760, 1989).

As a result of legal action, a new group of white firefighters with the lead name of Wilks, "filed suit against the city and the Board in District Court" (490 U.S. 755,760, 1989). Wilks alleged denial of promotion based on race, in which less qualified African Americans were promoted and which violated Title VII (490 U.S. 755,760, 1989). The Board and the city acknowledged race-conscious employment decisions but supported their action arguing that "the decisions were unassailable because they were made pursuant to the consent decrees" (490 U.S. 755,760, 1989). Martin was allowed to intervene in defense of the consent decrees. The defendants moved for dismissal, "claiming reverse discrimination based on impermissible collateral attacks on the consent decrees" (490 U.S. 755,760, 1989). The District Court denied the motion, and "ruled that the decrees provided a defense to claims of discrimination for employment decisions 'mandated' by the decrees" (490 U.S. 755,760, 1989). The District Court also held "that Wilks was precluded from challenging employment decisions taken pursuant to the consent decrees, even though they had not been parties to the proceedings when the decrees were entered" (490 U.S. 755,760, 1989). The Eleventh Circuit

Court of Appeals reversed and rejected the 'impermissible collateral attack' doctrine that immunizes parties to a consent decree from discrimination charges by nonparties for actions taken pursuant to the decree (490 U.S. 755, 1989). The case came before the Supreme Court after *writ of certiorari* was granted (490 U.S. 755,761, 1989).

In a 5-4 decision ( Rehnquist, White, O'Connor, Scalia, and Kennedy), the Supreme Court affirmed the ruling of the Court of Appeals. The opinion of the Court provided through Chief Justice Rehnquist, stated that "[i]t was a principle of general application in Anglo-American juris[-]prudence that one was not bound by a judgment *in personam* in a litigation which he was not designated as a party or to which he had not been made a party by service of process" (490 U.S. 755,761, 1989). Rehnquist wrote that it is a "deep-seated historical tradition, that everyone was entitled to their day in court" (490 U.S. 755,762, 1989). "A judgment or decree among parties to a lawsuit resolved issues among them, but it did not conclude the rights of strangers to those proceedings" (490 U.S. 755,762, 1989).

In addressing the issue of "impermissible collateral attack" the Court utilized Rule 19(b) of Federal Civil Procedures. "Federal Rule 19(b) provides that if a person cannot be made a party, the court shall determine whether in equity and good conscious the action should proceed among parties before it, or should be dismissed, the absent person being regarded as indispensable" (490 U.S. 755, 1989). The factors to be considered by the court follow in this discussion. "First, to what extent a judgment rendered in the person's absence might be prejudicial to the person or those already partners. Second, the extent to which, by protective provisions in the judgment, by shaping of relief or other measures, the prejudice can be lessened or avoided. Third, whether a judgment rendered in the person's absence will be adequate. And fourth, whether the plaintiff had adequate remedy if the action was dismissed for nonjoinder" (490 U.S. 755,764-765, 1989).

According to Rehnquist, that "...the system of joinder called for by the Rules is likely to produce more relitigation of the issues" (490 U.S. 755, 768, 1989). Rehnquist noted that the "voluntary settlement" by means of a consent decree between a group of employers and employees does not necessarily "settle" the claims of those not originally involved in the litigation (490 U.S. 755, 768, 1989).

Justices Stevens, with Brennan, Marshall, and Blackmun joining the dissenting opinion. The dissent began with the point, that "[a]s a matter of law there was a vast difference between persons who are actual parties to litigation and persons who merely had an interest that as a practical matter be impaired by the outcome of the case. Persons in the first category had a right to participate in a trial and to appeal from an adverse judgment; if they won or lost, their legal rights was enhanced or impaired" (490 U.S. 755,769, 1989). Stevens continued that individuals in the latter category are afforded the opportunity to participate in the litigation, if in a timely fashion or risk becoming involved as a party against their will. The individual could remain on the sidelines and risk the possibility of being harmed in a practical matter even though their legals rights were unaffected. If an individual maintained sideline-setting status, the individual in question forfeited the right to appeal (490 U.S. 755,769-770, 1989).

Justice Stevens' dissent discussed the parameters of the consent decree. He wrote, that "one of the effects of a decree was to curtail the job opportunities of nonparties, and this did not mean that nonparties had been deprived of legal rights or that they had standing to appeal from that decree without becoming parties" (490 U.S. 755,771, 1989). Stevens stated that individuals could collaterally attack a decision on narrow conditions when confronted with no right to appeal (490 U.S. 755,771, 1989). Justice Stevens outlined those conditions as including the absence of court jurisdiction over the subject matter, or judgment resulting from the production of corruption, duress, fraud, collusion, and mistake (490 U.S. 755,771, 1989). Stevens pointed out, that "the rule not only applied to parties of the original action, but allowed interested third parties collaterally to attack the judgments" (490 U.S. 755,771, 1987). Stevens reasoned that a person who envisioned a law suit paid a heavy price if they elected to remain on the sidelines rather than seeking intervention and "taking the risk that their legal rights would be impaired" (490 U.S. 755,772, 1989).

Stevens noted, the "race-conscious relief ordered in the consent decree was entirely consistent with the Court's approach to affirmative action" (490 U.S. 755,785, 1989). He reasoned that if evidence of racial discrimination was present, the guidelines of Title VII or the Equal Protection Clause of the Fourteenth Amendment provided no legal barriers preventing non-victims from legal protection. (490 U.S. 755, 785-786, 1989). Stevens concluded with the statement, that "in complex litigations, the Court had ruled that a sideline-sitter was bound as firmly as an actual party if he had adequate notice and a fair opportunity to intervene and if the judicial interest in finality was sufficiently strong" (490 U.S. 755,792, 1989).

In *Martin v. Wilks*, the Rehnquist Court opened a potential for numerous lawsuits challenging consent decrees that occurred in the past two decades. The Court, in essence, established legal justification for white employees to challenge without time limitations, affirmative action consent decrees pertaining to employee discrimination, resulting from Title VII. It now became possible for litigation to arise even if the litigants were not original parties to the consent decree (490 U.S. 755,770-772, 1989). The Court reduced the impact of affirmative action and consent decrees designed to eradicate historical racial discrimination in employment and promotional practice. The arguments of Stevens and the minority would be revisited in 1990 and 1991 in the congressional arena. In 1991, Congress passed a civil rights act that had the effect of nullifying some aspects of *Martin v. Wilks* and other 1989 cases.

### Price Waterhouse v. Hopkins, 490 U.S. 228 (1989)

The issue in this case was brought by Ann Hopkins, "a former employee at Price Waterhouse's Office of Government Services in Washington, D.C. of five years" (490 U.S. 228,231, 1989). At the time of her employment, "there were 662 partners with only seven women partners" (490 U.S. 228,231, 1989). Because Hopkins successfully secured "a $25 million contract with the Department of State, it was suggested she receive a recommendation for partnership in 1982" (490 U.S. 228,231, 1989). During that time, "88 persons were recommended, but Hopkins was the only woman" (490 U.S. 228,231-233, 1989). She was neither offered nor denied the partnership, instead, her candidacy was held for reconsideration the next year. Hopkins sued Price Waterhouse under "Title VII of the Civil Rights Act of 1964, 42 U.S.C. 2000e et seq., charging that the firm had discriminated against her on the basis of sex in deciding against the proposed partnership" (490 U.S. 228,231-232, 1989).

During the trial proceedings, evidence revealed that numerous remarks were made about Hopkins as a woman, along with her lack of interpersonal skills. The remarks included, "references such as macho, overcompensated for a woman, and in need of a course at charm school" (490 U.S. 228,235, 1989). It was suggested that the remarks demonstrated "gender bias" as it related to Hopkins (490 U.S. 228,235-236, 1989). During the course of the trial, testimony was presented which suggested that, "women in general were not deservant of a partnership because of their inability to function as a senior manager" (490 U.S. 228,236, 1989). The trial court judge decided that some of the remarks about Hopkins "stemmed from an impressibly cabined view of the proper behavior of women, and Price Waterhouse had done nothing to disavow a reliance on such comments" (490 U.S. 228,236-237, 1989). The trial court judge also held, that "Price Waterhouse had unlawfully discriminated against Hopkins on the basis of sex by consciously giving credence and effect to comments based on sexual stereotyping" (490 U.S. 228,237, 1989). The Court of Appeals affirmed the District Court ruling based on a different analysis of Title VII. The Court of Appeals reasoned, that "there was no violation of Title VII, however, if it was proven that the same decision absent an impermissible motive" was reached (490 U.S. 228,237, 1989).

In a 6-3 vote, the decision (Brennan, Marshall, Blackmun, Stevens, White, O'Connor), reversed the lower courts decision. The judgement of the Court was written by Brennan. They concluded, that "when a plaintiff in a Title VII case proved that gender played a part in an employment decision, the defendant avoided a finding of liability by proving by a preponderance of the evidence that it would have made the same decision even if the gender factor had not been given consideration" (490 U.S. 228,237-258, 1989).

Brennan stated, that "the balance between employee rights and employer prerogatives established by Title VII in eliminating certain bases for distinguishing among employees while otherwise preserving employer's freedom of choice was an important factor" (490 U.S. 228,239-240, 1989). The argument set forth by Brennan was, that "the preservation of an employer's freedom of choice meant that an employer was not liable if it proved that, if it had not taken gender into account, the same conclusion was reached" (490 U.S. 228,239-252, 1989). Interestingly, the majority advocated that "remarks made at work based on sexual stereotypes did not inevitably prove that gender played a part in the employment decision" (490 U.S. 228,251, 1989).

Justice Brennan pointed out that the decision of *Price Waterhouse* did not "traverse new ground." The Court had, in an earlier decision, "held that it was an employer's burden to justify decisions which resulted from the utilization of an illegal criterion to distinguish employees"(*Dothard v. Rawlinson*, 433 U.S. 321, 1977). The Court held "when a plaintiff in a Title VII case proved that her gender played a motivating part in an employment decision, the defendant avoided a finding of liability only by proving by a preponderance of the evidence it would have made the decision regardless of the employee's gender" (490 U.S. 228,258, 1989).

In his concurring opinion, Justice White wrote that the Court had an established precedent for supporting its decision in the case of *"Mt. Healthy City Board of Education v. Doyle*," 429 U.S. 274, 1977. The common denominator for both *Price Waterhouse* and *Mt. Healthy* was that "neither required proving that the illegitimate factor was the only principle or true reason for the petitioner's action" (490 U.S. 228, 259, 1989). White agreed the Court of Appeals applied the incorrect burden of proof standard. It was only necessary for Price Waterhouse to present a "preponderance of evidence" to substantiate that the decision was not premised on gender (490 U.S. 228, 260, 1989).

Justice O'Connor also presented a concurring opinion. She agreed, that "the facts presented in the case supported the conclusion that the burden of persuasion shifted from the employer to demonstrate by a preponderance of the evidence that it reached the same decision concerning Hopkins, absent gender consideration" (490 U.S. 228,261, 1989). She reasoned, that "the burden shift was proper as a part of the liability phase of the litigation" (490 U.S. 228,261, 1989).

Justice O'Connor expressed disagreement concerning the Court's conclusion regarding "the substantive requirement of causation under Title VII" (490 U.S. 228,261, 1989). Her attention focused on the issue of "disparate treatment as it relates to Title VII" (490 U.S. 228,270, 1989). O'Connor noted that in the past, "in an individual disparate treatment action, the plaintiff had the burden of persuasion throughout the litigation" (490 U.S. 228,270, 1989). However, in *Price Waterhouse*, the Court "narrowed the burden of proof" (490 U.S. 228,270, 1989). She stressed that the Court, prior to *Price Waterhouse*, had required that the plaintiff bear the burden of persuasion. According to O'Connor, "it was clear that Title VII tolerated no discrimination, subtle or otherwise, when using the required evidentiary standards" (490 U.S. 228,272, 1989). The rule "shifting the burden of proof to the defendant when the plaintiff had shown an illegitimate criterion as a substantial factor in the employment decision did not conflict with other congressional policies encumbered in Title VII" (490 U.S. 228,274, 1989). O'Connor believed that "there were significant differences between shifting the burden of persuasion to the employer in a case based strictly on statistical proof in a disparate impact case and shifting the burden of persuasion in the *Price Waterhouse* case, where the employee demonstrated that an illegitimate factor played a substantial role in an employment decision" (490 U.S. 228,275, 1989). She concluded by implying that the "deterrent purpose of Title VII was served well by a rule placing the burden of proof on the plaintiff regarding the issue of causation in all circumstances" (490 U.S. 228,278, 1989).

The dissenting opinion (Kennedy, Rehnquist and Scalia) was presented by Kennedy. Kennedy asserted that the decision of "the Court manipulated existing rules of employment discrimination and produced a confusing opinion" (490 U.S. 228,279, 1989). The pivotal point of the dissent was "the issue of causation as required under Title VII" (490 U.S. 228,281, 1989). Kennedy pointed out that "Title VII was not concerned with the mere presence of impermissible motives but rather employment decisions resulting from the motives" (490 U.S. 228,282, 1989). He disagreed that Title VII liability contained no "but-for causation" as inferred by the Court (490 U.S. 228,283, 1989). Kennedy pointed out that the confusion created by the Court was a result of "internal inconsistency." He wrote, "Title VII unambiguously stated that an employer who made decisions because of sex had violated the statue" (490 U.S. 228,285, 1989).

*Price Waterhouse* was important because "the burden of proof now shifted to the plaintiff and the employer merely had to prove by a preponderance of the evidence that the decision was made absent any gender consideration" (490 U.S. 228,261, 1989). This case now made it difficult to bring other cases involving discrimination predicated on gender. *Price Waterhouse* required legal considerations in defining discriminatory intent.

### Lorance v. AT&T Technologies, Inc., 490 U.S. 900 (1989)

The petitioners (Patricia Lorance, Janice King, and Carol Bueschen) were female hourly wage employees for AT&T Technologies, Inc., (AT&T) who began work in the early 1970s (490 U.S. 900,914, 1989). "Until 1979, all hourly wage earners accrued competitive seniority exclusively on the basis of years spent in the plant. A worker promoted to the highly skilled and better paid 'tester' positions retained plant-wide seniority" (490 U.S. 900,901-902, 1989). However, a collective-bargaining agreement enacted in July, 1979 changed the method of calculating tester seniority. The new method determined seniority by "time actually spent as a tester" (490 U.S. 900,902, 1989). However, an employee could attain "plant-wide seniority" by spending "five years" as a tester or upon completion of a proscribed training program (490 U.S. 900, 902, 1989).

When the new seniority system was implemented, Lorance worked as a tester but received a demotion four years later due to the new system. "King and Bueschen became testers several months after the implementation of the new seniority system. They were not affected by the restructured system until 1982" (490 U.S. 755, 914, 1989). An important factor in the case was that Lorance, King and Bueschen, under "the plant-wide seniority system," would not have been demoted (490 U.S. 900,902, 1989). Because of the new seniority system, "Lorance, King, and Bueschen filed charges with the Equal Employment Opportunity Commission in 1983, and upon receiving the right-to-sue letters, filed legal action in Federal District Court for the Northern District of Illinois," alleging violation of Title VII of the Civil Rights Act of 1964 (490 U.S. 900, 902, 1989). The allegation was that the new seniority system's purpose and effect resulted in the "protection of incumbent testers" (men) from female employees who had greater plant-wide seniority, and constituted increasing numbers of testers (490 U.S. 900,903, 1989). "The seniority system at issue was a 'competitive seniority' one designed to allocate entitlement to limited benefits such as promotions or non-demotion" (490 U.S. 900,902, 1989).

The District Court granted judgment in favor of AT&T on the judicial grounds that the women had "failed to file their complaints with the EEOC within the applicable period of limitations" (490 U.S. 900,903, 1989). The District Court used the time-frame outline in 42 U.S.C. Section 2000e-5(e), "which provided that a charge must be filed with EEOC within 180 days of the alleged unfair employment practice, unless the complainant had first instituted proceedings with a state or local agency, in which case the period was extended to a maximum of 300 days" (490 U.S. 900,903, 1989). The Court of Appeals for the Seventh Circuit affirmed the ruling, "noting that the relevant discriminatory act that triggered the period of limitations occurred at the time an employee was subjected to a facially neutral but discriminatory seniority system that the employee knew, or reasonably had known, was discriminatory" (490 U.S. 900,903, 1989). The Supreme Court granted *certiorari* to resolve the conflict regarding the statute of limitations.

In a 5-3 decision the opinion of the Court (Scalia, Rehnquist, White, Stevens and Kennedy) began by focusing on the wording of 42 U.S.C. Section 2000e of the Civil Rights Act of 1964. Justice Scalia wrote for the Court. It was the Court's view, that "the statute provided that a charge shall be filed with the EEOC within an applicable period after the alleged unlawful employment practice occurred" (490 U.S. 900, 904, 1989). Therefore, in assessing timeliness, Scalia noted, that "it required the Court to identify precisely the unlawful employment practice complaint" (490 U.S. 900, 904, 1989). According to Scalia, "the provision meant that absent discriminatory purpose, the operation of a seniority system cannot be an unlawful employment practice even if the system had some discriminatory consequences" (490 U.S. 900,905, 1989). The Court reasoned that "for liability to incur," there had to exist a finding of "actual intent to discriminate on proscribed statutory grounds on behalf of those implementing the seniority system" (490 U.S. 900,905, 1989). Scalia emphasized that Lorance, King and Bueschen argued that the new seniority system was founded on the "differential impact it had on the sexes as an unlawful" practice because it hinged on sexual discrimination (490 U.S. 900,905, 1989). Their claim was based on "intentional discrimination" resulting from an amendment to their contract (409 U.S. 900,905, 1989).

Scalia continued the rationale for the Court, asserting that Lorance, King and Beuschen's "claims of discriminatory conduct occurred beyond the period of limitations and therefore did not constitute a continuous violation" (490 U.S. 900,908, 1989). He wrote that proof of discriminatory intent was required in a Title VII challenge to seniority systems (490 U.S. 900,908, 1989). Scalia indicated that the existence of a seniority system containing discriminatory impact was not sufficient of itself to invalidate the system; however, "actual intent to discriminate must be proven" (490 U.S. 900,909, 1989). It was the Court's viewpoint that Lorance, King, and Bueschen's claim "depended on proof of intentional discrimination occurring outside the period of limitations" (490 U.S. 900,909, 1989). The Court, according to Scalia, held that the signing date of the contract governed the limitation period. It was "the alleged discriminatory adoption that triggered the limitations period" (490 U.S. 900,911, 1989). Scalia concluded with the rationale that allowing a "facially neutral system to be challenged years after its adoption violated the premises of Title VII" (490 U.S. 900,912, 1989).

The dissenting opinion was written by Marshall, with Brennan and Blackmun joining. Justice O'Connor, the only female on the Court, took no part in the consideration or decision of the case involving the three women. Marshall expressed failure at comprehending how the Court's conclusion that a seniority system designed to discriminate, which was a violation of Title VII, 42 U.S.C. Section 2000e-5(e), began immediately upon the adoption of the system (490 U.S. 900,913, 1989). It was Marshall's contention that in order to adhere to the criteria set forth by the Court, one had to know in advance that discrimination was a possibility (490 U.S. 900,913-914, 1989). The view of the Court, according to Marshall, created a surprise regarding congressional intent, "since the goal in enacting Title VII, certainly never included conferring absolute immunity on the discriminatory adopted seniority systems that survive their first 300 days" (490 U.S. 900,914, 1989). Marshall reasoned that the harsh reality of the majority opinion was that "it required an employee to anticipate discrimination, or forever hold their peace" (490 U.S. 900,914, 1989). The Court majority, according to Marshall, concluded that Lorance, King and Bueschen were denied legal action because "they failed to anticipate discriminatory practices within the first 300 days of the new system's adoption" (490 U.S. 900,914, 1989).

Justice Marshall presented a retrospective analysis of the Court's dealing with the issue of the legality of seniority systems under Title VII. He noted that the Court had previously held, that "absent a discriminatory purpose, the operation of a seniority system cannot be a lawful employment practice, even if the system had some discriminatory consequences" (490 U.S. 900,915, 1989). "The Court held by a narrow margin that 42 U.S.C. Section 2000e protected those seniority systems put into place after the passage of Title VII" (490 U.S. 900,916, 1989). Finally, Marshall's analysis set forth the legal theory that the Court had created a situation "rewarding those employers ingenious enough to cloak their acts of discrimination in a facially neutral guise which was identical to a facially discriminatory seniority plan" (490 U.S. 900,917, 1989).

The case was important because it dealt with the issue of seniority systems and discrimination. A key issue was whether a facially discriminatory employment practice disguised as facial neutral system met the constitutional muster of Title VII. The Court allowed the implementation of such an employment practice. This provided another hindrance for those seeking to establish affirmative action programs. Another key issue in this case was the question of when did the statute of limitations requirement take effect regarding the implementation and complaints against such a practice. The Court was now requiring that anyone seeking to bring charges of discriminatory practices must anticipate when and if the discriminatory practice occurred prior to filing charges alleging a discriminatory employment practice. The Court majority ruled, that the time factor began with the adoption of the seniority system.

## Patterson v. McLean Credit Union, 491 U.S. 164 (1989)

Brenda Patterson was an African American female employed by McLean Credit Union from 1972 to 1982 as an accounting clerk. Her primary employment entailed filing and sometimes working as a back-up teller. Patterson was laid off after having been employed by McLean Credit Union for ten years. She alleged that during her employment she was harassed, denied a promotion to an accountant clerk position, and was laid off because of her race.

During trial testimony, Patterson asserted that unlike other workers, she was given "the menial task of dusting and sweeping the office" (491 U.S. 164, 1989). She indicated, that "she was criticized publicly and received repressive work loads" (491 U.S. 164, 1989). Her testimony revealed that "numerous complaints pertaining to her work ethic contained racial overtones" (491 U.S. 164,165, 1989). Patterson alleged that "McLean Credit Union denied her employment training and salary increases" (491 U.S. 164,165, 1989). After her termination, she began legal action in the United States District Court for the Middle District of North Carolina under 42 U.S.C. Section 1981 of the Civil Rights Act of 1866, alleging racial discrimination (491 U.S. 169, 1989).

The scope of *Patterson v. McLean Credit Union* (491 U.S. 164, 1989) centered around "the Civil Rights Act of 1866 which focused on racial discrimination in contract performance" (491 U.S. 164,165, 1989). That act is codified as Title 42, Section 1981. Section 1981 provided:

> " 'All persons within the jurisdiction of the United States shall have the same right in every State and Territory to make and enforce contracts, to sue, be parties, give evidence, and to the full and equal benefit of all laws and proceedings for the security of persons and property as is enjoyed by white citizens, and shall be subject to like punishment, pains, penalties, taxes, licenses, and exactions of every kind, and to no other,' Revised Stat. Section 1977," (491 U.S. 176).

The case focused on two interpretations of Section 1981. The first issue was whether the Civil Rights Act of 1866 covered discrimination predicated on race in a private contract. Second, did the Act prohibit discriminatory practices during the formation of the contract or conditions that arose from the contract (491 U.S. 164,176-177, 1989).

In *Patterson v. McLean Credit Union* (491 U.S. 164, 1989) the Court majority (Kennedy, Rehnquist, White, O'Connor and Scalia), in a 5-4 decision ruled in favor of the defendant-employer. Justice Kennedy wrote for the Court. Justice Brennan concurred in part and dissented in part with Justice Marshall and Blackmun joining and Stevens joining part of the concurrence. Stevens also wrote a separate concurring and dissenting opinion (491 U.S. 164,167, 1989).

Justice Kennedy began the opinion by pointing out that the case considered the meaning and coverage of one of the oldest civil rights statutes, 42 U.S.C. Section 1981. The Court majority provided the following legal rationale for its decision:

(1) "Racial harassment relating to the conditions of employment was not actionable under Section 1981, because that provision did not apply to conduct that occurred after the formation of a contract and which did not interfere with the right to enforce established contractual obligations" (491 U.S. 164,175-185, 1989); (2) "Since Section 1981 was restricted in scope to forbidding racial discrimination in the making and enforcement of contracts, it cannot be construed as a general proscription of discrimination in all aspects of contract relations" (491 U.S. 164,175-185, 1989). Section 1981 did not extend beyond the conduct by an employer which impaired an employee's ability to enforce through legal processes the establishment of contractual rights (491 U.S. 164,176-178, 1989); (3) Patterson's racial harassment claim was not actionable under Section 1981. The Court pointed out, that with "the possible exception of her claims that respondent's refusal to promote her was discriminatory, none of the alleged conduct involved either a refusal to make a contract with her or her ability to enforce established contractual rights" (491 U.S. 164, 178-182, 1989). "The alleged conduct was past formation conduct exercised by the employer relating to the terms and conditions of continuing employment, which had credence under an expanded interpretation of Title VII"; (4) "The fact that there was no merit to the contention that Section 1981's same right must be interpreted to incorporate state contract law, such that racial harassment in the conditions of employment was actionable when, and only when, it amounted to a breach of contract under state law"(491 U.S. 164,176-182, 1989).

Kennedy wrote, that this "theoretical interpretation unjustifiably federalized all state-law breach of contract claims where racial *animus* was alleged, since Section 1981 covered all types of contracts" (491 U.S. 164,182-185, 1989).

The dissenting opinion written by Brennan with Marshall, Blackmun, and Stevens joining, stated that "what the Court declined to snatch away with one hand, it took with the other" (491 U.S. 164,189, 1989). Brennan noted, that "the Court's failure to apply Section 1981 to private conduct gave the landmark civil rights statute a needlessly cramped interpretation" (491 U.S. 164,189, 1989). He stated, that the Court strained hard to justify the narrowest interpretation and ignored powerful historical evidence, and instead provided a parsimonious interpretation of Section 1981 (491 U.S. 164,189, 1989).

Justice Brennan asserted, that "Patterson had just claim for a cause of action under Section 1981 predicated on allegations of racial discrimination" (491 U.S. 164,205, 1989). Brennan presented, "the viewpoint that the Court's denial was based on a historical analysis, ignoring the premises for establishing Section 1981" (491 U.S. 164,205, 1989). The Court may not take a narrow view of what was meant by the "same right to make and enforce contracts as white citizens," (491 U.S. 164,205-206, 1989). He pointed out that "the statutory language of Section 1981, clearly imposed limitations on the type of harassment claims that were cognizant under Section 1981" (491 U.S. 164,207, 1989). Hence, "the statute prohibited discrimination in the making and enforcement of contracts" (491 U.S. 164,207. 1989). Justice Brennan wrote, "that the Court's interpretation of Section 1981 undermined Title VII as not only judicial begging, but was misleading" (491 U.S. 164,210, 1989). It was Brennan's view, "that Section 1981 was a statute of general application, extending not just to employment contracts but to all contracts" (491 U.S. 164,210, 1989). He pointed out that the coverage of employment discrimination in Section 1981 and Title VII were different. "Section 1981, on the one hand, contained no limitations in scope and had a longer statute of limitations" (491 U.S. 164,211, 1989). Whereas Title VII, "on the other hand, was limited to employment discriminatory practices by businesses with 15 or more employees" (491 U.S. 164,211, 1989). Justice Brennan asserted that "given the extent and nature of the evidence produced by Patterson, and the importance of credibility determinations in assigning weight to that evidence, the jury may well have concluded that petitioner was subject to such serious and extensive racial harassment" that she was denied the benefits that a white employee would have received under similar circumstances (491 U.S. 164,215, 1989).

Justice Stevens, in supporting the dissenting opinion, wrote that a contract was "not just a piece of paper." "Whenever significant new duties were assigned to the employee, the contract was amended and a new contract was made" (491 U.S. 164,221, 1989). McLean's requirement of Patterson, "to work in a hostile environment denied the employee the same opportunity for advancement available to white citizens" (491 U.S. 164,221, 1989). Hence, this created an employment situation covered under Section 1981 of the Civil Rights Act of 1866. Stevens disagreed with the Court's narrow construction of "to make" a contract (491 U.S. 164,222, 1989).

The decision of the Court gave a narrow interpretation of Section 1981. The case impacted affirmative action by failing to establish the precedent that racial discrimination applied only to discrimination in the "formation of a contract" (491 U.S. 164,175-185, 1989). As a result, this opened the potential for allowing discrimination once the contract had been formulated. It may be suggested that the Court was granting the formation of a legal system for discrimination which resulted from continued employment. It was Justice Kennedy's position, "that racial harassment during the performance of a contract was neither the making nor the enforcement of a contract" (491 U.S. 164,172, 1989). Therefore, racial harassment in contractual performance was not unlawful discrimination under Section 1981.

In a commentary to *Patterson v. McLean Credit Union*, Burton (1990) argued that "the Rehnquist Court"was unaware that the law had envisioned a racially just society in all respects. Rather, the Court assumed that Congress envisioned a racially just society only in some respects - those enumerated in Section 1981 and other federal statutes - and left other matters to state law and private conscience. Burton theorized that the dissenting opinion was not persuasive in the quest to bring racial discrimination in contract performance within the realm of contract formation (Burton, 1990).

## Supreme Court and Other Federal Court Decisions Since 1989

During the 1990s, the judicial system continued to experience legal confrontations regarding the legitimacy of affirmative action programs.

The issues of preferential treatment in the areas of college admission's, awarding of contracts, set-asides for Minority Business Enterprises (MBE's), scholarship programs, as well as numerical employment goals based on race provided the order of business for the Courts. Consequently, it is important to discuss cases that will influence the future of affirmative action in the United States. Even though some of the following cases did not reach the United States Supreme Court, it can be argued that each case presents serious legal considerations regarding affirmative action and the manner in which the Supreme Court may resolve future affirmative action cases. Hence, their inclusion in the discussion of how the courts have impacted affirmative action is both relevant and necessary.

### Milwaukee County Pavers Assn. v. Fiedler, 922 F.2d 419 (7th Cir. 1991)

"An association of highway contractors in Wisconsin brought suit to enjoin as a form of affirmative action or reverse discrimination that violates the equal protection clause of the Fourteenth Amendment, programs by which the State of Wisconsin sets aside certain highway contracts for firms that are certified as 'disadvantaged business enterprises'.." (922 F.2d 419, 421, 1991). The program required highway contractors to give preferential treatment to subcontractors certified as a "disadvantaged business enterprise."

The Court's decision was written by Justice Posner of the Seventh Circuit Court of Appeals. Posner held, that the "program under which Wisconsin set-aside certain exclusively state-funded highway contracts for firms certified as 'disadvantaged business enterprises' racially discriminates in favor of blacks and other minorities in violation of the equal protection clause in the absence of showing that discrimination was necessary..." (922 F.2d 419, 1991). The federal program in which Wisconsin was the administrator was not a violation unless the state exceeded the federal law.

Posner found that harm existed in the programs because contractors were required to award some contracts to non low bidding subcontractors. They also were hurt in being limited in their competition for subcontractors (922 F.2d 419, 421, 1991). Wisconsin argued, that they did not discriminate because the program was based on disadvantaged enterprises. Posner reasoned that the mere racial presumption (a black is disadvantaged, but not a white male) was a form of racial discrimination and was unconstitutional unless it was remedial in nature (922 F.2d 419,421, 1991).

The case demonstrated that the issue of racial presumption was a pertinent issue before the court. The utilization of a program that provided economic assistance primarily to African American contractors was still challengeable under the argument of reverse discrimination in non remedial settings. This case shows the distinction between what kinds of programs state and local governments could constitutionally have and the federal government's permissionable programs which was developed in *Croson* guiding the lower courts.

### Northeastern Florida Chapter of the Associated General Contractors of America v. City of Jacksonville, Florida, 508 U.S. 656 (1993)

The focus of this case was the legality of Minority Business Enterprise (MBE's) resulting from a city ordinance. In this case, the litigants Northeastern Florida Construction Association did not meet the criteria of an MBE's and hence sought relief in the United States District Courts for the Middle District of Florida. Northeastern Florida construction company alleged that they would have bided successfully if it had not been for the set aside provisions (508 U.S. 656, 658-659, 1993). The focal point in this law suit was the question of whether "set asides violated the Fourteenth Amendment's Equal Protection Clause" (508 U.S. 656, 1993). The case came before the Supreme Court as a result of a *writ of certiorari*.

The original ordinance, implemented in 1984, was known as "Minority Business Enterprise Participation, and required ten-percent of the amount spent on city contracts set-aside each fiscal year for so-called Minority Business Enterprise," (508 U.S. 656,658, 1993). "An MBE was defined as a business whose membership was at least 51% minority or female" (508 U.S. 656,658, 1993). "A minority was defined as a person who considered himself to be African American, Spanish-speaking, Oriental, Indian, Eskimo, Aleut or handicapped" (508 U.S. 656,658, 1993). The ordinance did not require any degree of mathematical certainty, however, "the chief purchasing officer was required to make every attempt to come close to the ten-percent figure" (508 U.S. 656,658-659, 1993).

"On October 27, 1992, twenty-two days after the Supreme Court had granted *certiorari*, the City repealed its MBE ordinance and replaced it with an ordinance entitled African American and Women's Business Enterprise Participation" (508 U.S. 656,660, 1993). It was suggested that this ordinance differed from the previous one in three respects. First, "unlike the previous ordinance, the new ordinance applied only to women and African Americans" (508 U.S. 656,660-661, 1993). Second, "the new ordinance established a participating goal ranging from five to sixteen percent, depending upon the type of contract, the owner of the contract, and the fiscal year in which the contract was awarded" (508 U.S. 656,661, 1993). Third, "the new ordinance under its Sheltered Market Plan reserved contracts for the exclusive competition of certified African American and female-owned businesses" (508 U.S. 656,661, 1993). The key argument presented by the city was the repealing of the previous ordinance. The city advocated, that since "the ordinance had in fact been repealed, there remained no legal rationale for determining the constitutionality of a repealed ordinance. Therefore, the legal issue should be dismissed as moot" (508 U.S. 656,661, 1993).

The majority opinion was written by Justice Thomas and joined by Rehnquist, White, Stevens, Scalia, Kennedy, and Souter. In a 7-2 decision, "the Court reasoned that the issue was not moot" (508 U.S. 656,663, 1993). Thomas stated, that based on previous Court rulings, "it was well settled that the voluntary cessation of a challenged practice did not deprive a federal court of its power to determine the legality of the practice, simply because a defendant was not precluded from reinstating the said practice" (508 U.S. 656,662, 1993).

The Court reasoned that the set-aside program as found in *Croson* (488 U.S. 493, 1989) created an "injury in fact." The set-aside for certified African Americans and female owned businesses prevented equal competitive bidding opportunities (508 U.S. 656,662, 1993). The Supreme Court reversed the judgment of the Eleventh Circuit Court of Appeals and remanded the case for further proceedings.

The dissenting opinion was delivered by Justice O'Connor with Blackmun joining. Justice O'Connor began with the statement, that "when a challenged statute expires, or is repealed or significantly amended pending review, and the only relief sought is prospective, the Court's practice had been to dismiss the case as moot" (508 U.S. 656,669, 1993). O'Connor set forth the rationale, "if the challenged statute no longer exists, there ordinarily can be no real controversy as to its continuing validity, and in order enjoining its enforcement would be meaningless" (508 U.S. 656,670, 1993). She pointed out, that "the new ordinance was narrowly defined compared to the previous one" (508 U.S. 656,673, 1993). She further reasoned that "the challenged statute was replaced by a narrowly drawn version pending review, and there was no indication that the legislature intended to reenact the prior provisions" (508 U.S. 656,674, 1993).

In this case the Court supported the precedent established regarding the set-aside principle in the awarding of contracts. The Supreme Court again affirmed the view that "race-conscious preferential treatment was unconstitutional." It could be argued that this case provided a precedent for cases with similar legal issues coming before the Court during the 1990s.

### Podberesky v. Kirwan, 838 F. Supp. 1075 (D. Md. 1993)

The Benjamin Banneker Scholarship Program created by the University of Maryland at College Park in 1978 was the issue in this case (838 F. Supp. 1075,1077, 1993).    The program provided a merit-based scholarship for African Americans (838 F. Supp. 1075,1077, 1993). Members of other racial minorities were ineligible to apply.    The scholarship program was, "designed by the University for the purpose of overcoming historical racial discrimination with a specific emphasis on the exclusion of African Americans" ( 838 F. Supp. 1075,1076, 1993).

Daniel Podberesky, a Hispanic student, applied to the Banneker Scholarship Program. His application was denied because he was not African American. Consequently, "Podberesky filed suit in the United States District Court for the District of Maryland alleging that his denial constituted reverse discrimination as prohibited by the Fourteenth Amendment of the United States Constitution" (838 F. Supp. 1075, 1993).

The District Court, "upheld the legality of the scholarship program" (838 F. Supp. 1075, 1993). "The Fourth Circuit Court of Appeals reversed the ruling of the District Court" (838 F. Supp. 1075-1077, 1993). The Court of Appeals ruled, that "the district judge had failed to make specific findings of the present effects of past discrimination" (956 F.2nd 52 [4th Cir.]). The District Court on remand, "made specific findings and reaffirmed the original decision that the program was constitutional" (838 F. Supp. 1075, 1993).

Upon appeal to the Fourth Circuit Court of Appeals, from the District Court, a unanimous decision was given by the three judge panel. The judgement of the Court was written by Judge Widener, Jr.  The key question presented in this case was, "whether a public university, racially segregated by law for almost a century and actively resistant to integration for at least twenty years, could voluntarily remedy the problem by implementing a scholarship designed to improve African American attendance" (838 F. Supp. 1076, 1993). It was noted that, "the District Court had failed to properly analyze the arguments set forth by the University of Maryland justifying its program" (838 F. Supp. 1075,1076, 1993). Judge Widener reasoned, that "the present effects cited by the university as a rationale for the program were not grounded in past discriminatory practices of the university" (838 F. Supp. 1075,1092, 1993).

The three judge panel of the Fourth Circuit Court of Appeals decision reaffirmed the principle that race-based remedial measures must be judged according to the "strict scrutiny" standard (838 F. Supp. 1075, 1083, 1993). The strict scrutiny standard required, that "a program must serve a compelling state interest and it must be narrowly tailored" (838 F. Supp. 1075,1083, 1993). Hence, regarding affirmative action, "the compelling state interest must be substantiated by demonstrating the present effects of racial discrimination which the designated program attempts to rectify was predicated on past discrimination" (838 F. Supp. 1075,1083, 1993). As a result, applying the strict scrutiny principle, "Judge Widener concluded that the present effects of discrimination remedied by the Banneker Program were not tied to past discriminatory practices by the university" (838 F. Supp. 1075,1083, 1993).

Judge Widener stated that the "mere knowledge of historical fact was not the kind of present effect that can justify a race-exclusive remedy" (838 F. Supp. 1075,1083, 1993). Widener suggested, that "accepting this type of argument would result in claims being brought predicated on findings in history books" (838 F. Supp. 1075,1092, 1993). It was concluded, that "the hostile climate effect presented insufficient argument to justify the scholarship program" (838 F. Supp. 1075,1092, 1993). "Even though there was hostility to African Americans on the Maryland campus, this demonstrated no connection between the institutions' past discrimination and present attitudes" (838 F. Supp. 1075,1093, 1993). The Court reason, that "insufficient means existed to distinguish hostility based on past discrimination and that of societal discrimination" (838 F. Supp. 1075,1093, 1993). "The Court declared the Banneker Scholarship Program unconstitutional and ruled that all students must be eligible to apply" (838 F. Supp. 1075,1093, 1993). The University of Maryland at

College Park was ordered, "to reconsider Podberesky's application without regard to race" (838 F. Supp. 1075,1096-1097, 1993).

The Court continued to apply the strict scrutiny principle and the idea that the program must be narrowly tailored in an affirmative action case. The Court continued to adhere to the precedent that an affirmative action program, in order to meet constitutional muster, must be designed to eradicate the present effects of racial discrimination resulting from historical practices. Consequently, "the Court exerted judicial authority to reduce affirmative action programs in universities even when the Court conceded that current racial hostility still existed" (838 F. Supp. 1075,1092, 1993).

### Maryland Troopers Association, Inc. v. Evans, 993 F.2d 1072 (4th Cir. 1993)

*Maryland Troopers Association, Inc. v. Evans* (1993) presented the question of what evidentiary foundation was required for a state to adopt a plan with numerical employment goals based on race. "The Maryland Troopers Association intervened to challenge a Consent Decree between the Coalition of Black Maryland State Troopers and the Maryland State Police, under which the MSP agreed to hire and promote certain percentages of black troopers at each state trooper rank" (993 F.2d 1072,1074, 1993). The Maryland Troopers Association contend, that "numerical goals violated the Equal Protection Clause of the Fourteenth Amendment and Title VII" (993 F.2d 1074, 1993).

The premises for the case was established in 1974, "when the United States sued the state of Maryland for racial discrimination in hiring state troopers" (993 F.2d 1072,1074, 1993). The matter was resolved between the United States and Maryland, with the implementation of a consent decree, "which provided that the MSP agreed to hire black applicants at a rate to achieve an overall percentage of 16% black troopers in five years" (993 F.2d 1072,1074, 1993). "In 1979, the consent decree was modified and changed the goal to 14% black troopers with an additional requirement that 33% of the entry level troopers hired would be black" (993 F.2d 1072,1074, 1993). "By 1980, 9.5% of the of the MSP troopers were black" (993 F.2d 1072,1074, 1993). However, "they were concentrated in the lower ranks because MSP did not hire laterally and promoted troopers no more than one rank per year" (993 F.2d 1072,1074, 1993). "In 1982, there were complaints of cronyism and rigid examinations within the promotion system" (993 F.2d 1072,1074, 1993).

The Attorney General of Maryland conducted an investigation to study the allegations of discriminatory practices. In response to the investigation, "MSP adopted an Affirmative Action Promotional Plan for Law Enforcement Personnel" (993 F.2d 1072,1074, 1993). The objective of the plan was to address two issues revealed in the Attorney General's investigation. "The findings revealed that tampering with promotional scores existed to favor chosen candidates of the MSP" (993 F.2d 1072,1074, 1993). Second, "the low representation of blacks in the upper ranks of the MSP suggested flaws in the promotional system" (993 F.2d 1072,1074, 1993). The implementation of the new plan was conducted by an outside consulting firm. The plan allowed, "the Superintendent of MSP to have authority and discretion over promotion and was allowed consideration for other factors which included exam scores, recommendations from supervisors, and special experiences of the candidate" (993 F.2d 1072,1074, 1993).

"In June of 1985, the Coalition of Black Maryland State Trooper's sued the MSP in United States District Court for Maryland based on allegations of ongoing racial discrimination in hiring and promoting state troopers" (993 F. 2d 1072,1075, 1993). Consequently, the Coalition and MSP entered into a consent decree. "The consent decree did not require the MSP to hire or promote anyone who was not otherwise qualified" (993 F.2d 1072,1075, 1993). "On January 11, 1991, the Maryland Troopers Association intervened, opposing the hiring and promotional goals of the consent decree" (993 F.2d 1072,1075, 1993).

"On August 11, 1992, the Federal District Court rejected the Maryland Troopers Association's challenge" (993 F.2d 1072,1075, 1993). The Federal District Court held, that "the evidence of racial discrimination was sufficient to warrant a race-conscious remedy" (993 F. 2d 1072,1075, 1993). The court's ruling was, "based on evidence presented in the 1985 findings of the Attorney General and the statistical comparison of the Maryland State Police and the African American composition of the relevant qualified labor pool" ( 993 F. 2d 1072,1075, 1993). The Maryland State Troopers Association appealed the decision to the Fourth Circuit Court of Appeals.

The opinion of the Fourth Circuit Court was delivered by Judge Wilkinson. Justice Wilkinson pointed out, that "racial and ethnic distinctions of any sort were inherently suspect, and thus called for the most exacting judicial examination" (993 F.2d 1072,1076, 1993). Wilkinson stated, that "the criteria of judging men and women by race presented a precarious situation" (993 F.2d 1072,1076, 1993). The use of race, according to Wilkinson, "as a reparational device risked perpetuating the very race-consciousness that such a remedy was designed to prevent" (993 F.2d 1072,1076, 1993). "The impact of the Fourteenth Amendment was to forbid states from classifying men and women on the basis of race" (993 F.2d 1072,1076, 1993). When using racial classifications, "the state must narrowly tailor any preferences based on race to meet remedial goals" (993 F.2d 1072,1077, 1993). "The preferences must remain in effect only long enough to remedy the discrimination" (993 F.2d 1072,1077, 1993). The Court pointed out, that "the proposed remedy was not allowed to take on a life of its own and the numerical goals were waived in the absence of qualified minority applicants" (993 2d. 1072,1077, 1993).

The Circuit Court of Appeals reasoned, "that race-conscious relief in the consent decree violated the guidelines of the Fourteenth Amendment" (993 F. 2d 1072,1077, 1993). The Court did not consider the issue of a "narrowly tailored" program because the state did not have the requirement to warrant a race-conscious remedy. The Court acknowledged that problems existed because of test score tampering. However the Court indicated, "only when there are gross statistical disparities between the racial composition of the employer's workforce and the racial composition of the relevant qualified labor pool may a court infer that the employer has racially discriminated" (993 F.2d 1072,1077, 1993).

Regarding the implementation of race-conscious programs to resolve past historical discrimination, the Court held that these programs violated the guidelines of the Fourteenth Amendment. The Court continued its adherence to the utilization of the strict scrutiny principle and the narrowly tailored requirement for race-preference programs.

### Adarand Constructors, Inc. v. Pena, 115 S. Ct. 2097 (1995)

The focus of the case was, "a Colorado-based general contracting firm which had sought to obtain a highway construction project funded by the federal government" (115 S. Ct. 2097,2102, 1995). "The construction firm (Mountain Gravel), based on the terms of the federal government's contract, was entitled to increase compensation if it hired subcontractors certified as small business that were controlled by socially and economically disadvantaged individuals" (115 S. Ct. 2097,2102, 1995). There was a presumption, implied by the Small Business Act, that "socially and economically disadvantaged individuals included all people of color and any other individual found to be disadvantaged by the Small Business Administration (SBA)" (115 S. Ct. 2097,2102, 1995). The lowest bid from a subcontractor was submitted by Adarand. However, "Mountain Gravel subcontracted to a higher bidder which was a Hispanic-controlled business known as the Gonzales Construction Company" (115 S. Ct. 2097,2102, 1995). Consequently, Adarand filed suit against the government officials and claimed, that "the SBA's presumption of a disadvantaged business owned by people of color was unconstitutional under the Equal Protection Clause of the Fifth Amendment because the presumption discriminated on the basis of an illicit racial classification" (115 S. Ct. 2097, 2102, 1995).

In a 5-4 decision, the Supreme Court overturned the decision of the District Court. Justice O'Connor wrote the judgement with some parts of it speaking for the Court, and focused on "the issue of whether or not Congress had wider discretion than state and local governments to authorize race-based affirmative action programs" (115 S. Ct. 2097,2098, 1995). The Court (Justices O'Connor, Rehnquist, Scalia, Kennedy and Thomas) held, "that congressionally enacted affirmative action programs, such as those administered by state or local governments, must satisfy strict scrutiny as required under the Equal Protection Clause" (115 S. Ct. 2097,2098, 1995).

In reaching their decision, "the Court's plurality utilized *stare decisis* and the history of equal protection cases, by interpreting them to establish three central propositions related to skepticism, consistency, and congruence" (115 S. Ct. 2097,2100, 1995). The concept of "skepticism stressed that any preferences based on racial classifications were inherently suspect, even when intended to aid a historically disadvantaged class" (115 S. Ct. 2097,2100, 1995). "Consistency referred to the requirement that all racial classifications must be strictly scrutinized, regardless of whether the classification at issue was invidious or benign" (115 S. Ct. 2097,2100, 1995). And the term "congruence required that Equal Protection analysis under the Fifth Amendment must be given the same legal analysis as Equal Protection under the Fourteenth Amendment" (115 S. Ct. 2097,2100, 1995).

Based on the previously mentioned rationale, the plurality of the Court went on to establish the argument that the *Metro Broadcasting* decision had two major flaws. First, "in refusing to apply consistent standards to benign and invidious discrimination, the Court had in essence turned it's back on the precedent established in *Croson*" (488 U.S. 469, 1989). This was important because, "it provided an explanation as to why strict scrutiny of all governmental racial classifications were essential" (115 S. Ct. 2097,2100, 1995). Second, "the decision of *Metro Broadcasting* violated the congruence principle by holding that Congress' benign racial classifications were subject only to intermediate scrutiny" (115 S. Ct. 2097,2100, 1995). The Court refuted, "the notion that strict scrutiny could not be strict in theory but must be strict in fact" (115 S. Ct. 2097,2101, 1995). Justice O'Connor writing for the plurality noted, that "race-based remedies would sometimes be acceptable, even under the strict analysis, as long as they satisfied the narrowing test set forth by the Court" (115 S. Ct. 2117-2126, 1995).

Justices concurred in part and concurred in the judgement. Justice Scalia stressed, the principle of absolute color-blindness as the litmus test for Equal Protection cases. Scalia reasoned, that "government never had a compelling interest in discriminating on the basis of race designed to compensate for past discrimination" (115 S. Ct. 2097,2118, 1995). Thomas wrote, "against racial paternalism as an exception to the principle of Equal Protection" (115 S. Ct. 2097,2119, 1995). His assessment was that all racial classifications, "whether overtly invidious or purportedly benign, was subjected to strict scrutiny" (115 S. Ct. 2097,2119, 1995).

One dissenting opinion was given by Stevens with Ginsburg joining. The dissenting opinion rejected "the Court's requirement of consistency based on the argument that there was no moral or constitutional equivalence between benign and invidious discrimination" (115 S. Ct. 2097,2120, 1995). Justice Stevens expressed disagreement with "the plurality's requirement of congruence, advocating that there were important practical and legal differences between federal and state and local decision makers" (115 S. Ct. 2097,2121-2127, 1995). Stevens pointed out, that "the federal government must be the primary defender of people of color against states inclined to oppress such people" (115 S. Ct. 2097,2131, 1995).

An additional dissent was written by Souter with Ginsburg, and Breyer joining, which "focused on the issue that the Court's new standard of strict scrutiny did not necessarily invalidate all congressionally enacted programs" (115 S. Ct. 2097,2131-2133, 1995). In a separate dissent, Ginsburg reasoned, "that given the long history of racial discrimination in the United States, affirmative action programs provided an appropriate means for achieving real equality" (115 S. Ct. 2097,2134, 1995).

The Supreme Court demonstrated in this case that any effort designed to aid those classified as "socially and economically disadvantaged" gain economic productivity was deemed unconstitutional. The Supreme Court utilized strict judicial analysis in assessing affirmative action plans predicated on a race-conscious formula. The Court reaffirmed again the judicial concept of strict scrutiny in reviewing race-based classifications. In conclusion, the Court continued to reduce the viability of affirmative action programs as result of *Adarand*.

Welch (1996), in a commentary on the *Adarand* case, suggested that the Court had ruled correctly. According to Welch, *Adarand* (115 S. Ct. 2097, 1995) was a challenge to the authority of the United States government to treat some citizens differently because of their race (Welch, 1996). He implied that *Adarand* solidified the principle that racial or ethnic discrimination was legally and morally wrong. Welch postulated that the *Adarand* decision ensured that any program making race the basis for granting or denying privileges to citizens of the United States would be limited in impact and duration (Welch, 1996). According to Welch (1996), the main result of the *Adarand* opinion was that "free people whose institutions were founded upon the doctrine of equality, should tolerate no retreat from the principle that government may treat people differently because of their race only for the most compelling reasons." It was held in *Adarand* (1995), that all racial classifications imposed by federal, state, or local government actors would be analyzed under strict scrutiny (Welch, 1996).

Welch concluded his assessment of the *Adarand* case with the inference that *Adarand* protected society, and made it difficult for government officials to discriminate against any individual on the basis of race or ethnicity (Welch, 1996). The decision, when properly applied, assured that governmental benefits or burdens cannot be granted nor denied any citizen because of race or ethnicity (Welch, 1996).

### Taxman v. Board of Education of Township of Piscataway, 91 F.3d 1547 (3rd Cir. 1996)

The Taxman case focused on the issue of lay-offs as a part of an affirmative action plan. "The Board of Education accepted a recommendation from the Superintendent of Schools to reduce the teaching staff in the Business Department at Piscataway High School by one. At the time, two of the teachers in the department were of equal seniority and began employment with the Board on the same day nine years earlier" (91 F.3d 1547, 1551, 1996). Sharon Taxman, a white employee, and Debra Williams, an African American, were the two parties involved. Williams was the only African American teacher among the faculty in the Business Department.

Rules regarding layoffs in New Jersey were outlined according to state law. The policy of layoffs, as required by law, "required that non-tenured faculty must be laid off first, and layoffs among tenured teachers in the affected subject area or grade level proceeded in reverse order of seniority" (91 F.3d 1547,1551, 1996). "The local school board lacked the discretion to choose between employees for layoffs, except in a rare instance of a tie in seniority between two or more employees eligible to fill the vacancy" (91 F.3d 1547,1551, 1996). "In prior decisions involving the layoff of employees with equal seniority, the board had broken the tie through a random process which included drawing numbers out of a container, drawing lots, or a lottery" (91 F.3d 1547,1551, 1996). This was the first time the involved employees were of a different racial background.

During this period, the board had in place an affirmative action policy. The policy  contained no "remedial purpose" provisions (91 F.3d 1547,1550, 1996). The purpose of the affirmative action policy was "to provide equal educational opportunity for students and equal employment opportunity for employees as well as prospective employees" (91 F.3d 1547,1550, 1996). "The policy was not adopted with the intention of remedying the results of any prior discrimination, nor did it identify under-representation of people of color within the Piscataway School System" (91 F.3d 1547,1550, 1996). Williams, however, as mentioned earlier, was the only African American teacher in the Department of Business and the board decided to terminate the contract with Taxman in the interest of "cultural diversity" and retained Williams (91 F.3d 1547,1551, 1996). The retention of Williams was viewed as sending a positive message to the students.

Consequently, "Taxman filed a charge of employment discrimination with the Equal Employment Opportunity Commission (EEOC)" (91 F.3d 1547,1552, 1996). The federal legal issue centered on Title VII. The Act made it unlawful for an employer "to 'discriminate against any individual with respect to their compensation, terms, conditions, or privileges of employment' or 'to limit, segregate, or classify employees... in any way which would deprive or tend to deprive any individual of employment opportunities or otherwise effect his status as an employee on the basis of race, color, religion, sex, or national origin,' " (91 F.3d 1547,1553, 1996).

Judge Mansmann writing for the Third Circuit Court of Appeals began by analyzing Title VII and the Supreme Court cases that had interpreted the permissibility of racial considerations in employment decisions. It should be noted that this case was reargued *En Blanc*. The Court of Appeals explained that the Supreme Court had only allowed affirmative action plans to exist where the plan's purpose mirrored the purpose of Title VII (91 F.3d 1547,1557, 1996). According to Mansmann, Title VII was "enacted to ... remedy the segregation and underrepresentation of minorities that discrimination had caused in our Nation's workforce" (91 F. 3d 1547,1557, 1996). An affirmative action plan that had been formerly approved by the Supreme Court included the requirement that it did not unnecessarily trammel the interests of the group of employees (91 F. 3d 1547,1564, 1996).

Judge Mansmann "explained that the requirement which barred consideration of race from the workplace was Congress' primary objective for the enactment of Title VII" (91 F.3d 1547,1558, 1996). Mansmann explained, that "the Supreme Court and Congress at that time had never addressed the racial diversity purpose but merely sought to combat discrimination in places of learning" (91 F.3d 1547,1558, 1996). The Court of Appeals rejected the board's reliance on case law interpreting the Fourteenth Amendment's Equal Protection Clause and explained that the Supreme Court had not yet ruled that an affirmative action purpose which satisfied the Constitution necessarily satisfied Title VII (91 F. 3d 1547,1559, 1996).

Mansmann rationalized, that the board's effort and intent were laudable, and that the benefits flowing from diversity in the educational context were significant indeed. However, it did not sufficiently meet the congressional standard that affirmative action programs and policies must be remedial in their design (91 F. 3d 1547,1560, 1996). The Court held that the board's policy unnecessarily trammeled the interest of whites (91 F. 3d 1547,1565, 1996). The Court noted that the policy had no definition or structure, it did not define racial diversity, nor did it specify what would be the sufficient degree of racial diversity. Therefore, the Board's plan violated the guidelines of the Fourteenth Amendment and Title VII.

One dissenting opinion was given by Judge Scirica with Chief Justice Sloviter joining. This dissenting opinion noted that the educational system presented a unique concern. Scirica and Sloviter stated that "the board implemented a program that, in limited circumstances, allowes consideration of race as a factor in employment decisions" (91 F.3d 1547,1576, 1996). According to Scirica and Sloviter, "the board did not countenance the layoff of a more-qualified teacher in the place of a less-qualified one" (91 F.3d 1547,1576, 1996). The dissenters pointed out, that the board had not preferred teachers with junior seniority against those more experienced. Rather the board "concluded that when teachers are equal in ability and in all other respects- and only then-diversity of the faculty is a relevant conclusion" (91 F.3d 1547,1577, 1996). Judge Scirica stated, "I do not believe Title VII prevents a school district, in the exercise of its professional judgement, from preferring one equally qualified teacher over another for a valid educational purpose" (91 F.3d 1547,1577, 1996).

Another dissent was presented by Justice Lewis with McKee joining. Their rationale was that "while the majority holds that Title VII only allows race to be considered in remedying a history of intentional discrimination or a manifest imbalance..." (91 F.3d 1547,1577, 1996). "This conclusion is fundamentally at odds with the overriding goals of the statute" (91 F.3d 1547,1577, 1996). "The real-life impact of the majority's unprecedented construction of Title VII is readily apparent when one contemplates the myriad of different decisions that employers across the nation faced every day" (91 F.3d 1547,1577, 1996). Consequently, "it was suggested that the majority's decision eviscerated the purpose and goal of Title VII" (91 F.3d 1547,1578, 1996).

A third dissenting opinion was written by Circuit Judge McKee with Chief Judge Sloviter and Lewis joining. It was McKee's position that the Court had come full circle. "A law enacted by Congress in 1964 to move this country closer to an integrated society and away from the legacy of 'separate-but-equal' is being interpreted as outlawing this Board of Education's good faith effort to teach students the value of diversity" (91 F.3d 1547,1578, 1996). McKee asserted, that "given the interpretation of Title VII", there was "no reason why the employer has any duty, prior to granting a preference to a qualified minority employee, to determine whether his past conduct might constitute an arguable violation of Title VII" (91 F.3d 1547,1578, 1996). McKee did not believe that "what the board attempted to do, nor the individualized manner in which it was attempting to do it, runs afoul of congressional enactment cloaked in the legislative history recounted herein, and in the opinions of my colleagues" (91 F.3d 1547,1579, 1996).

An interesting development took place prior to the scheduled adjudication of the Taxman case before the United States Supreme Court in January of 1998. The *New York Times* (1997) reported that the landmark affirmative action lawsuit of *Taxman v. Board of Education of Township of Piscataway* (1996) was settled out of court. The *New York Times* stated that the case was settled out of court because civil rights groups feared the Supreme Court might use the case to outlaw the widespread use of voluntary racial preference plans to promote diversity (*New York Times*, 1997). The surprised settlement was viewed by many as evidence that a shifting political and legal consensus in America was developing, moving away from affirmative action and toward "neutral" policies in addressing race and gender issues (*New York Times*, 1997).

The case was settled as a result of a $308,500 contribution from a national coalition of civil rights groups, the Piscataway, New Jersey School Board granted Taxman $433,500 in damages that she had demanded. According to David Rubin, the attorney for the Piscataway Board of Education, "a number of national civil rights organizations expressed to the board their genuine concern that an adverse ruling in this case could gut the infrastructure of affirmative action across the country" (*New York Times, p. B4*, 1997).

The decision, according to Jesse Jackson, gave new life to the forces of resegregation and states rights. Jackson commented that "a civil rights coalition, which included the NAACP Legal Defense Fund, the Black Leadership Forum and the Southern Christian Leadership Conference, helped to raise the money for the settlement in order to stop the misrepresentation of the issue of affirmative action in this particular case" (*New York Times, p. B4*, 1997). Jackson suggested that the *Taxman* case was riddled with problems. He argued that the case was distorted on the issues and it was an important maneuver to remove the case from hearing before the United States Supreme Court (*New York Times*, 1997).

Hugh Price, president of the National Urban League, asserted that civil rights advocates claimed the particular circumstances in Piscataway made it the wrong case to establish a precedent on affirmative action. However, he fully expected another attempt from a different direction, but agreed that *Taxman* was not the strongest case to send before the Supreme Court at this time (*New York Times*, 1997). On the other hand, the decision was viewed by Clint Bolick as heartening the interests of those opposed to affirmative action. Bolick argued that the defenders of racial preferences were running for the hills. He expressed delight in the payment made by civil rights groups to a victim of reverse discrimination (*New York Times*, 1997).

Similarly, Don Livingston, former General Counsel of the U.S. Equal Employment Opportunity Commission and a specialist in civil rights law, argued that the facts of the *Taxman* case were overwhelmingly in favor of *Taxman* and thus ran the risk of slamming the door shut on affirmative action (*New York Times*, 1997). Livingston reminded the country, that the Supreme Court had restricted the use of racial preferences in a series of cases involving government contracting and political redistricting in recent years. In those cases, as pointed out by Livingston, the Court said the use of race and sex in matters of public policy were justified only where a specific pattern of discrimination needed to be redressed, and then only if the affirmative action plan was narrowly tailored (*New York Times*, 1997). The Supreme Court had not extended restrictions to the implementation of voluntary affirmative action plans adopted under Title VII by businesses, colleges, and other institutions that wanted diversity in their work force or student bodies. Past rulings on Title VII by the Supreme Court indicated that employers at times discriminated against white people when adopting affirmative action plans that addressed the under-representation of people of color.

The foes of affirmative action had sought the *Taxman* case to persuade the high court to overrule past decisions on Title VII and expressed disappointment in the settlement of the case. William Mellor, President of the Washington-based Institute for Justice, stated with regard to *Taxman v. Piscataway* that "the Supreme Court would have put the final nail in the coffin of race- and gender-based affirmative action" (*New York Times, p. B5*, 1997). He further surmised that those supporting race- and gender-based programs presented very weak legal arguments. It was his contention that supporters of affirmative action had lost the moral high ground and were fighting a rear-guard action politically (*New York Times*, 1997). In support of the *Taxman v. Piscataway School Board* case, Anne Bryant, Executive Director of the National School Boards Association, stated that the School Board made a thoughtful and courageous decision in 1989. She suggested that diversity in faculties served a compelling educational purpose in promoting tolerance. Bryant suggested it was one thing to tell a white student that people were equal regardless of race, but it is far more powerful to expose the students to teachers of all races (*New York Times*, 1997).

*Taxman v. Piscataway* was more amenable to settlement than many other cases because it involved solely a money judgment rather than any broader adjustment or rights or relationships. The school board had rehired Ms. Taxman within two years, so the only question was that of payment for her two years of back pay, lost pension contributions and seniority, as well as lawyer's fees. She had received $144,000 in a judgment in 1993, which was appealed by the school board (*New York Times*, 1997).

The settlement at the time was only the latest development in the public debate over whether the nation should abandon affirmative action practices which provided African Americans and other people of color along with women preference in some aspects of employment, school admissions and other competitive situations. Earlier that month (January, 1997), Houston voters saved the city's affirmative action program with a public vote that rejected a referendum designed to eliminate affirmative action programs. A week later, a federal judge struck down the city transit authority's affirmative-action program, stating that "basing government action on race offends the American Constitution" (*New York Times, p. B5*, 1997).

## Hopwood v. State of Texas 78 F.3d 932 (1996)

"The University of Texas School of Law implemented a policy that provided racial preferences for African Americans and Mexican Americans for the purpose of correcting perceived racial imbalances in the student body" (78 F.3d 932,934, 1996). "The applications submitted by African Americans were reviewed in a different manner and separately from applications of white applicants" (78 F.3d 932,934, 1996). "The admissions process allowed lower scores for students of color and review of the application by a specific subcommittee of color, as opposed to any one of the random subcommittees" (78 F.3d 932,937, 1996). "The subcommittee of color reviewed each application extensively" (78 F.3d 932,937, 1996).

Hopwood, a white applicant, was rejected and "filed charges against the law school for violation of the Equal Protection Clause of the Fourteenth Amendment" (78 F.3d 932,938, 1996). The District Court for the Western District of Texas ruled, that "the law school had violated the Equal Protection Clause of the Fourteenth Amendment, but refused to require removal of the race criteria" (78 F.3d 932,938, 1996). The District Court based its rationale on the fact that first, "a compelling government interest was met by overcoming the past effects of discrimination" (78 F.3d 932,938, 1996). Second, "the educational benefits that accrued from a racially and ethnically diverse student body did not justify the admission policy" (78 F.3d 932,938, 1996). "The requirement of separately evaluating the candidates of color was ruled a violation of the Equal Protection Clause" (78 F.3d 932,939, 1996).

The decision of the Court of Appeals, Fifth Circuit was delivered by Justice Smith. He stated, that "the University of Texas Law School's program of admissions for students of color discriminated in favor of African American and Mexican American applicants, and provided substantial racial preferences in their admission's program" (78 F.3d 932,934, 1996). The Court of Appeals addressed whether that policy violates the Fourteenth Amendment. The Court reasoned, that "the law school had presented no compelling justification under the Fourteenth Amendment, or Supreme Court precedent, that allowed the continuation of evaluating some races over others, even for the perceived purpose of a racially balanced student body" (78 F.3d 932,934, 1996). The evaluation process of the law school placed applicants into three categories. "These categories were presumptive admission, presumptive deny, and middle discretionary zone" (78 F.3d 932,935, 1996). Smith pointed out that "within this system most, but not all, applicants were placed in the presumptive admit categories" (78 F.3d 932,935-936, 1996). This process provided different treatment for the application of African American and Mexican American applicants.

Smith continued that the process in essence created a "segregated application evaluation process" (78 F.3d 932,937, 1996). Once an application was received, it was in actuality "color-coded" according to race (78 F.3d 932 937, 1996). Therefore, according to the Circuit Court of Appeal, "race was always an overt part of the review process of any applicant's file" (78 F.3d 932,937, 1996). The review process also required extensive evaluation of African American and Mexican American applications.

The court reasoned, that "the central purpose of the Equal Protection Clause was to prevent the states from purposefully discriminating between individuals on the basis of race" (78 F.3d 932,939, 1996). "There was absolutely no doubt that courts were to employ strict scrutiny when evaluating all racial classifications, including those labeled as benign or remedial" (78 F.3d 932,940, 1996). Justice Smith pointed out, that "under the Fourteenth Amendment, a program that considered a host of factors including race were constitutional, even if the applicant's race tipped the scales among qualified candidates" (78 F.3d 932,943, 1996). However, "a school cannot compare applicants of different races to establish a strict quota on the basis of race" (78 F.3d 932,943, 1996). Therefore, "the use of race in admissions for diversity in higher education contradicted rather than furthered the aims of equal protection" (78 F.3d 932,945, 1996). The court disagreed with the position of the Law School, that "a diverse racial and ethnic student body created diversity of ideas and experiences, which enriched the learning experience" (78 F.3d 932,946, 1996). The court stated, that "the use of race, in and of itself, to select students merely achieved a student body that looked different" (78 F.3d 932,945, 1996).

In a special concurring opinion, Justice Weiner stated that the sole substantive issue in the appeal was whether the admissions process used by Texas met the constitutional muster required under the Equal Protection Clause of the Fourteenth Amendment (78 F.3d 932,962, 1996). It was Justice Weiner's opinion, that "the law school had failed to establish the existence of the present effects of past discrimination sufficient to justify the use of a racial-based classification" (78 F.3d 932, 962, 1996). Weiner disagreed with the majority's viewpoint, that diversity of a student body can never constitute a compelling governmental interest (78 F.3d 932,962, 1996). He pointed out that racial classifications can survive strict scrutiny requirements only when narrowly tailored (78 F.3d 932,963 1996). Justice Weiner stated, that "each applicant for admission to the law school was classified by race, and the application was treated differently based upon which racial category the application was filed" (78 F.3d 932,963, 1996). These classifications were subject to strict scrutiny. Justice Weiner asserted, that "the law school's race-based 1992 admissions process was not narrowly tailored to achieve diversity, and it violated the Equal Protection Clause and was unconstitutional" (78 F.3d 932,966, 1996).

## Summary of the Courts: 1989-1996

In 1989, the composition of the United States Supreme Court changed. Justice Powell, a Nixon appointee was replaced by Kennedy, a Reagan appointee. This change produced a significant shift in how the Court voted in cases involving affirmative action and reverse discrimination. Powell had become a generous supporter of affirmative action. Kennedy's appointment had an immediate impact on decisions reached by the Court. His views were revealed in the six cases decided by the

Supreme Court in 1989. In each of those cases, Kennedy voted on the side favorable to a reduction and reversal of affirmative action programs. His addition enabled the Court to move from mainly producing plurality decisions in this area to the formulation of many majority decisions.

In 1989, the Supreme Court addressed the issue of set-asides, which had been viewed as leading to the establishment of quotas. In *Croson* (1989) the Supreme Court narrowed the earlier decision of *Fullilove* (448 U.S. 448, 1980). *Fullilove* had led to the establishment of court-approved set-asides designed to improve the economic plight of contractor's of color (448 U.S. 448,498, 1980).

The focal point of *Croson* (1989) was the constitutionality of set-asides. The Court, in resolving this legal issue relied on the principle of strict scrutiny. A key area of concern was the lack of evidence demonstrating prior discrimination. The Court suggested that the set-aside plan lacked sufficient proof of discrimination in the construction industry.

It is important to note that the decision in *Croson* simplified the process for whites who were challenging set-aside provisions. "The Court now required that state and local governments must demonstrate a compelling state interest in order to establish a *prima facie*" case of past discrimination(488 U.S. 469, 1989). The Court also required that "race-neutral alternatives must be narrowly tailored so as to rectify the effects of past discrimination" (488 U.S. 469,472-473, 1989). The Court again held in *Croson* that quotas were unconstitutional.

Justice Marshall wrote in his dissent that "the Court's decision in *Croson* was a giant step backward in the realm of affirmative action" (488 U.S. 469,549, 1989). Marshall strongly suggested that "the Court had refused to accept documented proof of historical discrimination" (488 U.S. 469,656-657, 1989). He stated that "the Court exhibited judicial inconsistency in reaching this decision" (488 U.S. 469,656-657, 1989). Marshall asserted that "the decision of *Croson* was a reversal of *Johnson v. Santa Clara, Transportation Agency*" (480 U.S. 616) decided in 1987.

The decision handed down in *Wards Cove Packing Company v. Antonio* (490 U.S. 642, 1989) dealt a severe blow to affirmative action. *Wards Cove* presented the Court with the issue of disparate impact. The Court established the fact "that race-based statistical comparisons were not enough to prove disparate impact" (490 U.S. 642,653, 1989). The Court also held that "a statistical imbalance between jobs and employee groups was insufficient for employee groups supporting a *prima facie* case of illegal discrimination" (490 U.S. 642,650, 1989). Rather, "the appropriate statistical comparison, the Court surmised, was between the

racial composition of the at-issue jobs and the racial composition of the
qualified population in the relevant labor market" (490 U.S. 642,650,
1989). The ruling of the Court in *Wards Cove* (1989) made it difficult for
protected class individuals and groups to use statistics as support for
claims of illegal discrimination (490 U.S. 642,662, 1989). The Court was
concerned with what it considered the proper assessment of the burden of
proof. Thus, in *Wards Cove*, "the Court placed the burden of proof on the
plaintiff to win in a case involving a disparate impact" (490 U.S. 642,650,
1989).

One week later in *Martin v. Wilks* (490 U.S. 755, 1989) the Supreme
Court ruled on the constitutionality of a consent decree. The Court also
settled the issue of when one could become a party to an affirmative
action lawsuit. In *Martin v. Wilks* (1989) "it became apparent that the
Supreme Court had changed its judicial view of the mechanism utilized
in the implementation of affirmative action goals" (490 U.S. 755, 1989).

The Court in *Martin* reasoned that "a consent decree settled matters
among the immediate parties; it did not however, exclude the rights of
those that were strangers to the proceedings" (490 U.S. 755,762, 1989).
The decision in *Martin*, in effect, "opened the potential for large numbers
of lawsuits challenging consent decrees that had been implemented over
the past two years in affirmative action cases" (490 U.S. 755,770, 1989).
In essence, the Court held that under Title VII, white employers could
challenge, without time limitations, affirmative action consent decrees
settling employment disputes, even if the current litigants were not
original parties to the lawsuit. The decision in *Martin* reduced the impact
of consent decrees designed to eradicate historical racial discrimination
in employment and promotional practices.

In June of 1989, the Supreme Court's decision in *Price Waterhouse v.
Hopkins* (490 U.S. 228) sent a strong signal to employers to improve their
performance appraisal systems. In *Price Waterhouse*, the Court required
that an employee in a Title VII discrimination action demonstrate the
burden of proof by objective evidence (490 U.S. 228,258, 1989). "The
decision made it clear that employers must exercise legal and moral
propriety in the establishment of employee appraisal systems" (490 U.S.
228,258, 1989). Thus, the *Price Waterhouse* decision "shifted the burden
of proof to the plaintiff and the employer merely had to prove by a
preponderance of evidence that the major factor in the decision was made
absent gender consideration" (490 U.S. 228,261, 1989). The Court,
therefore, made if difficult to bring a successful case based on gender

discrimination.    The Court relied on the principle of intentional discrimination.  The Court asserted in *Price Waterhouse* that "when an employment decision was based on legitimate and impermissible facts such as gender, the employer still avoided liability if the same decision would have been made without the impermissible factor" (490 U.S. 228,251, 1989).  In short, gender discrimination could still play a role as long as it was a secondary rather than primary role.

The issue of the legality of seniority systems and the application of the statute of limitations was the focus in *Lorance v. AT&T* (490 U.S. 900). The key issue was "whether a discriminatory employment practice disguised as facially neutral met constitutional muster under Title VII" (490 U.S. 900, 1989). The Court in *Lorance* allowed "the implementation of such an employment practice, thereby serving as a hindrance for those seeking to establish affirmative action programs" (490 U.S. 900, 1989). The Court held that "the statute of limitations for challenging a discriminatory employment practice began when the practice was adopted rather than when the practice was applied to the harmed plaintiffs" (490 U.S. 900,911, 1989).

Justice Marshall stated that the decision of *Lorance* diminished the congressional intent of seniority systems under Title VII.  Marshall suggested, that "the Court in *Lorance* required an employee to anticipate discrimination or forever hold their peace" (490 U.S. 900,914, 1989). Marshall concluded with "the rationale that the Court in *Lorance* had created a situation that rewarded employers ingenious enough to cloak their acts of discrimination in a facially neutral guise identical to a facially discriminatory seniority plan" (490 U.S. 900,917, 1989).

The foundation of *Patterson v. McLean Credit Union* (491 U.S. 164) was the Civil Rights Act of 1866 (Section 1981).  The issue centered around discrimination in a private contract involving an African American woman.  The Court in *Patterson* had to resolve "the legal issue of whether or not the discriminatory practice was prohibited during the formation of the contract or the conditions that arose from the contract" (491 U.S. 164,176-177, 1989).  The allegation of racial harassment was also an issue in *Patterson*.

The Court held that "under Section 1981, the prohibition against racial discrimination in making and enforcing private contracts applied only to discrimination in the formation of the contract" (491 U.S. 164,175-185, 1989).  Thus, the Court reasoned that "Section 1981 did not extend protection against discriminatory conduct after the contractual relationship was initially established" (491 U.S. 164,175-185, 1989) . This, according to the Court, was "inclusive of a breach of contract or discriminatory work conditions after the establishment of the contract. Regarding the issue of racial harassment, the Court held that the conditions were not covered under Section 1981, because the provision did not apply to conduct occurring after the formation of the contract"(491 U.S. 164,175-185, 1989).

The dissenting opinion in *Patterson*, written by Brennan, suggested that the majority opinion had interpreted Section 1981 to undermine the purpose of Title VII. He pointed out that coverage of employment discrimination in Section 1981 and Title VII were different. The Court in *Patterson* established the potential to allow discrimination in a work setting after contract formulation. Hence, it may be argued that the Court was granting the formation of on the job practices allowing discrimination resulting from continued employment.

During the 1990s, the lower federal courts continued to address legal confrontations regarding the legitimacy of affirmative action programs. In *Milwaukee County Pavers Association v. Fiedler*, 922 F2d 419 (7th Cir. 1991) the legality of set-asides and the claim of reverse discrimination again revisited the courts. An association of highway contractors filed a claim of reverse discrimination in violation of the Equal Protection Clause of the Fourteenth Amendment, challenging the practice by the State of Wisconsin setting aside contracts for disadvantaged business enterprises. The Seventh Circuit Court of Appeals utilized the precedents established in *Croson* (1989) and *Bakke* (1978) in reaching its decision. The Circuit Court of Appeals held that programs involving set-aside contracts for firms identified as disadvantaged violated the Equal Protection Clause of the Fourteenth Amendment. The Seventh Circuit Court of Appeals reasoned that racial presumption was a form of racial discrimination established *a'la Bakke* (1978) constituted reverse discrimination (922 F2d 419, 421). *Milwaukee County Pavers Association* clearly demonstrated that the utilization of a program designed to provide economic assistance primarily to African American contractors could still be challenged under the argument of reverse discrimination in Federal Court.

The legality of set-aside contracts confronted the Supreme Court again during the 1993 term. As noted earlier, the Supreme Court resolved the issue of set-asides in *Croson* (1989). In *Northeastern Florida Chapter of the Associated General Contractors of American v. City of Jacksonville, Florida* (508 U.S. 656, 1993) the issue was set-aside contracts for

Minority Business Enterprises. The legal question was whether the practice violated the Equal Protection Clause of the Fourteenth Amendment. The facts in *Northeastern* differed from *Croson* (1989) in that prior to adjudication by the Supreme Court, the City of Jacksonville repealed the MBE ordinance and replaced it with an ordinance that set-aside contracts for certified African American and female owned businesses. Hence, the city argued that the case was moot.

The Court's response was that it was settled legal principle that the voluntary cessation of a challenged practice did not deprive a federal court of the power to determine the legality of the practice simply because a defendant was not precluded from reinstating the said practice" (508 U.S. 662, 1993). The Court noted that "the city's new ordinance allowed preferential treatment in the awarding of contracts, thus violating the Equal Protection Clause of the Fourteenth Amendment" (508 U.S. 662, 1993). The Supreme Court again in 1993 affirmed the view that race-conscious preferential treatment was unconstitutional.

Also in 1993, a federal district court was asked to decide the legality of a scholarship program created by the University of Maryland at College Park in 1978 for African Americans. The purpose of the scholarship was to overcome historical racial discrimination. It should be noted that members of other racial minorities were ineligible to apply. Poderesky, a Hispanic student, applied for the Banneker Scholarship and was denied one because of his ethnicity. Hence, the case of *Podberesky v. Kirwan* (838 F. Supp. 1075 (D.MD. 1993) landed in the courts. The issue of reverse discrimination as alleged in *Bakke* (1978) in higher education again required adjudication. The underlying issue in the case was whether the restriction in awarding of the scholarship was justified based on the historical discrimination exhibited toward African Americans.

The Federal District Court upheld the legality of the scholarship on the premise that it was designed as a remedy for historical discriminatory practices. However, "the Fourth Circuit Court of Appeals held that the lower court had failed to support its findings of the present effects of past discrimination" (956 F.2d [4th Cir.]). The decision of the Court of Appeals reaffirmed "the principle that race-based remedial measures must be judged according to the standard of strict scrutiny" (838 F. Supp.1075,1083, 1993). The program must serve a compelling state interest and must be narrowly tailored.

The Court therefore held that the Banneker Scholarship was not tied to past discrimination by the University. The Court argued that "the mere knowledge of a historical fact was not the kind of present effect that justified a race-exclusive remedy" (838 F. Supp. 1075,1083, 1993). The Court continued to apply the precedent that an affirmative action program, in order to met constitutional muster, must be designed to eradicate the present effects of racial discrimination resulting from historical practices. "The Banneker Scholarship Program was declared unconstitutional and the Court continued to reduce affirmative action programs in universities even when the Court conceded that racial hostility continued to exist" (838 F. Supp. 1075,1092, 1993).

In 1993, the Court was requested to determine the legality of numerical goals based on race, race-conscious remedies, consent decrees, and racial preference. These issues were the foundation for the case of *Maryland Troopers Association, Inc., v. Evans* (993 F.2d 1072 [4th Cir. 1993]). The Court held that "in order to support a race-conscious remedy in a Title VII action, the state must present more than a general history of societal discrimination and must specify racial discrimination that was the target of the plan" (993 F.2d 1072, 1993). The Court pointed out that "race-conscious remedies must be narrowly tailored and may not take on a life of it's own" (993 F.2d 1072, 1993). The Court reasoned that "race-conscious relief in a consent decree violated the guidelines of the Fourteenth Amendment"(993 F.2d 1072,1077, 1993). The Court again applied the established criteria that a remedial affirmative action program must adhere to the requirements of strict scrutiny and must be narrowly tailored.

In 1995, the Supreme Court adjudicated cases with the issues of race-based classifications, strict scrutiny, and affirmative action programs. In *Adarand Constructors, Inc. v. Pena* (1995) "the Supreme Court held that race-based classifications were subject to strict scrutiny regardless of whether enacted by Congress or other governmental decision makers" (115 S. Ct. 2097,2112-13, 1995). "The Court, in reaching this decision, imposed an artificial symmetry on equal protection jurisprudence using the concepts of congruence and consistency" (115 S. Ct. 2097,2100, 1995) . The concepts of congruence and consistency were incorporated by the Court into an analysis of the Fifth Amendment Due Process Clause. It may be argued that the Court disregarded the text of the Fourteenth Amendment, as well as the historical relationship between federalism and race, along with current social and political realities. The Court argued that "all racial classifications, whether overtly invidious or purportedly benign, were subject to strict scrutiny" (115 S. Ct. 2097,2119, 1995).

The dissenting opinion argued that the decision given in *Adarand* created a new meaning for strict scrutiny, but suggested that it would not invalidate congressionally enacted programs. Justice Ginsburg wrote that "the Court should consider the fact that affirmative action has been a vital tool in the quest for real equality"(115 S. Ct. 2097,2134, 1995). In the *Adarand* decision the Court continued to reduce the viability of affirmative action programs.

During the judicial term of 1996, the Circuit Court of Appeals was presented with a case from Piscataway, New Jersey. The case of *Taxman v. Board of Education of Township of Piscataway* 91 F.3d 1547 (3rd Cir. 1996) contained the issues of employee layoffs, employment discrimination, the legality of a remedial affirmative action policy and what value should be given to race in employment decisions. As noted earlier, the Board of Education for Piscataway High School had implemented an affirmative action policy without remedial purpose designed to afford students with diversity among the faculty. The Business Department, in order to comply with the policy, laid off Taxman (the white teacher). As a result, Taxman filed an employment discrimination case with the Equal Employment Opportunity Commission. The focal issue in the case was Title VII. It should be noted that "Title VII made it unconstitutional for an employer to discriminate against an individual with respect to their compensation, terms, conditions, privileges of employment, or to segregate or classify employees in any manner which would deprive any individual of employment opportunities or otherwise effect employment status on the basis of race, religion, sex, or national origin" (91 F.3d 1547,1553, 1996).

The Third Circuit Court of Appeals held that the requirement barring consideration of race from the workplace was the primary objective of Title VII. Therefore, the Circuit Court of Appeals rejected the board's reliance on case law interpreting the Fourteenth Amendment and the Equal Protection Clause. The Circuit Court of Appeals argued that even though the board's actions were laudable, it nevertheless did not meet the requirement for a remedial purpose. The plan utilized by the Board violated the guidelines of the Fourteenth Amendment and Title VII.

Prior to the scheduled adjudication of the *Taxman* case before the United States Supreme Court in January of 1998, an interesting development took place. As reported in the *New York Times* (1997) the potential landmark case was settled out of court. The case was settled because civil rights groups feared the Supreme Court might use the case to outlaw the widespread use of voluntary racial preferences to promote diversity. The settlement was viewed by many as evidence that a shifting political and legal consensus in America was developing for a movement away from affirmative action and toward policies that are neutral in addressing race and gender.

In 1996, a similar issue that had once been resolved in *Bakke* (1978) was again the subject of judicial interpretation. The case of *Hopwood v. Texas* (1996) involved the challenge of racial preferences in admission policies for a university. The issue again was consideration of race as a factor in admissions. The legal challenge involved the question of whether racial preferences was a violation of the Equal Protection Clause of the Fourteenth Amendment.

The Federal District Court ruled that the Law School had presented no compelling justification, under the Fourteenth Amendment, that allowed the continuation of evaluating one race over another (78 F. 3d 934, 1996). The Federal District Court reasoned that the central purpose of the Equal Protection Clause was the prevention of purposeful discrimination against an individual based on race. The Federal District Court utilized the concept of strict scrutiny as established in earlier court cases.

The cases presented during the years from 1989-1996 arguably demonstrated a continuous reduction in decisions favorable to proponents of affirmative action. The out of court settlement of *Taxman v. Piscataway* (1996) revealed that proponents of affirmative action developed the tactic of selectively deciding which cases to send before the Court. In view of the discussed judicial proceedings, it can be argued that many companies will question their commitment to affirmative action as well as their approach. The Civil Rights Act of 1991 was an effort to rectify the effects of the sweeping decisions made by the Court during 1989. However, it was suggested that the struggle between the Court's view of affirmative action and that of the United States Congress continues. In view of the decisions reached during the period from 1989-1996, American corporations, as well as the public sector, must develop strategies for affirmative action during the 1990s that meet the test of strict scrutiny exhibited by the conservative philosophy of the United States Supreme Court (Scott and Little, 1991).

The scope of this Chapter focuses on the role of the Supreme Court and affirmative action. A review of trends established relating to affirmative action since 1989 suggests that the Court tightened the noose around the neck of affirmative action. In addition, it may be suggested that the Supreme Court decisions have gone full circle in the area of affirmative action.

# CHAPTER VI

# METHODOLOGY

Often research on affirmative action has been based on anecdotal case studies (Kellough and Kay, 1986). However, another technique related to qualitative research-- analysis of time-ordered archival data-- provides an excellent opportunity to specify the relationship between affirmative action and public sector employment. The methodology for this research utilizes a longitudinal analysis of state government affirmative action employment data. Data are analyzed to assess the impact of affirmative action on employment diversity by analyzing hiring and employment-related data of state personnel boards in the seven southern states from the inception of the 1964 Civil Rights Act to 1995. Time-ordered employment data from Arkansas, Georgia, Mississippi, North Carolina, Oklahoma, South Carolina and Tennessee are examined to assess variations in employment. This research design allows for intrastate as well as interstate comparisons to assess how states compare with each other, as well as how far each state has come with regard to occupations that are representative of African Americans in the available workforce and state population as a whole. While this is primarily a qualitative investigation of affirmative action in select southern states, the analysis of these data provide for additional insights.

Data collection for this research began in the Winter of 1996. Letters of inquiry were sent to the state personnel directors of the thirteen southern states of the Old Confederacy. States included were Alabama,

Arkansas, Florida, Georgia, Louisiana, Mississippi, North Carolina, Oklahoma, South Carolina, Tennessee, Texas, Virginia, and West Virginia. The letters requested personnel data related to affirmative action policies from 1964 to the present. Specifically, the request was for data that related to the status of African Americans, women, affirmative action requirements and equal employment opportunity reports. It was emphasized that the data would be used only for analyzing employment patterns and opportunities during this time period, and that the research was for a dissertation. The letter of inquiry explained that the research would focus on employment diversity for mid-level and upper-level management for the prospective states. It was pointed out that the data would be utilized to develop an impact assessment of affirmative action from 1964-1995. An executive summary was offered in the letter of the final study for those states that supplied the data if they requested one.

The letters of inquiry were sent out in January of 1996. As of August 1996, data had been received from seven of the thirteen states. Ideally, data from all thirteen states would have provided the best outcome. Nevertheless, this does represent a 54% response rate. Follow-up letters were sent to those states that did not respond, but this did not improve the response rate. In both the initial and follow-up letters, the Major Professor/Dissertation Director assisted in the draft and co-signed each one. Telephone calls were used after the follow-up letters, but the response rate still remained the same.

Alabama, Florida, Louisiana, Texas, Virginia and West Virginia did not reply to several queries. Data were received from Arkansas, Georgia, Mississippi, North Carolina, Oklahoma, South Carolina and Tennessee. As a result, the analysis is confined to the selected states. Thank you letters were sent to those states that provided data. All of those states providing the requested data supplied the investigator with the necessary contact person in case there was a need for additional communication.

Participating states provided Equal Employment Opportunity Act statistical data taken from EEO-4 job reports. This classification is primarily white-collar and constitutes the mid- to upper-level management positions. The reference period for the data is from 1973 until the 1995. In some instances, the data include pertinent statutes and provisions for employment diversity for that particular state. Demographic information for whites, African Americans/Blacks, Hispanics, Asian, and American Indian was also provided. The break-down of ethnicity is cross-classified by gender. This research and analysis focuses primarily on the progress of African Americans (male/female) by comparing them with other protected groups and whites.

The data also provide statistical information differentiated by job category. Those delineations are as follows: official/administration, professional, technicians, protective services, para-professional, administrative support, skilled-craft, and service maintenance. These categories are defined by guidelines established by the Equal Employment Opportunity Commission (EEOC) and are uniform across all seven states of the study. For this research, only those classified as full-time employees are included in the analysis.

According to the EEOC categorical codes, officials and administrative occupations include employees involved in setting broad policies and exercising overall responsibility for the execution of such policies. These employees are responsible for directing individual departments or special phases of the agency's operations. Officials and administrators have the responsibility of providing specialized consultation on a regional, district, or area basis. The agency operations included within this category are: department heads, bureau chiefs, division chiefs, directors, deputy directors, controllers, wardens, superintendents, sheriffs, police and fire chiefs, and inspectors. The examiner's function entails bank, hearing, motor vehicle and warehouse examiners. Inspectors include fire, alcohol beverage control board, license, diary, livestock, and transportation. This category encompasses assessors, tax appraisers, and investigators, coroners, farm managers, and kindred workers (EEOC Report).

Employees in the professional category are required to have specialized or theoretical knowledge which is usually acquired through college training or through work experience and other training which provides comparable knowledge. This category includes personnel and labor relations workers, social workers, doctors, psychologists, registered nurses, economists, dieticians, lawyers, systems analysts, accountants, engineers, employment and vocational rehabilitation counselors, teachers or instructors. The professional category also includes police and fire captains and lieutenants, librarians, management analysts, airplane pilots and navigators, surveyors and mapping scientists, and kindred workers (EEOC Reports).

Employees in the protective service category are those workers entrusted with public safety, security and protection from destructive forces. Protective service workers include police patrol officers, fire fighters, guards, deputy sheriffs, bailiffs, correctional officers, detectives, marshals, harbor patrol officers, game and fish wardens, park rangers (except maintenance), and kindred workers (EEOC Reports).

The category of para-professionals is composed of employees who perform some of the duties of a professional or technician in a supportive role, which usually requires less formal training and or experience normally required for professional or technical status. Such positions may fall within an identified pattern of staff development and promotion under a "New Careers" concept. Included in this category are positions such as research assistants, medical aids, child support workers, policy auxiliary welfare service aids, recreation assistants, homemakers aides, home health aides, library assistants and clerks, ambulance drivers and attendants, and kindred workers (EEOC Reports).

Technicians are those employees required to have a combination of basic scientific or technical knowledge and manual skills that can be obtained through specialized post-secondary school education or through the equivalent of on-the-job training. Occupations within this category are computer programers, drafters, survey and mapping technicians, licensed practical nurses, photographers, radio operators, technical illustrators, highway technicians, technicians (medical, dental, electronic, physical sciences), police and fire sergeants, inspectors (production or processing inspectors, testers, and weighers) and kindred workers (EEOC Reports).

Administrative support employees are responsible for internal and external communication, recording and retrieval of data and or information and other paperwork required in an office. Included with the administrative support category are bookkeepers, messengers, clerk-typists, stenographers, court transcribers, hearing reporters, statistical clerks, dispatchers, license distributors, payroll clerks, office machine and computer operators, telephone operators, legal assistants, sales workers, cashiers, toll collectors, and kindred workers (EEOC Reports).

Skilled craft employees perform job tasks which require special manual skills and a thorough and comprehensive knowledge of the processes involved in the work which is acquired through on-the-job training experience or through apprenticeship or other formal training programs. Occupations included in the category of skilled craft include mechanics and repairers, electricians, heavy equipment operators, stationery engineers, skilled machining occupations, carpenters, compositors, typesetters, power plant operators, water and sewage treatment plant operators, and kindred workers (EEOC Reports).

The employees included in the category of service maintenance are employers that perform duties which result in or contribute to the comfort, convenience, hygiene or safety of the general public or which contribute to the upkeep and care of buildings, facilities or grounds of public property. Employees in this group may operate machinery. The employees within this category include chauffeurs, laundry and dry cleaning operatives, truck drivers, bus drivers, garage laborers, custodial employees, gardeners and ground keepers, refuse collectors, construction laborers, park rangers (maintenance) farm workers (except managers) craft apprentices (trainers, helpers,) and kindred workers (EEOC Reports).

Data supplied by the state of Arkansas covered a time span from 1988 to 1997. The date from the state of Georgia spanned from 1973 to 1995. The state of Mississippi supplied data for the years of 1988, 1989, 1990, 1991, 1993, and 1995. The State Personnel Director stated that for the years of 1992 and 1994, Mississippi did not file the EEO-4 reports (Appendix). The state of North Carolina provided data for the years from 1977 to 1995. However, the state of Oklahoma only supplied data for the years of 1984, 1994, and 1996. Assistant Administrator, Janice Wadkins informed the researcher via telephone (January 12, 1998) that a change in administrative personnel had resulted in data for the previous years not being stored. Therefore, the time period of study for Oklahoma is limited to the three years reported above. The state of South Carolina gave data for the period of 1987 to 1994. And the state of Tennessee supplied employee data for the years of 1983-1996. All of the data submitted utilized the eight EEO-4 categories. The statistical information collected was for state level employees as reported by the State Personnel Director. It is important to note that obtaining data from EEOC presents a difficult task due to the legal requirements and the issue of confidentiality. Also, the EEOC reflect only what information is reported as was discussed regarding Mississippi.

In order to assess the impact of the 1964 Civil Rights Act and the 1965 Voting Rights Act on employment diversity in the seven southern states, political data were obtained for each state during the previously mentioned time periods. The political data included the total population and the total African American population of each state in order to obtain the percentage of African Americans in each state. The political data also included the number of African Americans in the state legislators for each of the seven selected states. The rationale here was to provide data to analyze what relationship may exist between the number African

American legislators and increases in employment hiring of African Americans. These data provide a means for the statistical analysis in Chapter VII. The political party of the governor for each reported year was also analyzed to study what effect, if any, the party of the governor had on hiring practices for that state. The analysis of the Supreme Court and Federal Court decisions were studied to see what effect, if any, the judicial decisions at that time had on state level employment. It could be argued that a negative or anti-affirmative action decision would have a similar affect on state level employment practices. On the other hand, the argument could be set forth that a positive or pro-affirmative action judicial decision would produce a positive correlation in employment hiring for African Americans. These factors and their effects will be discussed in the data analysis chapter. It should be noted, however, that since public policies are incremental in nature, the effects of an election or Supreme Court decision may not be immediately apparent.

The political data for each of the seven states were compiled by researching material provided by the Joint Center for Political Studies for each of the corresponding years in which data were collected. This information was supplemented by information obtained from *Information Please Almanac* (1994-1997) along with *Statistical Abstract of the United States*(1982-1983, 1994, 1995, 1996, and 1997). Political data were also obtained from information provided by *State Elective Officials and The Legislatures* (1987-1988).

The collected state employee data were reported for full time employees and the respective fiscal years. These data were analyzed for descriptive purposes as well as to provide recommendations at the end of the study.

# CHAPTER VII

# DATA ANALYSIS

A major objective of this study was to develop an impact assessment of affirmative action and employment diversity in the southern states known as the Old Confederacy. The pivotal point of the research was to analyze over a period of time based on actual data the progress of African Americans since the inception of affirmative action. These states were Arkansas, Georgia, Mississippi, North Carolina, Oklahoma, South Carolina and Tennessee. The analysis was based, in part, upon a longitudinal intrastate and interstate study of the selected states. While the analysis of these data focuses on the top two policy making categories, discussion addresses those occupations in which African Americans have made dramatic increases, on the one hand, or almost no increases, on the other hand.

In assessing the status of affirmative action, the impact of the judicial branch with decisions handed down by the United States Supreme Court and other federal courts require analysis because of their potential impact on hiring and promotion practices by management. As previously discussed, the court system has had an effect on the state of affirmative action as it relates to employment hiring and promotional practices. The role of the Supreme Court and other courts in the area of affirmative action led to the development of two hypothetical propositions. The first query was whether decisions reached by the judicial system have led to an increase in hiring and promotional practices. The second query was whether judicial rulings have led to a decrease in the hiring and promotion of African Americans in the state workforce; or has it created a leveling effect or even neutralized diversified employment and promotional practices in several selected states. However, it should be noted that public policies are incremental in nature; therefore, the effect of a Supreme Court decision may not be immediately apparent.

In order to address the two hypothetical propositions, the study assessed over time, the actual numbers of African Americans employed during this period in each of the selected states. The research assessed the actual number of African Americans in the state workforce for those occupations involved in policy making. It should be kept in mind that some states provided data over a longer period of time. Hence, the tables for the respective states reflective of collected data.

## African American Employment in Southern State Governments

### Arkansas

As shown in Table 2, Arkansas had a total of 4,045 (21%) African American employees in state level positions in 1988. By the mid-term of the reported data, 1992, there were 4,727 (22%). By the end of the reported time period of 1997, there were 5,952 (25%) African Americans. This represents a total increase over nine years of 1,907 (4%) in African American's share in state government in Arkansas. African Americans made only a small increase in the workforce in Arkansas during this period. In the Administrative-Official category beginning in 1988, there were 84 (9%) African Americans employed as reported in Table 2. By 1992, the number increased to 114 (11%), reflecting a modest gain of two-percent. In 1997, the total of African Americans in the Administrative-Official position increased to 133 (13%). The data revealed in Table 2 that in this top category of policy making, African Americans gained a net increase of four percent. In the area of Protective Services, African Americans began with 590 (29%) in 1988 and increased to 1,445 (42%). This category is not included in the policy making realm of state employment, nevertheless it reveals that African Americans in the protective services category increased thirteen percent. When assessing the job classification of Professionals, the data reported 1,080 (14%) African Americans employed in 1988.

Table 2

African American Workers in Arkansas

| Jobs | 1988 | 1989 | 1990 | 1991 | 1992 | 1993 | 1994 | 1995 | 1996 | 1997 |
|------|------|------|------|------|------|------|------|------|------|------|
| Adm.[1] | 84 9% | 98 10% | 114 11% | 113 11% | 114 11% | 125 12% | 122 13% | 134 13% | 139 13% | 133 13% |
| Pro.[2] | 1080 14% | 1173 16% | 1246 16% | 1371 16% | 1428 17% | 1458 17% | 1562 17% | 1700 18% | 1623 18% | 1686 19% |
| Prot.[3] | 590 29% | 665 31% | 738 32% | 786 31% | 825 30% | 908 32% | 1045 34% | 1218 42% | 1395 41% | 1445 42% |
| Para.[4] | 790 30% | 802 30% | 797 30% | 742 32% | 767 32% | 777 32% | 775 32% | 695 31% | 857 33% | 849 34% |
| Tech.[5] | 152 15% | 160 13% | 188 15% | 187 15% | 183 14% | 192 15% | 196 15% | 157 15% | 182 14% | 185 15% |
| Ad-S.[6] | 949 24% | 1017 25% | 1048 25% | 1058 25% | 1060 25% | 1044 25% | 1105 26% | 983 27% | 1263 26% | 1280 27% |
| Craft[7] | 21 8% | 32 8% | 42 11% | 34 9% | 28 8% | 25 8% | 27 9% | 23 9% | 35 9% | 36 9% |
| Serv.[8] | 379 28% | 365 29% | 339 28% | 330 27% | 322 28% | 319 28% | 331 29% | 272 29% | 360 32% | 338 31% |
| Total | 4045 21% | 4312 21% | 4512 22% | 4621 21% | 4727 22% | 4848 22% | 5163 23% | 5182 24% | 5854 25% | 5952 25% |

Numbers equal total African Americans in each job category.
Percentages equal percent in each category that are African American.
Data collected from EEO-4 Reports.
[1]   Administrative-Officials
[2]   Professionals
[3]   Protective-Services
[4]   Para-Professionals
[5]   Technicians
[6]   Administrative Support
[7]   Skilled Craft
[8]   Service-Maintenance

In 1992, the number increased to 1,428 (17%), thus showing an increase of three percent in the African American share of jobs. As witnessed in Table 2, in 1997 the number of African Americans employed as Professionals increased to 1,686 (19%). Over a nine year time period, African Americans in the state workforce of Arkansas increased five percent for those classified as Professionals. The job classification of Technicians found that African American employment remained an average of fifteen percent over the nine year period.

## Georgia

According to the data supplied by the state of Georgia, there were 7,438 (18%) African American employees in state government as of 1973. By 1978, the number of African Americans employed increased to 12,093 (24%). The number of African Americans employed by the state increased by 4,655. Table 3 demonstrated an increase of six percent for African American employees in state government occupations. In 1983, the number of African American employees increased to 15,130 (29%) in the state workforce of Georgia. This revealed a five percent increase in African American employment since 1978. This also reflected an actual increase of African American employees of 3,037. The number of African American employees in the Georgia state workforce increased in 1987 to 19,158 (32%) which represents an increase of 4,028 employees. Thus, by 1987, there was a three percent increase in employment for African Americans in the state of Georgia since 1983. The data showed that employment for African Americans increased by 1993 to 26,881 (35%) in the workforce. This was an increase of African American employees by 7,723, a three percent increase for the time period of 1987 to 1993. By the end of the reported data, 1995, the number of African Americans employed in the state workforce was 30,714 (37%) of the total workforce in Georgia. From the time span of 1993 to that of 1995 the actual increase was 3, 833, which resulted in a two percent increase in employment for African Americans. Over a period of twenty-two years (1973-1995) the overall total of African Americans in the state workforce increased from 7,438 (18%) in 1973 to 30,714 (37%) in 1995. The overall employment for African Americans increased 23,276, which represented a nineteen percent increase in African American employment for the state of Georgia and represented more than a fourfold increase, or more than a 400%, over the 1973 totals.

In 1973, the number of African Americans employed as administrative-officials was 2 (.5%) for this category. In 1978, the number increased to 11 (2%), which was an increase of nine employees. This represented an increase of 1.5% job share held by African Americans. By 1984, the number increased to 45 (6%), an increase of thirty-four African Americans since 1978 employed as administrative-officials and this reflected a four percent increase.

As of 1989, African Americans employed as administrative-officials increased from 45 (1984) to 115 (10%), an increase of seventy employees as shown in Table 3. This reflected a four percent increase from 1984 to 1989. Table 3 revealed an increase in 1993 of 149 (12%) of the number of African Americans employed as administrative-officials. In short, from 1989 to 1993, the number of African Americans increased from 115 (10%) to 149 (12%), reflecting a gain of thirty-four in the category of administrative officials. The actual gain of thirty-four employees represented a two percent increase in African American job share. In 1995, the total number of African Americans employed as administrative-officials increased to 173 (12%). This time period witnessed a leveling effect resulting in an average of twelve percent African American employee workforce in the category of administrative-officials. It should be noted that over a time period of twenty-two years, the number of African Americans employed as administrative-officials increased from 2 (.5%) in 1973, to 173 (12%) by 1995, a 11.5% increase in the share of African Americans employed as administrative-officials in the state of Georgia.

In assessing the number of African Americans employed as professionals in the state of Georgia, Table 3 revealed that in 1973 there were 735 (7%) African Americans. As of 1979, the number of African American professionals in state government increased to 2,106 (12%), which meant 1,371 additional employees. This amounted to a five percent increase of job share. As of 1984, the number of African Americans employed as professionals in the state government increased to 3,022 (17%), which reflected an increase of 919 employees and a five percent increase in African Americans employed as professionals. By 1989, there were 4,968 (21%) African American professionals, providing an increase of four percent from the previous year of 1984. The increase of African Americans in the professional category was 1,946. In 1992, the employment of African American professionals in state government reached 6,505 (23%). This was a two percent increase over 1989, though the actual number of African American professionals employed in state government increased by 1,151. The number of African Americans employed as professionals in the state of Georgia in 1995 was 7, 693 (25%). In sum, there was an increase of 6,958 African American professionals in state government in Georgia from 1973 to 1995.

Table 3 shows that African Americans employed in the category of para-professional started in 1973 with 2,739 (44%) employees and increased to 5,175 (54%) by 1995, amounting to a ten percent increase.

## Table 3

### African American Workers in Georgia

| Jobs | 1973 | 1974 | 1975 | 1976 | 1977 | 1978 | 1979 | 1980 | 1981 |
|------|------|------|------|------|------|------|------|------|------|
| Adm.[1] | 2<br>.5% | 2<br>.5% | 5<br>.8% | 9<br>1% | 14<br>2% | 11<br>2% | 20<br>3% | 27<br>4% | 27<br>4% |
| Pro.[2] | 735<br>7% | 1016<br>8% | 1136<br>8% | 1439<br>10% | 1646<br>11% | 1748<br>11% | 2106<br>12% | 2460<br>14% | 2601<br>14% |
| Prot.[3] | 164<br>5% | 210<br>6% | 219<br>7% | 328<br>10% | 467<br>11% | 474<br>13% | 623<br>16% | 585<br>15% | 868<br>20% |
| Para.[4] | 2739<br>44% | 3175<br>44% | 3435<br>46% | 3505<br>53% | 3652<br>54% | 2761<br>44% | 2841<br>48% | 3058<br>47% | 3142<br>48% |
| Tech.[5] | 368<br>8% | 447<br>10% | 502<br>11% | 536<br>12% | 621<br>13% | 292<br>8% | 241<br>7% | 292<br>9% | 327<br>11% |
| Ad-S.[6] | 745<br>9% | 1184<br>13% | 1385<br>14% | 1422<br>15% | 1596<br>16% | 2178<br>21% | 2048<br>21% | 2231<br>23% | 2364<br>24% |
| Craft[7] | 239<br>11% | 301<br>13% | 390<br>15% | 428<br>16% | 477<br>18% | 193<br>17% | 236<br>18% | 261<br>18% | 278<br>19% |
| Serv.[8] | 2446<br>42% | 2750<br>45% | 3426<br>44% | 2786<br>50% | 2742<br>49% | 4436<br>52% | 4680<br>53% | 4746<br>55% | 4715<br>56% |
| Total | 7438<br>18% | 9085<br>20% | 10497<br>21% | 10453<br>22% | 11215<br>22% | 12093<br>24% | 12795<br>25% | 13660<br>26% | 14321<br>27% |

Number equal total African Americans in each job category.
Percentages equal percent in each category that are African American.
Data collected from EEO-4 Reports.

[1]   Administrative-Officials
[2]   Professionals
[3]   Protective-Services
[4]   Para-Professionals
[5]   Technicians
[6]   Administrative Support
[7]   Skilled Craft
[8]   Service-Maintenance

## Table 3 (continued)

| Jobs | 1982 | 1983 | 1984 | 1985 | 1986 | 1987 | 1988 | 1989 |
|------|------|------|------|------|------|------|------|------|
| Adm.[1] | 23<br>3% | 33<br>4% | 45<br>6% | 47<br>6% | 51<br>7% | 57<br>7% | 68<br>8% | 115<br>10% |
| Pro.[2] | 2755<br>15% | 2796<br>16% | 3022<br>17% | 3364<br>18% | 3620<br>18% | 3950<br>19% | 4444<br>20% | 4968<br>21% |
| Prot.[3] | 1020<br>22% | 1252<br>24% | 1356<br>25% | 1558<br>28% | 1664<br>29% | 1815<br>30% | 1830<br>30% | 2054<br>31% |
| Para.[4] | 3179<br>48% | 3185<br>49% | 3231<br>49% | 3290<br>49% | 3370<br>50% | 3855<br>50% | 4050<br>51% | 4348<br>50% |
| Tech.[5] | 325<br>11% | 347<br>12% | 370<br>13% | 424<br>15% | 485<br>16% | 576<br>18% | 640<br>20% | 771<br>22% |
| Ad-S.[6] | 2538<br>26% | 2480<br>27% | 2599<br>28% | 2835<br>30% | 2880<br>30% | 3052<br>31% | 3502<br>33% | 3837<br>34% |
| Craft [7] | 286<br>19% | 276<br>19% | 271<br>19% | 314<br>21% | 339<br>22% | 360<br>22% | 354<br>21% | 376<br>22% |
| Serv.[8] | 4685<br>57% | 4761<br>55% | 4831<br>56% | 5103<br>56% | 5210<br>58% | 5493<br>57% | 5444<br>56% | 5784<br>57% |
| Total | 14811<br>28% | 1510<br>29% | 15725<br>30% | 16935<br>31% | 17619<br>31% | 19158<br>32% | 20332<br>32% | 22253<br>33% |

Numbers equal total African Americans in each job category.
Percentages equal percent in each category that are African American.
Data collected from EEO-4 Reports
[1]  Administrative-Officials
[2]  Professionals
[3]  Protective-Services
[4]  Para-Professionals
[5]  Technicians
[6]  Administrative Support
[7]  Skilled Craft
[8]  Service-Maintenance

Table 3 (continued)

| Jobs | 1990 | 1991 | 1992 | 1993 | 1994 | 1995 |
|------|------|------|------|------|------|------|
| Adm.[1] | 117<br>10% | 136<br>11% | 135<br>12% | 149<br>12% | 153<br>12% | 173<br>12% |
| Pro.[2] | 5564<br>22% | 6112<br>22% | 6119<br>23% | 6505<br>23% | 7067<br>24% | 7693<br>25% |
| Prot.[3] | 2507<br>32% | 2762<br>33% | 2789<br>33% | 3246<br>35% | 3963<br>40% | 4465<br>42% |
| Para.[4] | 4449<br>51% | 4822<br>51% | 4981<br>52% | 5417<br>53% | 4827<br>52% | 5175<br>54% |
| Tech.[5] | 811<br>23% | 868<br>25% | 888<br>26% | 889<br>26% | 1685<br>33% | 1821<br>35% |
| Ad-S.[6] | 3545<br>32% | 3836<br>33% | 3927<br>34% | 4154<br>35% | 4542<br>35% | 4695<br>36% |
| Craft [7] | 407<br>22% | 383<br>22% | 375<br>22% | 391<br>23% | 406<br>23% | 430<br>23% |
| Serv.[8] | 6139<br>62% | 6039<br>58% | 5862<br>57% | 6130<br>60% | 6121<br>61% | 6261<br>62% |
| Total | 23539<br>34% | 24958<br>34% | 25076<br>34% | 26881<br>35% | 28764<br>36% | 30714<br>37% |

Numbers equal total African Americans in each job category.
Percentages equal percent in each category that are African American.
Data collected from EEO-4 Reports.
[1]   Administrative-Officials
[2]   Professionals
[3]   Protective-Services
[4]   Para-Professionals
[5]   Technicians
[6]   Administrative Support
[7]   Skilled Craft
[8]   Service-Maintenance

It should also be noted that a large percent of the state workforce for African Americans were in the occupational category of service maintenance. In 1973, there were 2,446 (42%) African American employees and by 1995 6,261 (62%) state employees were African Americans. African Americans employed in the category of service maintenance experienced a twenty percent growth over a twenty-two year time span.

## Mississippi

In the state of Mississippi, African Americans employed in the state workforce totaled 6,283 (30%) in 1988. Two years later, in 1990, the number of African Americans employed by the state of Mississippi rose to 8,858 as reported in Table 4. In two years the African American share of the state employee workforce increased five percent. In 1993, African Americans employed by the state continued to increase. The number of African Americans employed by the state of Mississippi grew to 9,683 (39%). This was reflective of a four percent increase in employment gains for African Americans employed in the state labor force from 1990-1993. The total number of African Americans employed by the state experienced a decrease beginning in the 1990s. The number of African Americans employed decreased from 9,683 (39%) in 1993 to 8,507 (36%) in 1995. For the years reported by Mississippi, the total number of African Americans went from 6,283 (30%) in 1988 to 8,507 (36%) in 1995. In 1993 the highest number for African American employment reached 9,683 (39%).

In the occupational category of administrative-officials for the state of Mississippi, were 135 (12%) African Americans employed in 1988. In 1990, the number of African Americans employed as administrative-officials increased to 192 (15%). This increase was representative of a three percent increase. As of 1993, African American administrative-officials reached 200 (15%), which reflected another increased of three percent.

The number of African American administrative-officials increased to 228 (16%) by 1995. Based on the data reported by the state of Mississippi, African Americans employed in the occupational status of administrative-officials rose from 135 (12%) in 1988 to 228 (16%) in 1995. Overall, this represented a four percent increase in job share for African Americans in the state labor force in the category of administrative-officials.

An analysis of African Americans employed by the state of Mississippi as professionals revealed that in 1988 there were 1,056 (17%) such employees. The number of African American professionals rose in 1990 to 1,340 (19%) employees, a two percent increase. Employment gains for African American professionals continued in 1993.

During this period, African American professionals increased to 1,651 (22%), representing a five percent increase from 1988 (17%) to 1993 (22%) as shown. As of 1995, African American professional employees equaled 1,888 (24%) of the state labor force. An assessment of the data reveals that African American professionals rose from 1,056 (17%) in 1988 to 1,888 (24%) in 1995, seven percent total increase.

Further study of the Mississippi data revealed two interesting facts. First, in the category of protective services, African American employment grew from 1,217 (46%) in 1988 to 1,914 (58%) in 1995, an increase of twelve percent. Second, the data show that the number of African American para-professionals were 1,047 (68%) in 1988, and maintained a sixty-four percent average for 1991 (3,262) and 1993, (3,358).

However, a dramatic decrease was reported in 1995. During this time, the number of African American para-professionals dropped to 1,708 (47%). Based on the data in Table 4, there was a twenty-one percent reduction in African Americans employed as para-professionals. It is important to note that Mississippi did not report data for 1992 and 1994.

Mississippi was unlike the other two states that experienced a decline in African American employment population. While the other states were experiencing a decline, Mississippi continued to have an increase in the two policy making categories. The only decline in African American employment was in one category, that of para-professionals, which was not a policy making employment category.

Table 4

African American Workers in Mississippi

| Jobs | 1988 | 1989 | 1990 | 1991 | 1993 | 1995 |
|---|---|---|---|---|---|---|
| Adm.[1] | 135 12% | 160 13% | 192 15% | 203 16% | 200 15% | 228 16% |
| Pro.[2] | 1056 17% | 1177 18% | 1340 19% | 1457 21% | 1651 22% | 1888 24% |
| Prot.[3] | 1217 46% | 1324 45% | 1339 46% | 1613 53% | 1720 56% | 1914 58% |
| Para.[4] | 1047 68% | 3233 63% | 3161 62% | 3264 64% | 3358 64% | 1708 47% |
| Tech.[5] | 761 23% | 836 25% | 803 25% | 789 25% | 806 27% | 901 29% |
| Ad-S [6] | 884 29% | 875 30% | 931 31% | 872 31% | 899 33% | 878 36% |
| Craft [7] | 175 22% | 195 26% | 188 24% | 184 23% | 196 24% | 208 26% |
| Serv.[8] | 1008 51% | 948 55% | 904 50% | 876 53% | 853 52% | 782 55% |
| Total | 6283 30% | 8747 36% | 8858 35% | 9258 37% | 9683 39% | 8507 36% |

Numbers equal total African Americans in each job category.
Percentages equal percent in each category that are African American.
Data collected from EEO-4 Reports.
[1]  Administrative-Officials
[2]  Professionals
[3]  Protective-Services
[4]  Para-Professionals
[5]  Technicians
[6]  Administrative Support
[7]  Skilled Craft
[8]  Service-Maintenance

## North Carolina

African American workers in North Carolina during the year of 1977 equaled 13,626 (22%) of the total state employment labor force as recorded in Table 5. In 1982, the total number of African Americans employed by the state rose to 16,222 (25%). Beginning in 1983, the number of African American state employees maintained a level of 26% through 1994. As of 1995, state-employed African Americans totaled 22,363 (27%). In summary, African American employees went from 13,626 (22%) in 1977 to 22,363 (27%) in 1995 in state government in North Carolina. The increase for African Americans employed by the state of North Carolina over an eighteen year time frame was five percent.

In North Carolina, African American administrative-officials for 1977 numbered 91 (7%) of those employed in this category. The time period from 1978 to 1984 reflected a very small African American increase and a constant share of the work force. However, starting in 1985, there were 135 (9%) African American and they maintained this level through 1990. By 1993, the number of African American administrative-officials rose to 220 (12%). And in 1994, the state of North Carolina employed 239 (13%) African Americans as administrative-officials. In 1995, 257 (14%) of the administrative-officials were African Americans. Over an eighteen year period starting with only 91 (7%) employees in 1977, African Americans increased to 257 (14%) in 1995. The number of African Americans employed as administrative-officials increased by 166 and a total of seven percent over the period in question.

An assessment of African Americans employed as professionals in state government revealed that in 1977 there were 1,086 (12%) African Americans in the state labor force. From 1981 through 1983, professional African Americans employed averaged 13%. During the time period of 1984 through 1991, African Americans employed as professionals remained constant at fourteen percent and reached 2,399 (15%) in 1994. A year later in 1995, the number of professional African Americans increased to 2,632 (16%) in the state of North Carolina. Over an eighteen year time period, there was an overall gain of four percent of the employment share of African American professionals. There were 1,086 (12%) in 1977 and grew to 2,632 (16%) for the year of 1995. North Carolina had an unusually high percentage of African Americans in the category of service maintenance in the state.

## Table 5

### African American Workers in North Carolina

| Jobs | 1977 | 1978 | 1979 | 1980 | 1981 | 1982 | 1983 | 1984 |
|------|------|------|------|------|------|------|------|------|
| Adm.[1] | 91 7% | 106 7% | 110 8% | 107 8% | 116 8% | 109 7% | 112 7% | 116 7% |
| Pro.[2] | 1086 12% | 1222 13% | 1213 12% | 1222 12% | 1252 13% | 1303 13% | 1366 13% | 1531 14% |
| Prot.[3] | 903 18% | 1033 19% | 1200 21% | 1264 21% | 1330 22% | 1433 23% | 1595 24% | 1656 24% |
| Para.[4] | 370 8% | 397 8% | 487 9% | 530 10% | 527 11% | 534 11% | 574 11% | 635 12% |
| Tech.[5] | 2788 31% | 3019 33% | 3277 34% | 3393 35% | 3453 36% | 3499 36% | 3443 37% | 3632 37% |
| Ad-S.[6] | 2448 18% | 2677 19% | 2805 20% | 2908 20% | 2929 21% | 2996 22% | 3101 22% | 3265 23% |
| Craft[7] | 2016 16% | 2173 17% | 2347 19% | 2381 19% | 2330 20% | 2407 20% | 2497 21% | 2634 22% |
| Serv.[8] | 3924 64% | 3904 65% | 3980 65% | 4032 65% | 3936 66% | 3941 66% | 3965 66% | 3840 65% |
| Total | 13626 22% | 14531 23% | 15419 24% | 15837 24% | 15873 25% | 16222 25% | 16653 26% | 17309 26% |

Numbers equal total African Americans in each job category.
Percentages equal percent in each category that are African American.
Data collected from EEO-4 Reports.
[1]  Administrative-Officials
[2]  Professionals
[3]  Protective-Services
[4]  Para-Professionals
[5]  Technicians
[6]  Administrative Support
[7]  Skilled Craft
[8]  Service-Maintenance

Table 5 (continued)

| Jobs | 1985 | 1986 | 1987 | 1988 | 1989 | 1990 |
|------|------|------|------|------|------|------|
| Adm.[1] | 135 9% | 133 8% | 142 9% | 145 9% | 160 9% | 165 9% |
| Pro.[2] | 1581 14% | 1602 14% | 1703 14% | 1760 14% | 1838 14% | 1866 14% |
| Prot.[3] | 1747 25% | 1806 26% | 1823 25% | 2073 26% | 2360 27% | 2636 28% |
| Para.[4] | 623 13% | 610 12% | 649 13% | 706 13% | 722 13% | 758 13% |
| Tech.[5] | 3716 35% | 3725 35% | 3810 36% | 3884 35% | 3870 35% | 3925 35% |
| Ad-S.[6] | 3366 23% | 3451 23% | 3674 24% | 3836 24% | 3923 25% | 3996 25% |
| Craft [7] | 2582 22% | 2516 22% | 2456 22% | 2324 21% | 2328 21% | 2233 20% |
| Serv.[8] | 3783 65% | 3704 66% | 3652 66% | 3617 64% | 3605 64% | 3499 63% |
| Total | 17533 26% | 17547 26% | 17909 26% | 18345 26% | 18806 26% | 19078 26% |

Numbers equal total African Americans in each job category.
Percentages equal percent in each category that are African American.
Data collected from EEO-4 Reports.
[1]   Administrative-Officials
[2]   Professionals
[3]   Protective-Services
[4]   Para-Professionals
[5]   Technicians
[6]   Administrative Support
[7]   Skilled Craft
[8]   Service-Maintenance

## Table 5 (continued)

| Jobs | 1991 | 1992 | 1993 | 1994 | 1995 |
|------|------|------|------|------|------|
| Adm.[1] | 168 10% | 181 10% | 220 12% | 239 13% | 257 14% |
| Pro.[2] | 1968 14% | 2098 15% | 2187 14% | 2399 15% | 2632 16% |
| Prot.[3] | 2793 28% | 3083 29% | 3317 30% | 3649 31% | 3977 32% |
| Para.[4] | 784 14% | 820 14% | 945 15% | 1055 16% | 1107 17% |
| Tech.[5] | 3906 34% | 3968 33% | 4097 33% | 4252 34% | 4511 35% |
| Ad-S.[6] | 4017 25% | 4184 25% | 4243 26% | 4380 27% | 4368 27% |
| Craft[7] | 2178 20% | 2158 20% | 2397 20% | 2394 20% | 2309 20% |
| Serv.[8] | 3452 63% | 3433 63% | 3391 63% | 3296 62% | 3202 62% |
| Total | 19266 26% | 19925 26% | 20797 26% | 21664 26% | 22363 27% |

Numbers equal total African Americans in each job category.
Percentages equal percent in each category that are African American.
Data collected from EEO-4 Reports.
[1] Administrative-Officials
[2] Professionals
[3] Protective-Services
[4] Para-Professionals
[5] Technicians
[6] Administrative Support
[7] Skilled Craft
[8] Service-Maintenance

A review of the data revealed that the percent of African Americans in the category of service maintenance remained in the mid-sixties range during the time period under analysis.

## Oklahoma

An accurate assessment over a long period of time of employment gains for African Americans employed by the state of Oklahoma is limited. As previously discussed, the data that were supplied included only three years of 1984, 1994, and 1996. Nevertheless, although the data is limited, it still provides for an assessment over a 12 year period. As shown in Table 6, there were 3,777 (11%) African American employees labor force in 1984. In 1994, the number decreased to 3,728 (11%) a drop of 49, African Americans employed in state government. The total number of African Americans working as state employees continued to decline in 1996 to 3,564 (10%). Hence, for both interval periods the number of African Americans decreased, with the last two years demonstrating a precipitous drop of 164 African Americans in state government.

African Americans employed in the administrative-official category in state government in Oklahoma was 123 (5%) in 1984 as witnessed in Table 6. By 1994, however, the actual numbers decreased to 81, yet actually increased one percent (6%). In 1996, the number increased by only six employees making a total of 87 (6%) African Americans employed as administrative-officials in Oklahoma state government. However, the reported data reflected gains for African Americans in the occupational category of professionals in state government. As indicate in Table 6, there were 709 (6%) African Americans employed as professionals in 1984. The number of African American professional state level employees rose to 934 (7%) 10 years later in 1994, an increase of 1%. As of 1996, the number of African Americans employed as professionals were 1,146 (9%), an increase of 212 (3%).

The Oklahoma data demonstrates that the higher percentages of African Americans employed by the state were in the categories of para-professional (20% in 1996), administrative support (15%), and service maintenance (16%) in 1984. This trend continued in 1996. It is worth noting that a disproportionate percentage of African Americans employed in state government are in non-policy making occupations in the state of Oklahoma. But these shares have decreased slightly over time, accounting for the overall drop in African American state employees.

Table 6

African American Workers in Oklahoma

| Jobs | 1984 | 1994 | 1996 |
|------|------|------|------|
| Adm.[1] | 123<br>5% | 81<br>6% | 87<br>6% |
| Pro.[2] | 709<br>6% | 934<br>7% | 1146<br>9% |
| Prot.[3] | 217<br>7% | 262<br>7% | 314<br>8% |
| Para.[4] | 738<br>20% | 755<br>19% | 653<br>19% |
| Tech.[5] | 308<br>11% | 292<br>8% | 249<br>8% |
| Ad-S.[6] | 964<br>15% | 945<br>14% | 742<br>13% |
| Craft [7] | 112<br>8% | 53<br>5% | 51<br>4% |
| Serv.[8] | 606<br>16% | 406<br>14% | 322<br>13% |
| Total | 3777<br>11% | 3728<br>11% | 3564<br>10% |

Numbers equal total African Americans in each job category.
Percentages equal percent in each category that are African American.
Data collected from EEO-4 Reports.
[1] Administrative-Officials
[2] Professionals
[3] Protective-Services
[4] Para-Professionals
[5] Technicians
[6] Administrative Support
[7] Skilled Craft
[8] Service-Maintenance

Employment has risen slightly in more important occupations. Nevertheless, Oklahoma is a state which has shown few gains for African Americans.

## South Carolina

The total number of African Americans employed by the state of South Carolina were 18,638 (35%) in 1987. A review of these data reveals that from 1987 to 1994, a total of 8 years, the number of African Americans employed remained fairly steady at between 35 and 37%. The actual number of African American employees for 1991, according to Table 7 reached 21,759 (36%) the high point in the study. In 1992, African American employment experienced a one percent increase even though the actual numbers decreased to 21,458 for that particular year. However, in 1993, the actual number of African Americans employed by the state of South Carolina slightly increased by 28 employees to 21,486 (36%) and continued fluctuating in 1994 with a downturn of 167 employees to a total of 21,319 (37%). The data showed a one percent increase for 1994, even though the actual numbers for African Americans employed by the state declined. Over a seven year time period, African American state government employee job share increased two percent. The number of African American employees began with 18,638 (35%) in 1987 and reached 21,319 (37%) in 1994.

When analyzing the job classification for African Americans employed as administrative-officials, Table 7 demonstrated that in 1987 there were 208 (10%) African Americans in this particular category. The number of African American administrative-officials for South Carolina increased to 292 (12%) in 1990. As of 1992, the number of African American administrative-officials increased to 323 (14%). By 1994, the number of administrative-officials that were African American increased to 378 (15%). Over a seven year period in North Carolina, the number of administrative-officials that were African American increased from 10% to 15%, a net increase of 5%.

There were a large number of African Americans employed as professional state employees in South Carolina. As witnessed in Table 7, in 1987 there were 3,342 (21%) African Americans employed in this category. In 1990, the number of African Americans employed as professionals increased to 4,082 (22%). This was representative of a one percent increase over a three year period.

Table 7

African American Workers in South Carolina

| Jobs | 1987 | 1988 | 1989 | 1990 | 1991 | 1992 | 1993 | 1994 |
|------|------|------|------|------|------|------|------|------|
| Adm.[1] | 208 10% | 246 11% | 251 11% | 292 12% | 328 13% | 323 14% | 357 14% | 378 15% |
| Pro.[2] | 3342 21% | 3560 21% | 3817 22% | 4082 22% | 4410 23% | 4511 23% | 4531 23% | 4864 24% |
| Prot.[3] | 2116 42% | 2290 44% | 2757 47% | 2850 48% | 3046 48% | 2900 48% | 2895 49% | 2968 50% |
| Para.[4] | 4235 61% | 4269 64% | 4379 63% | 4533 62% | 4647 63% | 4702 63% | 4580 61% | 4518 61% |
| Tech.[5] | 765 21% | 839 20% | 867 20% | 939 21% | 967 21% | 975 21% | 1035 22% | 1082 24% |
| Ad-S.[6] | 2915 29% | 3013 29% | 3059 30% | 3109 31% | 3181 32% | 3119 33% | 3210 33% | 3100 34% |
| Craft[7] | 807 28% | 819 29% | 837 29% | 885 29% | 898 29% | 854 29% | 893 29% | 858 29% |
| Serv.[8] | 4250 70% | 4227 70% | 4178 69% | 4239 69% | 4282 68% | 4074 67% | 3985 65% | 3551 64% |
| Total | 18638 35% | 19263 36% | 20145 36% | 20929 36% | 21759 36% | 21458 37% | 21486 36% | 21319 37% |

Numbers equal total African Americans in each job category.
Percentages equal percent in each category that are African American.
Data collected from EEO-4 Reports.
[1]  Administrative-Officials
[2]  Professionals
[3]  Protective-Services
[4]  Para-Professionals
[5]  Technicians
[6]  Administrative Support
[7]  Skilled Craft
[8]  Service-Maintenance

By 1992, there were additional gains made for African Americans in the category of professionals, in which they increased to 4,511 (23%). By 1994, the number of African Americans employed in this category reached 4,864 (24%). Overall, the number of African American job share of professionals in South Carolina increased three percent over a ten year time period, going from 3,342 (21%) in 1987 to 4,864 (24%) African American employees in 1994, an increase of 1,522.

Even though the category of protective service is not a policy making occupation, there was a large increase in African American employment in this category. As noted in Table 7, in 1987 there were 2,116 (42%) African Americans employed in the category of protective services. As of 1994, the number of African Americans employed in protective services increased to 2,968 (50%), an increase of 952. A large number and percentage of African Americans employed by the state of South Carolina were found in the category of para-professionals as well. In 1987, there were 4,235 (61%) African Americans employed as para-professions as reflected in Table 7. The actual number and percent of African Americans increased temporarily only slightly and dropped to 61% again by 1994, although the actual numbers increased by almost 300. In the area of service maintenance in 1987, there were 4,250 (70%) African Americans employed. However, it is important to note that as of 1994, 3,551 (64%) African Americans were employed as service maintenance employees in which they experienced a decline of 6%.

## Tennessee

The total African American work population for state government employees in Tennessee was 6,709 (19%) in 1983, as noted in Table 8. During the years from 1984 to 1988, the number of African American state employees increased from 7,141 to 7,995. Even though the total number of African American employees increased, the total percentage for African Americans in the state workforce remained at twenty percent until 1988. Beginning in 1989 and continuing to 1994, the number of African Americans employed in state government in Tennessee increased, but the percentages remained constant at twenty-one percent for African Americans. In 1988, there were 7,995 (20%) African American employees and by 1994, the number rose to 8,715 (20%) African Americans in the public sector. Beginning in 1995, the numbers and percentages decreased from the reported employment figures for 1994.

In 1995, there were 8,203 (20%) African American employees in the total state work force. In 1996, there were 8,309 (20%) African Americans in state government in Tennessee. Over a thirteen year period, the total African American employee workforce increased by one percent from 6,709 (19%) in 1983 to 8,309 (20%) in 1996, but showed a net increased of 1600.

The number of African Americans employed as administrative-officials for Tennessee in 1983 was 130 (5%), and dropped in 1984 to 95 (5%), with a further decline in 1985 to 89 (5%) for African Americans employed in this category. By 1989, the number of administrative-officials that were African American increased to 149 (8%), and continued showing a steady increase through 1996. For example, as of 1993, the number grew to 176 (9%) for African Americans employed in the category of administrative-officials. By 1996, they increased to 197 (9%) for African Americans that were employed at the administrative-officials level in state government in Tennessee. Over a thirteen year time period, the number of African Americans employed at the state level as administrative-officials increased from 130 (5%) African Americans in 1983 to 197 (9%) African Americans in 1996. This was a four percentage increase for African Americans employed at the administrative-official level in the state of Tennessee

In the category of professionals, Table 8 reveals that there were 1,606 (14%) African Americans employed in 1983. As of 1988, the number increased to 2,198 (16%) for African Americans employed as professionals in the public sector.

During the time frame from 1989 through 1994, the percentage of African Americans employed as professional state employees held constant at seventeen percent. The actual numbers for African Americans employed as professionals, however, continued to show increases. In 1996, the population for African Americans employed at the professional level was 2,357 (16%). Over a thirteen year period, African Americans experienced a 2% gain in the ranks of professionals.

In observing other categories of state level employment for Tennessee, it is clear that a significant decrease in technicians occurred from 1983 to 1996. In 1983 there were 1,747 (26%) African Americans employed as technicians for the state of Tennessee, whereas in 1996 there were only 364 (14%), thus showing a decrease of 1,383 (12%). At the same time, a substantial increase in numbers in the category of para-professional took place.

Table 8

African American Workers in Tennessee

| Jobs | 1983 | 1984 | 1985 | 1986 | 1987 | 1988 | 1989 |
|------|------|------|------|------|------|------|------|
| Adm.[1] | 130 5% | 94 5% | 89 5% | 91 5% | 115 6% | 128 7% | 149 8% |
| Pro.[2] | 1606 14% | 1712 14% | 1845 15% | 1993 15% | 2076 15% | 2198 16% | 2281 17% |
| Prot.[3] | 652 17% | 681 20% | 756 20% | 807 20% | 827 20% | 818 20% | 885 20% |
| Para.[4] | 325 24% | 1766 41% | 1809 39% | 1681 39% | 1733 40% | 1716 41% | 1766 41% |
| Tech.[5] | 1747 26% | 369 12% | 370 12% | 372 11% | 414 12% | 407 12% | 453 13% |
| Ad-S.[6] | 1085 19% | 1347 20% | 1368 20% | 1410 20% | 1451 21% | 1434 21% | 1494 22% |
| Craft[7] | 142 7% | 305 15% | 293 15% | 309 15% | 290 14% | 282 14% | 299 15% |
| Serv.[8] | 1022 34% | 867 26% | 905 27% | 1024 29% | 966 28% | 1012 29% | 1025 30% |
| Total | 6709 19% | 7141 20% | 7435 20% | 7687 20% | 7872 20% | 7995 20% | 8352 21% |

Numbers equal total African Americans in each job category.
Percentages equal percent in each category that are African American.
Data collected from EEO-4 Reports.
[1]   Administrative-Officials
[2]   Professionals
[3]   Protective-Services
[4]   Para-Professionals
[5]   Technicians
[6]   Administrative Support
[7]   Skilled Craft
[8]   Service-Maintenance

Table 8 (continued)

| Jobs | 1990 | 1991 | 1992 | 1993 | 1994 | 1995 | 1996 |
|------|------|------|------|------|------|------|------|
| Adm.[1] | 160<br>8% | 159<br>8% | 165<br>9% | 168<br>9% | 176<br>9% | 174<br>8% | 197<br>9% |
| Pro.[2] | 2302<br>17% | 2306<br>17% | 2273<br>17% | 2320<br>17% | 2461<br>17% | 2292<br>15% | 2357<br>16% |
| Prot.[3] | 971<br>21% | 947<br>20% | 895<br>20% | 914<br>20% | 966<br>21% | 923<br>21% | 966<br>21% |
| Para.[4] | 1766<br>42% | 1761<br>42% | 1757<br>43% | 1743<br>42% | 1787<br>37% | 1774<br>37% | 1737<br>35% |
| Tech.[5] | 453<br>13% | 467<br>14% | 459<br>14% | 459<br>14% | 337<br>14% | 328<br>13% | 364<br>14% |
| Ad-S.[6] | 1405<br>21% | 1369<br>21% | 1343<br>21% | 1346<br>21% | 1557<br>23% | 1310<br>21% | 1300<br>21% |
| Craft [7] | 300<br>15% | 294<br>15% | 282<br>15% | 294<br>16% | 293<br>17% | 278<br>17% | 265<br>16% |
| Serv.[8] | 975<br>29% | 929<br>29% | 934<br>29% | 971<br>29% | 1138<br>30% | 1124<br>29% | 1123<br>29% |
| Total | 8332<br>21% | 8232<br>21% | 8108<br>21% | 8215<br>21% | 8715<br>21% | 8203<br>20% | 8309<br>20% |

Numbers equal total African Americans in each job category.
Percentages equal percent in each category that are African American.
Data collected from EEO-4 Reports.
[1]   Administrative-Officials
[2]   Professionals
[3]   Protective-Services
[4]   Para-Professionals
[5]   Technicians
[6]   Administrative Support
[7]   Skilled Craft
[8]   Service-Maintenance

The number of African Americans employed as para-professional increased from 325 (24%) in 1983 to 1,737 (35%) in 1996, an increase of 1,412 (11%). The largest gain for African Americans in state government was in the para-professional ranks.

The category of service maintenance experienced a decline over the 13 year period in question. There were 1,022 (34%) African American employees in 1983 but by the year 1991, they had dropped to 929 (29%). However, beginning in 1993, the number of African Americans employed in the category of service maintenance dropped to a low point of 971 (29%) but again increased to 1,123 (29%) by 1996. Even though the number of African Americans employed as service maintenance workers demonstrated numerical gains, the percentages in this category revealed a decrease. As of 1983, the percentage of African Americans employed as service maintenance workers was thirty-four, but as of 1996, the percentage declined to twenty-nine, a five percent decrease in the African American job share of service maintenance workers for the state of Tennessee over a thirteen year period.

## A Comparative Analysis of State Employment

In order to conduct a comparative assessment of employment regarding the progress of African Americans in state government, it is beneficial to analyze the years that demonstrated either substantial increases or decreases for African American employment in the selected states. The years of 1988, 1991, 1994, and 1995 demonstrated years in which African American state level employees had either attained increased employment or experienced a reduction in state level employment. This time frame was used to assess the impact of employment hiring practices for African Americans in the seven selected states.

Beginning in 1988, Arkansas had 4,045 (21%) African American employees in state government. As noted in Table 9, in 1988 Arkansas had a population of 2,349,000 with a total African American population of 364,095 (15%) as reported by the *Joint Center for Political Studies* in 1988. The African American state employment percent was six percent above the percent of the state population at this point. During this same time period, the number of African Americans employed in state government in Georgia totaled 20,332 (32%) for the total state workforce. The state of Georgia population in 1988 was 5,837,000 with an African American population of 1,587,664 (27%) of the total population (*Joint*

*Center for Political Studies*, 1988). Like Arkansas, the percent (32%) of African Americans in state government exceeded the state population percent, which in this case was 27%. During this same time period, Mississippi had a total African American state employed workforce of 6,283 (30%) with a total state population of 2,598,000. The total African American population for the state of Mississippi in 1988 was 897,869 (35%) as reported by the *Joint Center for Political Studies*. The total African American percent in state government was lower than the percent of the state population, in this case by 5%. Compared to its counterparts, Arkansas and Georgia, the percent of African Americans in state government was not as representative.

The state population for North Carolina in 1988 was 6,165,000, with an African American population of 1,380,960 (22%) of the total (*Joint Center for Political* Studies, 1988). The reported data revealed at this time that African Americans constituted 18,345 (26%) of the state government employees. The percent of African Americans in state government exceeded the state population by 4% at this time. While six states had data for the year of 1988, Oklahoma supplied data starting in 1984 but not in 1988. The state population during that time was 3,025,290 with an African American population of 204,674 (7%) as reported by the *Joint Center for Political Studies* (1984). The total African American state government workforce for Oklahoma during that year was 3,777 (11%). The rate of employment (11%) for state level employees was higher than the percent African American population (7%) in 1984.

South Carolina had an African American state government workforce of 19,263 (36%), in 1988. During this time period, the state of South Carolina had a total state population of 3,300,000, with an African American population of 996,600, which comprised thirty percent of the state population (*Joint Center for Political Studies*, 1988). Thus, South Carolina experienced progress with the total percentage of African American population in 1988, 6% less than the total African American state employee total. The total state population for Tennessee in 1988 was 4,717,000 with a total African American population of 735,852, which was sixteen percent of the total population (*Joint Center for Political Studies*, 1988). The total African American state government employee workforce at this time was 7,995 (20%), or 4% higher than the percent of the state population of 16%.

In summarizing the totals for 1988 (except Oklahoma) the data revealed that South Carolina had the highest amount of African American state employees with thirty six percent.

Table 9

African Americans in State Government and in
Southern Population as a Whole

| | YEAR | | | | | | | | | | | |
| | 1988 | | | 1991 | | | 1994 | | | 1995 | | |
| State | Gov. % | Pop. % | Diff. | Gov. % | Pop. % | Diff. | Gov. % | Pop. % | Diff. | Gov. % | Pop. % | Diff. |
|---|---|---|---|---|---|---|---|---|---|---|---|---|
| AR | 21 | 15 | 6 | 21 | 16 | 5 | 23 | 16 | 7 | 24 | 16 | 8 |
| GA | 32 | 27 | 5 | 34 | 27 | 7 | 36 | 27 | 9 | 37 | 27 | 10 |
| MS | 30 | 35 | -5 | 37 | 35 | 2 | --- | -- | -- | 36 | 36 | 0 |
| NC | 26 | 22 | 4 | 26 | 22 | 4 | 26 | 22 | 4 | 27 | 22 | 5 |
| OK | --- | --- | --- | --- | --- | --- | 11 | 7.5 | 3.5 | --- | --- | --- |
| SC | 36 | 30 | 6 | 36 | 30 | 6 | 37 | 30 | 7 | --- | --- | --- |
| TN | 20 | 16 | 4 | 21 | 16 | 5 | 21 | 16 | 5 | 20 | 16 | 4 |

Data for government percentages collected from EEO-4 Reports.
Data for African American percentage population collected from Join Center of Political
Studies (1988,1991,1994, and 1995).

Meanwhile, Tennessee had the lowest reported number of African
Americans in the state total workforce with twenty percent. Five of the
six states of the Old Confederacy had a higher percent African Americans
in the state workforce than the population as a whole. Arkansas and
South Carolina led with 6%. Mississippi was the only state with a lower
percentage of African American state government employees than the
population as a whole, with a decrease of 5%. Oklahoma which supplied
data for 1984 but not 1988, also had a negative relation between the
percent of African Americans in state government and the state
population, with a decrease of 4%.

A comparison of state level employees for 1991, found that Arkansas
had 4,621 (21%) African American state government employees. The
total population for the state of Arkansas for 1991 was 2,350,735, with an
African American population of 373,912 (16%), according to the *Joint
Center for Political and Economic Studies Press*, (1991). Hence, the

percentage of African Americans employed by the state of Arkansas demonstrated a close relationship with the actual African American population for the state with a plus 5%. The African American population for the total workforce for Georgia in 1991 was 24,958 (34%), while the total population for the state was 6,478,216, with an African American state population of 1,746,565 (27%). The percent of the African American state government employees was higher than the percent of the African American population as a whole within the state of Georgia.

At the same time, the state of Mississippi in 1991 had a total state population for African American employees of 9,258 (37%). This number appears significant because the African American population for the state of Mississippi in 1991 was 915,057, (35%). These data revealed a seven percent increase of African Americans employed by the state from 1988 to 1991 in the state of Mississippi.

North Carolina also exhibited a higher percentage of African Americans employed in state government than in the overall state population in 1991. North Carolina had 19,266 (26%) African Americans employed by the state. The African American population was 1,456,232 (22%) (*Joint Center for Political and Economic Studies Press*, 1991). These data reflected a higher percent of African Americans employed by the state than the percent of African Americans residing in the state of North Carolina.

The *Joint Center for Political Studies and Economic Press* (1991), reported that South Carolina had a total state population of 3,486,703 during this year with an African American population of 1,039,884 (30%). At the same time, the total number of African Americans employed by the state was 21,759 (36%). These data indicated that South Carolina had a higher percentage (6%) of African Americans employed by the state than in the total African American population for the state. In 1991, Tennessee's state population was 4,877,185, with an African American state population of 778,035 (16%) as reported by the *Joint Center for Political Studies and Economic Press* (1991). The total number of African Americans employed by the state in 1991 was 8,232 (21%). Like all of the other states of the Old Confederacy, Tennessee had a higher percentage (5%) of African Americans employed by the state than the number of African Americans comprising the state population. Of the southern states in the study, Oklahoma was the only one that did not report data for 1991. Mississippi, which had a negative relationship between African American state employees and the state population in 1988, became the lead state in government employment of this group in

1991 with 37%. Mississippi also experienced the highest percentage increase (7%) since 1988 in African Americans in state government. Because Mississippi had such a large African American population (35%) in 1991, it is also worth noting that they had the closest positive relationship between African American state employment and the state population, a difference of only 2%. Georgia had the largest difference (7%) between the percent of African Americans in the public sector and in the state population.

In Arkansas, the total number of African Americans employed by the state in 1994 was 5,163 (23%) as state level employees. The total state population for Arkansas was 2,350,725 with an African American population of 373,912 (16%) for the state (*Statistical Abstracts* 1994). The percentage of African Americans employed by the state was 7% higher in 1994 than the percentage of African Americans in the total population for Arkansas.

At the same time, the state of Georgia had a total African American state government work force of 28,764 (36%). The total state population (*Statistical Abstracts*) for Georgia was 6,478,216 with an African American population of 1,746,565 (27%). In 1994, the state of Mississippi did not submit any EEO-4 data. Consequently, there is no discussion of data for Mississippi for that year.

In 1994, North Carolina had a total of 21,664 (26%) African Americans employed in state government out of a total state population of 1,456,323 (22%) African Americans. The total state population at this time was 6,628,637. The percent (26%) of African Americans working in state government remained constant over the three year interval, with a plus percent of 4% over the state percent of the population.

In 1994, Oklahoma had a total African American workforce of 3,728 (11%) employed in state government. The total state population for Oklahoma in 1994 was 3,145,585 and the African American population was 233,801 (7.5% rounded off to the closest tenth), (*Statistical Abstracts*, 1994). While Oklahoma did not submit data for 1988, it is clear from the data that the state continued to have a higher percent of African Americans employed in state government than the percent of the population as a whole.

In the case of South Carolina, the total number of African American employees was 21,319 (37%). The total state population for South Carolina was 3,486,703 with an African American population of 1,039,884 (30%) (*Statistical Abstracts*, 1994). The percentage of African

Americans employed by the state actually increased by 1% while the population percent remained constant at 30% over the three year intervals since 1991.

In the case of Tennessee, the total number of African Americans in the total state workforce was 8,715 (21%) in 1994, with the percent remaining constant over 1991. The total state population for Tennessee was 4,877,185 while the African American population was 778,035 (16%), with the population percent also remaining constant over 1991 (*Statistical Abstracts*, 1994). Hence, Tennessee maintained a rate of employment in the public sector 5% higher than in 1991.

In summary the highest percentage of African Americans employed in the public sector in 1994 was South Carolina with thirty-seven percent, followed by Georgia with thirty-six percent. Oklahoma was the state with the lowest percentage of African Americans in state government at all levels in 1994. Georgia led the southern states with the highest percentage difference between African Americans employed in the public sector (36%) and the corresponding percent of the state population (27%), constituting a difference of 9%. Arkansas and South Carolina were both second with 9% more African Americans employed in state government positions than the population as a whole, followed by Tennessee with 5%.

After 1994, 1995 is the only other year in which five of the seven states may be compared to detect employment progress for African Americans, keeping in mind that this is only a one year interval. Arkansas, Georgia, Mississippi, North Carolina, and Tennessee were the states submitting data for 1995. After 1995, the data submitted are inconsistent. Arkansas is the only state that gave data for both 1996 and 1997. Oklahoma and Tennessee both submitted data for 1996. South Carolina did not submit any data past 1994. Keeping these limitations in mind, we move to a discussion of the 1995 data.

Arkansas had 5,182 (24%) African Americans in the state public sector in 1995, (*Statistical Abstracts*, 1995). The state population for Arkansas was 2,350,725, with an African American population of 373,912 (16%). Arkansas had 8% more African Americans in the public sector than in the population at-large in 1995, with an increase of 1% over the 1994 figure of 7%. Georgia had an African American state employment total of 30,714 (37%). The state population for Georgia during this time period was 6,478,216 with a total African American population of 1,746,565 (27%) (*Statistical Abstracts*, 1995). Like Arkansas, Georgia experienced a one percent increase of African Americans in the public sector, in this case going from a difference of 9% in 1994 to 10% in 1995, and moving from 36% African American employees in 1994 to 37% in 1995. The state of Mississippi had a total African American employment of 8,507 (36%) compared to a total African American state population of 915,057 (36%) (*Statistical Abstracts*, 1995). The percent of African Americans in state government over a four year period (no data were submitted in 1995) actually decreased 1% in Mississippi. Parity was achieved between the percent in the public sector (36%) and the state population (36%).

North Carolina had a total African American state employment total of 22,363 (27%). The total African American population in the state of North Carolina was 1,456,323 (22%) while the total state population was 6,628,637 (*Statistical Abstracts*, 1995). The percent of African Americans working in state government increased by 1% over 1994, going from 26% of the total to 27%. The state of Tennessee during this time had an African American employment rate of 8,203 (20%) in the public sector. The total African American population was 778,035 (16%) and a total state population of 4,877,185 (*Statistical Abstracts*, 1995). While Tennessee continued to have a higher percent of African Americans in state government (20%) compared to the population as a whole (16%), the difference decreased by 1%, moving from 5% in 1994 to 4% in 1995.

In 1995, the state of Georgia exhibited the highest percent of African Americans employed in state government with thirty-seven percent followed by Mississippi with thirty-six percent. North Carolina (27%), Arkansas (26%), and Tennessee followed in that order. Much of these differences reflect the differing state level of African Americans in the state population and labor pools.

From 1988 to 1994, Arkansas experienced an incremental gain in the percent of African Americans working in the state government of two percent. The total for 1988 was twenty-one percent for the job share of African Americans, by 1994 the percent of African Americans working in government had increased to twenty-three percent, and one year later in 1995, it had increased to 24%, for a total 3% increase. In the case of Georgia the rate of African American employment in state government went from thirty-two percent in 1988 to thirty-seven percent in 1995, an increase of five percent for the state of Georgia. In the state of Mississippi during this time span the numbers increased from thirty percent African Americans in state government in 1988 to thirty-six percent in 1995. In actuality, the percent of African Americans in state government dropped from 36% in 1989 to 35% in 1990, although the numbers continued to climb. By 1993, African Americans working in state government peaked at 9,683 (39%), and dropped dramatically two years later to 8,507 (36%). During this same time period, the state of North Carolina remained fairly consistent with 26% of the positions in state government occupied by African Americans from 1988 to 1994, with a one percent increase the following year in 1995. Nevertheless, in actual numbers, African Americans increased from 18,345 in 1988 to 22,363 in 1995, an increase of more than 4,000 employees. Oklahoma had 11% of the positions in the public sector held by African Americans in 1984 with a slight decrease (3,728) in 1994, although maintaining a total of 11% (3,777). Two years later in 1996, the number dropped to 3,564 (10%) African Americans employed in state government. African Americans in state government in South Carolina had 19,263 (36%) in 1988 and increased to 21,319 (37%) in 1994, an increase of 1% and more than 2,000 employees.

In the case of Tennessee, the employment rate for African Americans in state government was 20% (7,995) in 1988, and while continuing to increase in actual numbers to a high of 8,715 (21 %) in 1994, dropped by more than 500 African American employees the following year to 8,203 and to 20%.

Of the states that supplied data, Georgia was the most progressive with regard to African Americans in state government. Georgia began with a total African American workforce of 7,438 (18%) in 1973 and increased to 30,714 (37%) by the year of 1995 quadrupling the 1973 numbers and more than doubling the percent over twenty-two years. The African American workforce for state employees for the state of Georgia increased 23,276 over a twenty-two year time period. The increase in African American hiring in Georgia represented a 19% increase. In this regard, Georgia was the most progressive of the states studied in the research. Further analysis of the data supported this conclusion. In the case of Mississippi, an increase of African Americans in state government employees of 6% was shown during a shorter time period. The number of African Americans in the state work population was 6,283 (30%) in 1988 and as of 1995, the total number of African American employees in the state workforce was 8,507 (36%) for Mississippi. The state of North Carolina exhibited a five percent increase for African Americans employed in state government in 1977 with 22% and 27% by 1995. Arkansas demonstrated a four percentage increase for African Americans employed by the state. There were 4,045 (21%) African Americans employed in state positions in 1988 and 5,952 (25%) as of 1997. South Carolina experience only a two percent increase. In 1987, there were

18,638 (35%) African Americans employed by the state and by the year 1994, there were 21,319 (37%) African Americans employed by the state. At the same time, Tennessee only demonstrated a one percent increase in employment for African Americans in the total state labor force. There were 6,709 (19%) African Americans employed by the state of Tennessee in 1983 and as of 1996, there were 8,309 (20%) African Americans in the public sector. Oklahoma actually experienced a one percent decrease. In 1984, there were 3,777 (11%) African Americans employed as state employees.    In 1996, there were 3,564 (10%) African American employees for the state of Oklahoma. Hence, in the case of Oklahoma, the actual numbers as well as the percent of African Americans employed in state level positions decreased.    In summary, while Georgia experienced the greatest gains in percent with 19%, Oklahoma was on the opposite end of the continuum, experiencing a 1% decrease.

## African American Administrative-Officials in Southern State Government

As previously noted, administrative-officials are the employees involved in setting broad policies and exercising overall responsibility for the execution of such policies.    Those employed as administrative-officials are also responsible for directing individual departments or special phases of the agency's operation.    Those employed in this category are involved in both decision making and policy making.    In order to assess the status of the Old Confederacy in this occupation the years of 1988, 1991, 1994, and 1995 were analyzed. These were the years that demonstrated either substantial increases or reductions for African Americans employed during this time period.

As noted in Table 10, in 1988, the state of Arkansas had 84 (9%) African Americans employed in the category of administrative-official. The state of Georgia had 68 (8%) African Americans employed in the occupational status of administrative-official. In the state of Mississippi, there were 135 (12%) administrative-officials that were African American. North Carolina had 145 (9%) African Americans employed as administrative-officials.    In South Carolina 246 (11%) African American employees were administrative-officials.    The state of Tennessee had 128 (7%) administrative-officials that were African American in 1988.

Nevertheless, South Carolina had the highest number of African Americans employed as administrative-officials with 246 (11%) compared to the other selected states. The state of North Carolina was shown to have the second highest number 145 (9%), African Americans employed as administrative-officials. It should be noted that Mississippi had 135 actual African Americans employed in the administrative-official category. However, Mississippi had the highest percentage (12%) of African Americans employed as administrative-officials for 1988 among the seven states. Georgia exhibited the lowest number of African Americans that were employed as administrative-officials with 68 (8%).

In 1991, Arkansas had 113 (11%) African Americans employed administrative-officials in the public sector. Georgia had 136 (11%) administrative-official state employees that were African American.

In Mississippi there were 203 (16%) African American employees that were in the administrative-official category. The state of North Carolina

Table 10

African Americans in Administrative-Officials Positions
in Southern State Government by Year

| YEAR | | | | |
|---|---|---|---|---|
| State | 1988 | 1991 | 1994 | 1995 |
| Arkansas | 84 (9%) | 113 (11%) | 122 (13%) | 134 (13%) |
| Georgia | 68 (8%) | 136 (11%) | 153 (12%) | 173 (12%) |
| Mississippi | 135 (12%) | 203 (16%) | ----- | 228 (16%) |
| North Carolina | 145 (9%) | 168 (10% | 239 (13%) | 257 (14%) |
| Oklahoma | ----- | ----- | 81 (5%) | ----- |
| South Carolina | 246 (11%) | 328 (13%) | 378 (15%) | ----- |
| Tennessee | 128 (7%) | 159 (8%) | 176 (9%) | 174 (8%) |

Data collected from EEO-4 Reports.

at this time had 168 (10%) African Americans employed in the same occupational category. South Carolina had 328 (13%) African Americans employed as administrative-officials in 1991, while Tennessee had 159 (8%) African Americans employed as administrative-officials in 1991.

For the year of 1991, South Carolina again had the highest number of African Americans employed in the position of administrative-officials with 328 (13%). Also, at this time, Mississippi had the second highest actual number of African Americans employed as administrative-officials with 203. Yet, the highest percentage (16%) was found in the state of Mississippi. Arkansas had the lowest number of African Americans employed as administrative-officials with 113 employees. However, the lowest percentage (8%) of African Americans employed as administrative-officials in 1991 was in Tennessee.

African Americans employed as administrative-officials in Arkansas for the year of 1994 was 122 (13%). Georgia had 153 (12%) African American employees classified in this category. As previously stated, Mississippi did not report any data for 1994. In the state of North Carolina, there were 239 (13%) African Americans employed in the position. Oklahoma had 81 (6%) African American employees in the same category. South Carolina had 378 (15%) administrative-official employees who were African American. In the state of Tennessee, there were 176 (9%) African Americans employed at the state level in this position.

A summary review of 1994 revealed that South Carolina continued to have the highest number of African Americans that were employed as administrative-officials with 378 (15%). North Carolina had the second highest amount with 239 (13%) African Americans employed in this category. The lowest number of African Americans employed policy making position was shown in Oklahoma with only eighty-one. In the absence of data from Mississippi in 1994, South Carolina had the highest percent (15%) of African Americans employed in the state government and Oklahoma the lowest with 6%.

In analyzing and comparing administrative-officials in 1995, the following conclusions became self-evident. In Arkansas during this period, there were 134 (13%) African Americans employed as administrative-officials, while Georgia had 173 (12%) policy making employees who were African American. Mississippi reported 228 (16%) African Americans who were employed in this critical position, while the state of Tennessee had 174 (8%) in this category who were African American. Unfortunately, the collected data for South Carolina ended with the year of 1994. And as reported earlier, Oklahoma only provided data for the years of 1984, 1994, and 1996. In 1995, North Carolina had the highest actual number (257) for African Americans employed as administrative-officials among the selected seven states. Mississippi had the second largest number (228) of African Americans employed in state government. Mississippi also had the highest percentage (16%) of African Americans employed in this position among the seven states. The state of Arkansas had the lowest number (134) of African Americans employed as administrative officials. Tennessee had the lowest percentage (8%) of African Americans employed as in this critical policy making category in 1995.

During the years of 1988, 1991, 1994, and 1995, the following growth patterns were revealed for African Americans employed as administrative-officials. In the case of Arkansas, from 1988 to 1991 there was an actual increase of African Americans employed with twenty-nine. However, from 1991 to 1994, Arkansas only experienced an increase of nine employees in this category. A year later in 1995, Arkansas added 12 African American employees who were administrative-officials. Arkansas witnessed a four percent increase for African Americans employed in this position. At the same time, Georgia from 1988 to 1991 demonstrated gains of sixty-eight African Americans employed as administrative-officials. Georgia, however, experienced an increase of only 17 actual African American employees classified in this policy making category from 1991 to 1994. And a year later (1995), employment numbers for African Americans employed in Georgia reflected an increase of twenty. Like Arkansas, Georgia experienced a four percent increase in this category.

In the case of Mississippi, from 1988 to 1991, there was an increase of sixty-eight African Americans employed in the category of administrative-officials. From 1991 to 1995, Mississippi experienced an increase of twenty-five. In the state of North Carolina, from 1988 to 1991, the actual number of African Americans employed as in this category increased by twenty-three, going from 145 to 168. Between 1991 and 1994, the actual number of African Americans employees classified as administrative-officials in the state of North Carolina increased by seventy-one. A year later in 1995, North Carolina experienced an additional eighteen African American employees in this position. North Carolina had a percentage increase of five percent from 1988 to 1995.

From 1988 to 1991, South Carolina experienced an increase of eighty-two African Americans employed as administrative-officials. Three years later in 1994, there was an increase of fifty African Americans employed in this state level position. In the case of Tennessee, between the years of 1988 and 1991, the actual number of African Americans employed as administrative-officials increased by thirty-one. During the period of 1991 to 1994, the number of African Americans employed in this critical position increased by an additional twenty-three. However, a year later in 1995, the actual number of African Americans employed as administrative-officials was reduced by two in the state of Tennessee.

Based on the limited data from Oklahoma, the number of African American employees classified as administrative-officials in 1984 was 123 (5%). In 1994, the stated of Oklahoma witnessed a reduction of forty-two African American employees in this occupation. Another reduction was experienced in 1996, which reflected an actual decrease of seven African Americans employed in this state level category. It should be noted that the percentages are consistently less than the African American percent of each state's population. It would be necessary to ascertain the African American percentage of college educated population in each state to assess whether African Americans are fairly represented among administrative leaders.

## African American Professionals in Southern State Government

Professionals in administrative capacities make policies as well as administrative-officials. Those employed in this category are required to have specialized or theoretical knowledge acquired through college training or work experience and other training that provides comparable knowledge. This section compares African Americans in this occupation and the progress they have made from 1988 to 1995. The years of 1988, 1991, 1994 and 1995 demonstrated either a substantial increase or decrease in employment for African Americans from the selected states, and years that provided some degree of uniformity for comparison.

As revealed in Table 11, African Americans employed as professionals for Arkansas in 1988 totaled 1,080 (14%) of the state government employment population. In the state of Georgia, African Americans employed at this level was 4,444 (20%). During this same time period, in the state of Mississippi the number of African Americans employed at the professional level was 1,056 (17%).

In the case of North Carolina, the number of professional state employees that were African American totaled 1,760 (14%). The state of South Carolina had 3,560 (21%) African Americans employed within the state. Professional employees who were African American and employed in the state of Tennessee were 2,198 (16%) in 1988. Georgia had the highest number of African Americans employed as professionals with 4,444 (20%) in 1988. South Carolina had the second highest number of African Americans employed as in this category with a total of 3,560 (21%). South Carolina also had the highest percentage (21%) of African Americans employed in state government.

African Americans employed at the professional level in 1991 in Arkansas totaled 1,371 (16%). The state of Georgia had 6,112 (22%) African Americans employed in this same occupational category. Mississippi employed 1,457 (21%) African Americans in state government in 1991. North Carolina had 1,968 (14%) professionals employees who were African American in 1991. In the state of South Carolina, there were 2,306 (17%) African Americans employed at the professional level during this same year.

Table 11

African Americans in Professional Positions
in Southern State Government by Year

| YEAR | | | | |
|---|---|---|---|---|
| State | 1988 | 1991 | 1994 | 1995 |
| Arkansas | 1080 (14%) | 1371 (16%) | 11562 (17%) | 1700 (18%) |
| Georgia | 4444 (20%) | 6112 (22%) | 7067 (24%) | 7693 (25%) |
| Mississippi | 1056 (17%) | 1457 (21%) | ---- | 1888 (24%) |
| North Carolina | 1760 (14%) | 1968 (14%) | 2399 (15%) | 2632 (16%) |
| Oklahoma | ---- | ----- | 934 (7%) | ----- |
| South Carolina | 3560 (21%) | 4410 (23%) | 4864 (24%) | --- |
| Tennessee | 2198 (16%) | 2306 (17%) | 2461 (17%) | 2292 (15%) |

Data collected from EEO-4 Reports.

In 1991, among the seven states in the study, Georgia had the highest actual numbers (6,112) of African Americans employed as professionals in state government. South Carolina had the second highest actual number (4,410) of African Americans who were employed as professionals in the public sector. The state of Arkansas, with 1,371, had the lowest number of actual employees who were African American employed as professionals and working for the state. At the same time, however, South Carolina had the largest percentage (23%) of African Americans employed in the category of professionals in state government. North Carolina, with fourteen percent, was the state among the seven with the lowest percentage of African Americans employed as professional workers in the workforce.

Professional level employees who were African American in 1994 employed by the state of Arkansas totaled 1,562 (17%) while Georgia, at this same time employed 7,067 (24%) professionals in state government who were African American. The state of Oklahoma reported 934 (7%) African Americans employees in professional positions in the state. African American state level employees totaled 2,399 (15%) for the state of North Carolina during this year. In South Carolina, the number of African Americans employed who were classified as professionals was 4,864 (24%) in 1994. In the case of Tennessee, the number of African American state government employees who were in the category of professional reached 2,461 (17%).

Thus, in 1994 the state of Georgia had the largest number of professionals (7,067) who were African American in the occupation of professional among the seven states. The state of South Carolina had the second largest number of African Americans employed at the professional level with 4,864. However, Georgia and South Carolina had the highest percent (24%) of African Americans professionals among the selected states. The lowest percentage (7%) of African Americans professionals was found in the state of Oklahoma.

A year later in 1995, Arkansas employed 1,700 (18%) African Americans in the category of professional in the state workforce. The state of Georgia had 7,693 (25%) of the state workforce that were African American professionals. During the same year, the Mississippi employment total for professionals who were African American equaled to 1,888 (24%). At the same time, the state of North Carolina had 2,632 (16%) African Americans in the category of professional. The state of Tennessee in 1995 had 2,292 (15%) African American employees in the category of professional.

Thus, for the year of 1995, Georgia, as in the previous years cited, again had the largest number (7,693) of actual African American employees that were in the classification of professional employees. The state of North Carolina at this time had the next largest number (2,632) of African Americans employed by the state that were classified as professional employees. During this time, Arkansas recorded the lowest number (1,700) of African American professionals in state government. Meanwhile, Tennessee reported the lowest percentage (15%) of African American professionals in state government. Georgia also had the largest percent (25%) of African Americans in professional positions, followed by Mississippi and South Carolina, both of whom had 24% African Americans in this category. The percent of African Americans among state professionals was generally higher than the percent of African Americans among state administrative-officials, which is presumably more racially representative of the state labor pool.

## The Supreme Court and Affirmative Action in Southern State Government

As previously cited in this study, the Supreme Court along with the federal court system makes judicial decisions that results in policy implementation. However, the actual effects of the policy or its impact into the American political system tends to be incremental in nature. There are often times when the necessary mechanisms required for implementation has to be set in place in order for a decision to take effect.

This discussion of Supreme Court cases is limited only to those affecting public personnel and state government. The Supreme Court in 1979, dealt with the issue of a voluntary affirmative action plan in the case of *United Steelworkers of American v. Weber*. The Court allowed the establishment of a voluntary affirmative action plan. The case of *Firefighters v. Stotts* (1984) was important in that the Court held that *bona fide* seniority systems were constitutional unless the seniority plan was intentionally discriminatory. Two years after *Stotts*, in 1986, the Court was confronted with the issue of reverse discrimination regarding to layoff provisions in the public sector. The Court in this instance, ruled that societal discrimination alone was insufficient justification for racial classification, because the end result was that of reverse discrimination.

The Supreme Court was confronted with the legal issue of whether or not the public sector could engage in continuous historical discriminatory employment practices. Hence, the Court in *Local 28 v. Equal*

*Employment Opportunity Commission* (1986) held that Title VII was designed to remove barriers that operated in the past to favor one racial group over another. The Court, thereby established the criteria for public sector employers to utilize mechanisms designed to eliminate the past effects of discrimination.

A key issue before the Supreme Court in 1987 was the issue of promotion of African Americans by those employed by state government. The case of *United States v. Paradise* (1987) provided the framework for public sector employers to avoid legal repercussion when confronted with the issue of egregious historical discrimination. *United States v. Paradise* (1987) demonstrated that the Supreme Court would uphold those affirmative action procedures designed to eliminate historical past discrimination. The Court also was concerned in this case, with the fact that the state of Alabama had consistently violated the orders of the district court. Also in 1987, the Supreme Court was confronted with the issue of sexual discrimination by a public sector employer. The case of *Johnson v. Transportation Agency* (1987) allowed the Court to set the parameter that in the hiring of state government employees consideration of race and gender were constitutional when bringing the workforce in line with the labor pool.

In 1989, the Supreme Court ruled on the issue of consent decrees. This case was pertinent to affirmative action, in that it dealt with state government employees who challenged an affirmative action program and they were not a party of the original judicial proceedings. *Martin v. Wilks* (1989), the Supreme Court held that white employers can challenge, without time limitations, affirmative action consent decrees settling employment discrimination disputes, even if they were not original parties to the consent decree.

Again, in 1989, the Court was confronted with the legality of seniority systems and the application of the statute of limitations. The case involved the legality of a collective bargained seniority system. This issue was pertinent to public personnel in that it focused on when a public employee must file a suit challenging a discriminatory employment practice. In the case of *Lorance v. AT&T* (1989), the Court held that a public employee challenging a discriminatory employment practice must recognize that the statute of limitations began when the employment practice was adopted rather than when the practice was applied to the harmed individual.

These court cases had an adverse effect on set-sides, hiring, and promotion policies in the public and private workplace. One year after these decisions, states of the Old Confederacy continued to increase the number of African American employees in state government. In fact, it is clear from the previous discussion that the progress of African Americans in state government continued into the mid-nineties as the Supreme Court continued to hand down decisions that had the effect of neutralizing or weakening affirmative action. Because many of these cases did not directly address affirmative action in hiring and promotion in the government sector, one would not expect any adverse effect on such personnel policies.

Based on the actual data, it could be argued that decisions reached by the United States Supreme Court and the Federal Circuit Court of Appeals did not directly impact employment practices for African Americans in the Old Confederacy states under examination. As indicated above, most of the selected states reflected continuous increases in hiring of African Americans in state government during the time period from 1989 to 1995 when the courts handed down decisions that were interpreted as having a negative impact on employment and hiring practices for African Americans. Southern states in this study are making a collective effort to overcome historical discriminatory employment hiring and promotion practices that were commonplace under the old system of *de jure* segregation. As mentioned earlier, this analysis must take into consideration other pertinent factors that may help explain the increases of African Americans in state government. These include the percentage of African Americans in the state population, the percent in the state labor force, elected African American state and federal representatives, and the political party of the governor of the states, as well as the legal issues before the judicial system.

## Statistical Analysis of Data

The objective of the study was to assess the hiring and employment practices of African Americans in state government. Based upon the collected data from the state personnel boards, it was necessary to formulate a statistical test to determine which variable(s) were responsible for explaining the hiring practices of the states in the study. Table 12 provides an overview of the variables used in the study and the sources from which the variables were collected. The statistical test was developed from a data set that included the actual state population and the number (percent) of African Americans in each of the seven states. The data included various political factors such as the percent of African Americans in the state legislature as a whole and the percent of African Americans in each state House and Senate. The party of the governor at the times when the state in question reported data were also included. The actual years of the collected data were included in the analysis. In assessing the status of affirmative action, the impact of the decisions handed down by the United States Supreme Court and other federal courts were analyzed to determine whether there was a positive or negative policy impact on employment practices for the states included in the study. The completed data set consisted of 747 cases with no missing data.

### Codification of the Data Set

The dependent variable was the actual percentage of African Americans in the state government labor force for the states of Arkansas, Georgia, Mississippi, North Carolina, Oklahoma, South Carolina, and Tennessee of the Old Confederacy. The label for African Americans workers was (AFRAM) and this included both African American males and females.

In developing a statistical assessment to determine the correlates of employment practices in the southern states, independent variables encompassing political effects were included. The variables for political effects included the percent of African Americans in the state legislature (ST.LEG), and represented the total percent of African Americans in the respective state legislatures. The percent of African Americans in the House of Representatives (ST.REP) was included as a variable in the political effects along with the percentage of African Americans in the state Senate (ST.SEN). Another independent variable for political effects was the party of the governor (GOVPTY) for each year of the reported state data. This was coded as 1 for Democrat and 2 for Republican. The years of the collected data were included in my examination of political effects. The unit of analysis consisted of the agency from which reported data was collected, the year of the reported data, and the state reporting the collected data.

The rationale for analyzing statistically the political effects was to determine the impact the percent of African Americans in the state legislature had on the percentage of African Americans in the state government labor force. The hypothetical question was whether the increase in African Americans elected in either the state House of Representatives or the state Senate had any significant relationship with the increased numbers of African Americans in the state government workforce. This statistical analysis was designed to test whether or not

Table 12

Data Sources for Variables Used in the Study

| Variables | Source of the Data |
| --- | --- |
| Percent of African Americans in Population | Joint Center for Political Studies (1974-1993) and Statistical Abstract (1982-83; 1994-1997) |
| Percent of African Americans in State Legislature | Joint Center for Political Studies (1974-1993) and Statistical Abstract (1982-83; 1994-1997) |
| Percent of African Americans in State House of Representatives | Joint Center for Political Studies (1974-1993) and Statistical Abstract (1982-83; 1994-1997) |
| Percent of African Americans in State Senate | Joint Center for Political Studies (1974-1993) and Statistical Abstract (1982-83; 1994-1997) |
| The Party of the Governor of the State | Joint Center for Political Studies (1974-1993) and Information Please Almanac (1994-1997) |
| Population of the Selected States | Joint Center for Political Studies (1974-1993), Statistical Abstract (1982-83; 1994-1997) and Information Please Almanac (1994-1997) |
| Years of Collected Data | EEO-4 Reports (supplied by State Personnel Boards) |
| Number of African American Workers | EEO-4 Reports (supplied by State Personnel Boards) |
| United States Supreme Court Cases | U.S. Reports and Supreme Court Reporter |
| Federal Circuit Court Cases | Federal Court Reporter |

the 1965 Voting Rights Act had any correlation with the increase in African American elected officials, and the increase in African American employment for the states in questionThe party of the governor during the time periods of collected data were analyzed to determine whether there were any significant relationships between the party of the governor and state government employment practices. The test was to determine, on the one hand, if a liberal Democratic governor was associated with increased African American employment, or if, on the other hand, a conservative Republican governor was associated with decreased hiring of African Americans as state employees. The rationale for including the year for statistical analysis was to determine if, as the years increased, the African American share of jobs in state government also increased after controlling for these political factors.

As previously noted, the court system has an effect on the state of affirmative action as it related to employment hiring and promotional practices.   Again, it must be kept in mind that public policies are incremental in nature.   Therefore, the effect of a Supreme Court or Federal Court decision may not be immediately apparent. The variable was coded by allowing a one year of implementation time before each court decision would be expected to have an effect.

As demonstrated in Table 13, a review of the court cases found that each case focused on one of nine key legal issues pertaining to affirmative action. The legal issues  and their codification were as follows: consent decrees (CONSENT), disparate impact (DISIMP), preferential treatment (PREFTR), racial discrimination (RACEDISC), reverse discrimination (REVDISC), seniority systems (SENSYS), set asides (SETASID), sexual discrimination (SEXDISC), and voluntary plan (VOLPLAN).   The statistical assessment utilized for assessing the impact of judicial decisions was coded as a positive one (+1) if the nature of the court's ruling suggested a positive impact on affirmative action hiring and employment policies and programs.  However, if the court ruling in question contained a negative or anti-affirmative action effect regarding employment practices, it was coded as a negative one (-1). Subsequent years received the same codes, unless a new court case in that legal area was decided, reflecting the continued ruling of that court case. As the years and court issues progressed, it became possible to have zero coding (which indicated no net effect of the court rulings during the previous years related to affirmative action), or a positive or negative two. This was possible if more than one court case pertaining to affirmative action

Table 13

Court Decisions in the Study

| Court Case | Legal Issue | Legal Impact |
|---|---|---|
| *DeFunis v. Odegaard* (1974) | Reverse Discrimination | +1 |
| *Regents of the University of California v. Bakke* (1978) | Reverse Discrimination and Racial Discrimination | -1 |
| *United Steelworkers v. Weber* (1979) | Voluntary Affirmative Action Plan | +1 |
| *Fullilove v. Klutznick* (1980) | Set Asides | +1 |
| *Firefighters v. Stotts* (1984) | Seniority Systems | -1 |
| *Wygant v. Jackson Board of Education* (1986) | Preferential Treatment | -1 |
| *Sheet Metal Workers v. EEOC* (1986) | Racial Discrimination | +1 |
| *United States v. Paradise* (1987) | Consent Decree | +1 |
| *Johnson v. Transportation Agency, Santa Clara* (1987) | Sexual Discrimination | +1 |
| *Richmond v. Croson* (1989) | Set Asides | -1 |

* Positive one (+1) denotes a pro-affirmative action court decision.
* Negative one (-1) denotes a anti-affirmative action court decision.
Data taken from U.S. Reports, Supreme Court Reporter, and Federal Court Reporter
This Table addresses the key issue as defined by the Supreme Court-other issues may have been involved as well.

Table 13 (continued)

| Court Case | Legal Issue | Legal Impact |
|---|---|---|
| *Wards Cove v. Antonio* (1989) | Disparate Impact | -1 |
| *Martin v. Wilks* (1989) | Consent Decree | -1 |
| *Price Waterhouse v. Hopkins* (1989) | Sexual Discrimination | -1 |
| *Lorance v. AT&T* (1989) | Seniority System | -1 |
| *Patterson v. McLean Credit Union* (1989) | Racial Discrimination | -1 |
| *Milwaukee County Pavers Assn. v. Fiedler* (1991) | Reverse Discrimination | -1 |
| *Northeastern Florida Chapter of General Contractors v. Jacksonville, Florida* (1993) | Set Aside | -1 |
| *Podberesky v. Kirwan* (1993) | Reverse Discrimination | -1 |
| *Maryland Troopers Asso. Inc. v. Evans* (1993) | Consent Decree | -1 |
| *Adarand Constructors, Inc. v. Pena* (1995) | Racial Discrimination | -1 |
| *Taxman v. Board of Education of Piscataway* (1996) | Racial Discrimination | -1 |
| *Hopwood v. Texas* (1996) | Reverse Discrimination | -1 |

* Positive one (+1) denotes a pro-affirmative action court decision.
* Negative one (-1) denotes a anti-affirmative action court decision.
Data collected from U.S. Reports, Supreme Court Reporter, and Federal Court Reporter.
This Table addresses the key issues as defined by the Supreme Court-other issues may have been involved as well.

were adjudicated during the same and previous time frame. This was to determine whether a particular legal issue had greater impact or influence affecting the hiring and promotion of African Americans in state government.

Another important factor in the statistical analysis was the percent of African Americans in the overall state population. Hence, the population statistics were collected for each corresponding year of data reported by each state. The objective here was to determine whether there was any statistically significant relationship between the percent of African Americans in the state population and the total percent of African Americans in the state government workforce. These total numbers were based on the actual reported population data for each year in question.

## Political Effects on African American Employment Practices

An important factor in discussing the impact of African American employment in the selected southern states was that of the political effects. The issue was whether or not the role of politics had any effect on the increased employment of African Americans in state government. The political variables included the population of the selected state, the percent of African Americans in the state legislature, the percent of African Americans in the state House of Representatives and Senate, along with the political party of the governor during the selected year in question. The political variables included the year in which the data were collected.

To determine the impact of each variable, a bivariate analysis was conducted using the Pearson R, with the dependent variable African Americans workers. As presented in Table 14, the bivariate analysis revealed that the most important variable was that of population (.36). Thus, it was likely that the African American population of the selected state was a determining factor in accounting for the increased employment of African Americans. This suggests that the higher the African American population for the selected state, then the higher the potential labor pool for African American employees. The next important factor was that of the number of African Americans in the state legislature of the state in question. It should be noted that House and Senate variables were dropped from later analysis, due to multicollinearity. The Pearson R for percentages of African Americans in the state house (STREP) and in state legislature (STLEG), as a whole was .98, and the Pearson R for percentage of African Americans in state senate (STSEN) and in state

Table 14

Bivariate Analysis of Political Effects on State Government Diversity

| Independent Variables | Pearson R | Level of Significance |
|---|---|---|
| African American Population in the selected state | .36 | 0 |
| Percent African Americans in the State Legislature of selected state | .29 | 0 |
| Party of the Governor for the selected state | .10 | .005 |
| The year of the collected data | .12 | .001 |
| The percent of African Americans in the state house chamber | .29 | 0 |
| The Percent of African Americans in the state senate chamber | .24 | 0 |

* Dependent variable = total number of African Americans in state government workforce

legislature as a whole was .83. The Pearson R with the state legislature was .29 for the state House of Representatives and .24 for the state Senate. The political effect of the state legislature had an importance of .29. When assessing the impact of the party of the governor, it became necessary to control for the influence of the geographical location of the selected southern states, which yielded a counter-intuitive plus significance (Republican governors related to more diversity in state workforce). Thus, it was necessary to re-code the South as (1- Deep South) and (2-Rim South). This resulted in the states of the study being coded as follows: (Arkansas =2), (Georgia = 1), (Mississippi = 1), (North Carolina = 2), (Oklahoma = 2), (South Carolina = 1) and (Tennessee = 2). The data revealed that the party of the governor had a partial effect of .13 on state workforce diversity, after controlling for Southern sub-region. It was also necessary to control for the year, suggesting that as the years increased, this may or may not have accounted for the increase or decrease in African American employment in state government. When controlling for the year, the governor's party had a partial effect of .07, with a significance level of .06, which suggested that the governor's party was not that important. In sum, it could be suggested that as time went on, the South elected more Republican governors, and racial diversity increased in the state workforce, but these two variables were not causally related.

## Court Case Effects and African American Employment

The role of the judicial branch and its decisions on the progress of African American hiring was analyzed utilizing a bivariate analysis. The dependent variable was the percent of African Americans in state government correlated with the year of the case in question. The bivariate analysis was conducted by assessing the impact of the basic legal issue in the case as it related to affirmative action and employment practices. As previously mentioned, the independent variables that included legal issues were consent decrees, disparate impact, preferential treatment, racial discrimination, reverse discrimination, seniority systems, set asides, sexual discrimination, and voluntary plans.

Table 15 demonstrated the bivariate analysis of court cases and their effects. The analysis revealed that those cases involving racial discrimination had the largest relationship (R=.09), with a level of significance of .01. Those cases involving the issue of racial discrimination, had a relationship affecting the number of African Americans hired by the state government. Even when controlling for year, racial discrimination court cases had a partial effect of .11 with a significance level of .002. Those court cases involving the issue of disparate impact, when the researcher controlled for the year the case was presented, reflected a partial effect on employment practices (.02) which was not significant. The legal issue of preferential treatment, when controlling for year, revealed an R of -.10, with a significance level of .005. This suggested a nonsensical result that when the legal impact of such cases was anti-affirmative action, the percentage of African

Table 15

Bivariate Analysis of Court Cases and their Effects

| Legal issues of the Court case | Pearson R | Level of Significance |
|---|---|---|
| Consent Decrees | .05 | .158 |
| Disparate Impact | -.09 | .018 |
| Preferential Treatment | -.15 | 0 |
| Racial Discrimination | .09 | .01 |
| Reverse Discrimination | -.02 | .504 |
| Seniority System | -.13 | 0 |
| Set Asides | .05 | .178 |
| Sexual Discrimination | .06 | .109 |
| Voluntary Plan | .11 | .002 |

* Dependent Variable = total number of African American employees and the year of the court case.
* Independent Variable= the legal issue involved in the court case in question.

Americans in southern state governments actually rose. The independent variable of seniority systems, on state diversity in the workplace when controlling for year, also resulted in a -.04, with a level of significance of .254, which was not significant. The independent variable of voluntary plan when controlling for year gave a partial Pearson R of .04, with significance level of .273, which was not statistically significant. So predictors had counter intuitive effects largely because of the fact that they were correlated with year. For the racial discrimination indicator, 76% of the cases fell into one particular category of zero. Racial discrimination was found in category zero during the years of 1975-1986 and 1990-1995. As mentioned earlier, a negative coding was used to study the projected impacts of the court case on diversity of hiring. As a result of this classification, only 1.1% of the cases had a -2 coding, while 3.5% had a -1 coding. During the study 19.3% of the cases had a +1 coding. The variance for this independent variable was only .252.

# CHAPTER VIII

# SUMMARY

A primary purpose of this research was to assess the impact of affirmative action on employment, hiring and advancement of African Americans in southern state governments since the 1964 Civil Rights Act and the 1965 Voting Rights Act. The research was designed to analyze, over a period of time based on primary data, the progress of African Americans since the inception of affirmative action. The study is, in part, an impact assessment of employment diversity from 1964-1995 that analyzed the patterns related to progress in administrative and managerial positions of African Americans.

The original intent of the study was to assess the progress of African Americans in all of the Old Confederacy. However, as previously noted, data could not be collected from all of the confederate states. Hence, the research focused on the states of Arkansas, Georgia, Mississippi, North Carolina, Oklahoma, South Carolina and Tennessee. The study focused on longitudinal data supplied by the state personnel boards of the selected states. The analysis examined those occupational categories, as defined by EEO-4 Reports that were involved in both decision making and policy making.

In assessing the progress of African Americans in southern state governments, the impact of the judicial branch, with specific focus on decisions handed down by the United States Supreme Court and other federal courts, was investigated. The court system was included in the discussion as an independent variable because it has had an effect on affirmative action in the public sector. The study incorporated those court cases that contain legal issues pertinent to affirmative action. This involved cases for both the United States Supreme Court and other federal courts from 1971-1996. Since the impact of court decisions on public policy are incremental in nature, their effect may not be immediately apparent.

The effect of political factors were studied to determine how they may have affected African American workers in southern state government. This included the percent of African Americans in the overall state population, the percent of African Americans in the state legislature as a whole, and the percent of African Americans in the House and Senate chambers of the state legislature. The party of the governor was assessed to determine if in fact, a Democratic or Republican governor was associated with any substantial increases or decreases in African American employment for state government employees. The effect of each of these independent variables were addressed in the data analysis chapter.

The research focused on southern states because the South has historically been the bastion of *de jure* racial discrimination and job inequality and resistance to laws to remedy racial inequality for African Americans. The study discussed the barriers and progress of African Americans in American and the southern states. The research analyzed the southern states in particular because African Americans have made advances in mid-level, upper level and executive positions of management and authority. The pivotal question in this regard was how much and why?

The topic of affirmative action was addressed because it is a natural extension of the struggle for equal rights in the United States. A key component of the quest for racial equality is that of equal treatment in the workplace. As noted by Burnstein (1994), one of the goals of affirmative action is to develop a workforce reflective of the racial and sexual composition of the population.

This study expands the body of knowledge regarding affirmative action focusing on the impact of affirmative action and voting in seven southern states. It is important to note that there are no academic studies comparing the southern states utilizing data supplied by the state personnel boards. This study provided the opportunity to determine how much progress the New South has made in the area of employment hiring and promotion practices. The literature in the field of affirmative action will be enhanced by the investigation of state governments in the Old Confederacy.

Chapter II of the dissertation discussed the origin of affirmative action. The chapter began with a synopsis of the formulation for affirmative action. It was noted that the political atmosphere that led to the enactment of affirmative action came on the heels of the turbulent Civil Rights Movement of the 1950s and 1960s. The actual concept of affirmative action began under the presidency of John Kennedy as the result of an Executive Order.

Chapter II outlined the legislative provisions of the 1964 Civil Rights Act (CRA) which was composed of eleven titles. The key components of the 1964 CRA relating to the study were Titles VI and VII, which established the foundation for affirmative action. Title VII was pertinent to the discussion of affirmative action in the dissertation. As indicated in the chapter, the 1964 CRA contained no criminal penalties or punitive damages for violations of Title VII. The study suggested that the omission of a penalty phase was, in part, due to the difficulties in getting the civil rights legislation passed. The issue of appeasement of a southern congressional constituency in procurement of such legislation may account for the omission of any penalty clauses in the Act. Title VII contains ambiguous language because it does not address the issue of non-intentional (structural or systemic) discrimination, thus making it possible for the courts to supply the necessary interpretative element. The role of the courts in interpreting affirmative action policies and programs was undertaken.

Chapter II explored the various definitions of affirmative action. In reviewing the current literature in the field, the study revealed the existence of numerous definitions for affirmative action. A common element within the various definitions was that the core objective of affirmative action was a commitment to fairly integrate traditionally disadvantaged groups into public institutions and processes. Thus, affirmative action is one aspect of the federal government's efforts to ensure equal employment opportunity.

In assessing the plethora of definitions for this initiative, the following summary of definitions were set forth. Taylor (1991) stated that affirmative action referred to specific steps beyond ending discriminatory practices designed to promote equal opportunity and ensure that discrimination will not recur. Swain (1996) defined affirmative action as the range of governmental and private initiatives which offered preferential treatment to members of designated racial and ethnic minority groups as a means of compensating for the efforts of past and present discrimination.   The general consensus of the literature was that affirmative action programs and policies were designed to compensate for past historical discriminatory practices.  As noted in Chapter II,  the literature suggests that affirmative action programs have been misinterpreted and viewed as encompassing quotas, which have been defined by the United States Supreme Court as unconstitutional.  Hence, as indicated in the literature, affirmative action programs have led to the allegation of reverse discrimination.  Yet, ironically, the United States Supreme Court has not developed or invoked a concise definition of the concept.

Chapter II noted that even though the Court has not been willing to establish strict and complete guidelines for affirmative action plans, there have been certain requirements that have withstood the scrutiny of the judicial system.  In reviewing the parameters of affirmative action, the literature suggested the inclusion of qualitative as well as quantitative goals for measuring progress.  The inclusion of such goals are pertinent to remedying past discriminatory practices.  Human resource personnel is a key component to study qualitative and quantitative goals related to affirmative action policies and programs.

The constitutionality of affirmative action was included in the discussion in Chapter II.  The constitutionality of affirmative action was tested by the Equal Protection Clause of the Fourteenth Amendment and the guidelines of Title VII of the 1964 CRA.  The question here was whether or not affirmative action created goals or quotas and gave rise to the concept of reverse discrimination.  As indicated in Chapter II, goals must be targets reasonably attainable by means of applying good faith efforts to make all aspects of the entire affirmative action program work.  As established by the Courts, goals must have flexibility.  The literature indicated that the constitutional argument against affirmative action was predicated on the notion that all governmental distinctions based on race are presumed illegal but in limited instances overcome this presumption by meeting the exact requirement of strict scrutiny.   In order for affirmative action programs to survive strict scrutiny, they must further a compelling state interest by the most narrowly tailored means available.  The Courts have clearly ruled that approval has never been given to race-conscious remedies absent judicial, administrative, or legislative findings of constitutional or statutory violations.   In discussing the origin of affirmative action, Chapter II focused on arguments for and against affirmative action. As noted in that particular chapter, numerous arguments were presented by both side of the issue. Those in support of affirmative action collectively argued that affirmative action is still needed in order to eliminate the lasting effects of invidious discrimination and discriminatory employment practices in both the public and private sector. Supporters of affirmative action suggested that this initiative was needed because it had provided enhanced employment opportunities for African Americans and other protected groups. Current congressional supporters of affirmative action argued that anti-discrimination efforts alone were insufficient to compensate for the effects of racial bias and intolerance in the past as well as the present. Supporters quickly point out that despite more than two decades of affirmative action, African Americans lag significantly behind white males in the area of employment and promotions. Thus, without affirmative action policies and programs, the plight of African Americans becomes even bleaker.

Those opposed to affirmative action have collectively set forth the viewpoint that this policy has led to quotas and reverse discrimination. This involves the argument that affirmative action promotes inequality rather than supporting equality. Opponents of affirmative action include Sowell, who argued that affirmative action created harm by giving incompetent people advantages, and thereby hindering the African American population. Many opponents argued that affirmative action implies that African Americans cannot succeed without some type of assistance. The argument against affirmative action included the view that affirmative action stigmatized African Americans and preferential treatment contributed to racial and ethnic polarization as well as reinforcing racial stereotypes.

The arguments against affirmative action can be summarized as follows. First, the philosophical view that affirmative action is simply another name for racial preferences. Second, the conservative Republican wing of Congress advocates that affirmative action has done more to divide Americans than to unite them. Third, that affirmative action is demeaning, degrading and stigmatizes African Americans and even suggest that it implies an inferiority complex associated with African Americans. Finally, the suggestion was made that affirmative action served to make any accomplishments by African Americans suspect, even those who are well qualified for positions.

The affirmative action initiative has even caused division in the United States Congress regarding the federal government's role in the implementation of affirmative action policies and programs. In 1995, a legislative effort was launched in an attempt to reduce or neutralize the impact of affirmative action in American society. During the 1995 legislative session, congressional subcommittees considered the Equal Opportunity Act of 1995 an anti-affirmative action initiative. The Senate version of the legislation was introduced by Senator Dole and the House version was introduced by Republican Representative Canady. The Dole-Canady measure endorsed programs aimed at broad recruiting efforts and expanded opportunities for competition. The measure included mechanisms designed to outlaw goals, timetables and set-asides as tools to remedy discrimination. The Dole-Canady legislation would have required the prohibition of government employees and agencies basing any hiring or promotion decisions partly or wholly on such factors as race, color, national origin, or gender. It was noted that this measure did not apply to existing anti-discrimination laws that allowed victims of racial and sexual discrimination to sue to recover lost wages or jobs.

The arguments given by supporters of the Dole-Canady measure included the view that it would restore the principles of equal protection for all Americans as embodied in the Fourteenth Amendment. Other arguments included the argument that affirmative action as a policy created divisions among its Americans. An argument in support of the Dole-Canady measure was that the Equal Opportunity Act of 1995 prohibited the federal government from providing preferential treatment on the basis of race and gender, and provided the means to prohibit the government from encouraging or requiring others to extend such preferences.

Opponents of the Equal Opportunity Act, suggested that many were opposed to affirmative action due to the focus on protected groups. Those opposing the Dole-Canady Act argued that this particular measure would roll back the clock on civil rights in the United States. There was agreement among the opponents of this measure that affirmative action policies are still critically needed to bring about equal opportunity in education and employment.

After extensive Judiciary Committee Constitutional Subcommittee hearings in both Houses, the plan to scale back the federal government's affirmative action programs got only as far as the subcommittee hearing stages in both Houses. The proposed legislation to end affirmative action on the federal government level was viewed as a political "hot potato" at this time. Congressional opponents of affirmative action had hoped to translate the momentum from federal court decisions regarding affirmative action into legislative success in 1995. Congressional abandonment to end affirmative action with the Equal Opportunity Act of 1995 demonstrated how difficult and complex the issue of affirmative action remains in American society.

The state level testing of affirmative action came in the form of the California Civil Rights Initiative, which became known as Proposition 209. This proposition provided the constitutional mechanism to eliminate public affirmative action in California, with the exception of court-ordered programs or those required to maintain federal funding. Proposition 209 was designed to prevent state courts from ordering public entities to engage in future affirmative actions, but it did not prohibit federal courts from doing so. California voters approved this controversial amendment in 1996 and effectively eliminated all preferential treatment in hiring, promotion and education.

As noted in Chapter II, in assessing the impact of affirmative action, consideration and discussion was devoted to the effects of the 1965 Voting Rights Act (VRA). The 1965 VRA was considered as an intervening variable in the discussion of affirmative action. The study suggested that the increased numbers of African American voters would have an impact or correlation with the increase of African Americans employed in state government in the selected southern states. The hypothetical inference was that as elected African American officials take office, this, in turn, provides the mechanism or leverage to encourage the hiring and promotion of African American employees. Four of the seven states in the study --Mississippi, South Carolina, Georgia, and North Carolina-- are included within coverage of the formula regarding the 1965 VRA. The effect of the VRA was expanded in the data analysis section.

Chapter III discusses the history of inequality and how it impacted the quest for equal employment. The discussion in this chapter began with the issue of inequality in the United States Constitution. The constitutional focus was on issues including the Three-Fifths Compromise and other constitutional areas covering the institution of slavery, leading up to the *Dred Scott* (1857) decision. The chapter addressed the implementation of such discriminatory practices as the Black Codes and Jim Crow laws and how these affected the African American quest for equality. The lack of sufficient congressional civil rights legislation was discussed as it related to the struggle of racial equality.

Chapter III also centered on the role of the Thirteenth and Fourteenth Amendments and their effect on the quest for racial equality. The impact of *Plessy v. Ferguson* (1896) and the legal principle of Separate-but-Equal was a legacy of the 19th century United States Supreme Court. This provided historical background to demonstrate how the Courts had now become involved as a mechanism in the move for equality. *Plessy v. Ferguson* was very important because this case, in essence, provided the legal foundation for Jim Crow laws and the implementation of the Black Codes.

The chapter devoted attention to the issue of suffrage as it related to equality. The main point of inference was that a people without the right to vote have few rights. The various legal barriers or means of circumventing the provision of the Fifteenth Amendment to the United States Constitution granting African American males the right to vote were presented. Those barriers included the grandfathers clause, the white primary, the poll tax, and literacy tests. As noted in the chapter, these barriers were removed only after intervention of the federal government and the federal judicial system.

Another key issue presented in Chapter III regarding the history of inequality was the struggle to overcome the effects of a segregated educational system in America. The problem of segregated schools was compounded by the legal precedent established in the case of *Plessy v. Ferguson* (1896). The National Association for the Advancement of Colored People (NAACP) became the vehicle for challenging segregated educational practices in particularly in the Old Confederacy. The attempt at desegregating educational institutions began with a series of graduate education cases. The graduate school desegregation cases included *Missouri ex rel. Gaines v. Canada* (1938), *Sweatt v. Painter* (1950), and *McLaurin v. Oklahoma State Regents* (1950).

As indicated in Chapter III, the issue of the constitutionality of racial segregation (as a practice) had not been tested before the courts. Thus, the importance of *Brown v. Board of Education* (1954) was of paramount importance. In an amazing 9-0 decision, the United States Supreme Court in Brown overturned the separate-but-equal precedent established in *Plessy v. Ferguson* (1896). The Court held that in the field of public education, the doctrine of separate-but-equal had no place. The *Brown* cases (I and II) completely altered the style, spirit, and stance of race relations in American society. With the advent of *Brown*, it was suggested that major strides were made in the quest for racial equality since the implementation of the original Constitution. Chapter III pointed out that a historical review of Supreme Court decisions, constitutional amendments, and congressional acts revealed that the problem of employment discrimination may still exist, more than four decades after the policy of racial neutrality stated in *Brown v. Board of Education* (1954) and more than three decades after the passage of Title VII of the Civil Rights Act. As noted in the study, even though African Americans are making progress, the movement for African Americans from low paying service worker and labor jobs to mid-level management is an incremental process in the nation as a whole.

Chapter IV, The Supreme Court and Affirmative Action: 1971-1988, encompassed the role of the judicial branch in the area of affirmative action during this period. A pertinent aspect of the discussion of the Supreme Court as presented at this time was the composition of the Court. Based on the discussion in the previous chapter, it was suggested that the federal courts had become the protector of African American rights. However, with the appointment of conservative Justices Rehnquist, O'Connor, Kennedy, Scalia, and Thomas, the Supreme Court is more hostile to affirmative action and unsympathetic toward the rights and concerns of African Americans.

Chapter IV presented those cases having legal significance in the area of affirmative action. The discussion began with the case of *Griggs v. Duke Power Company* (1971). This case established the legal precedent that any employee test must meet the requirement of business necessity. *Griggs v. Duke Power Company* established the first guidelines regarding affirmative action. In 1974, the Supreme Court would have its first request to adjudicate the issue of reverse discrimination. However, in *DeFunis v. Odegaard* (1974), the Court avoided the legal issue and decided that the issue of reverse discrimination was moot. This decision was due to the fact that at the time of appeal, DeFunis was already a student in law school. However, the issue of reverse discrimination would again confront the Court in 1978 in *Regents of the University of California v. Bakke*. This particular case involved two pertinent legal issues related to affirmative action. The case focused on the issue of reverse discrimination and that of racial classification. The Court, in essence, established two opinions in this case as discussed in detail in chapter three. The *Bakke* case established the precedent in the legal area of reverse discrimination. This case was viewed as having such an impact on the African American quest for equality, that Justice Marshall argued that the decision turned back the hands of time two hundred years.

As presented in Chapter IV, a year later in *United States Steelworkers' International v. Equal Employment Opportunity Commission* (1979), the

Court was requested to adjudicate the issue of a voluntary affirmative action plan. The Court held that a private voluntary affirmative action program designed to eradicate historical racial discrimination in employment was constitutional. In 1980, the court was confronted with the issue of set asides. *Fullilove v. Klutznick* (1980) witnessed the Court ruling that Minority Business Enterprise (MBE's) were constitutional, thereby upholding the legality of set aside programs. It was noted by the Court that set asides were legal, if in fact, they were narrowly tailored and did not unnecessarily trammel the interests of others. In 1984, the Court in *Firefighters Local v. Stotts* held that *bona fide* seniority systems, unless intentionally discriminatory to African American workers who demonstrated that they were individually victimized in hiring discrimination, were protected under the guidelines of Title VII. Two years later, in *Wygant v. Jackson Board of Education* (1986), the Court handed down a decision that seemed to say "yes" and "no" to racial preferences. Also in 1986, the Court ruled that racial discrimination that was egregious in nature was unconstitutional. Therefore, the Court allowed race-conscious relief as a remedy for past discrimination. The case of *Local 28 of the Sheet Metal Workers' International Association v. Equal Employment Opportunity Commission* (1986) had an impact on affirmative action and human resource personnel because it addressed the issue of union discriminatory practices, with an emphasis on continued intentional discrimination. Again, the Court applied the criteria of a race-based remedy aimed at rectifying the present effects of historical discriminatory practices.

As mentioned in Chapter IV, during the 1987 judicial term, the Court was presented with deciding whether the consideration of race and sex as a factor in employment hiring practices violated Title VII of the Civil Rights Act of 1964. During this term, the Court also considered the implementation of a voluntarily adopted affirmative action plan by a public agency. *Paradise v. United States* (1987) presented the legal issue of consent decrees. In this case, the Court handed down an important ruling. For the first time the Court held that judges may order strict racial promotional quotas to overcome long-term, open and pervasive discrimination. This case, as noted earlier, was an important affirmative action case because the Court set forth the precedent that strict racial quotas in promotions met constitutional muster in the public sector. Four weeks later, in *Johnson v. Transportation Agency, Santa Clara County* (1986), the Court rendered what was regarded as the most significant affirmative action/reverse discrimination decision since *Bakke* (1978), and ruled that it was permissible to take gender and race into account in employment decisions. The Court held that African Americans and women could receive limited preferential treatment.

Chapter IV revealed that during the years from 1971-1988, the Supreme Court was generally protective of the rights of the employee. The Courts decisions were viewed as protecting those advocating affirmative hiring and promotional practices. The ideological composition of the Court was an important factor in determining the outcome of the cases. During this time period there was a clear liberal bloc composed of Justices Brennan, White, Marshall, and Blackmun. The judicial philosophy of these justices championed the rights of protected groups. The dissolution of the liberal bloc resulted in anti-affirmative action decisions emanating from the Supreme Court in the late eighties.

Chapter V, the Supreme Court and Affirmative Action: 1989-1996, continued the discussion of how the Supreme Court has impacted affirmative action. Chapter V suggested that a change in the composition of the court led to a more conservative philosophical interpretation of affirmative action programs. The impact of the appointment of Kennedy to the Supreme Court was felt immediately and his vote clearly affected the Court's deliberation of six cases in 1989. In 1989, the Court handed down six crucial decisions regarding affirmative action and reverse discrimination that were the pivotal point in anti-affirmative action decisions.

The Court's view of affirmative action moved to a more employer friendly interpretation, the main theme of the chapter. Earlier, the Court had adopted an employee friendly judicial philosophy before 1989. In the six crucial cases discussed earlier, the Court handed down decisions that tremendously impacted affirmative action and narrowed its scope. The Court's decisions in the six case of 1989, which included, *Richmond v. Croson, Wards Cove Packing Company v. Antonio, Martin v. Wilks, Price Waterhouse v. Hopkins, Lorance v. AT&T Technologies*, and *Patterson v. McLean Credit Union*, had a direct impact on personnel and the composition of the workforce in the public and private sector.

As outlined in Chapter V, during the 1989 session the Court began to utilize judicial phrases such as "strict scrutiny," "*prima facie* case of past discrimination" and "disparate impact" to turn back the clocks. The 1989 Supreme Court decisions overturned earlier Supreme Court decisions that were favorable toward affirmative action programs and policies. *Ward Cove* exemplified the employer friendly judicial perspective, because the

Court made it difficult for protected class individuals and groups to use statistical support for claims of illegal discrimination. The burden of proof was now placed on the plaintiff to win a disparate impact case. The burden of proof was also shifted to the plaintiff in *Price Waterhouse v. Hopkins*, since, the employer merely had to establish a preponderance of evidence when the legal issue involved gender discrimination. As pointed out in the text of Chapter V, the Court in *Lorance v. AT&T* held that the statute of limitations for challenging a discriminatory employment practice began when the practice was adopted rather than when the practice was applied to the harmed plaintiffs. Since the issue of when discrimination in a contract began was of paramount importance, the Court held that discrimination in a private contract applied only to the formation of the contract and not those conditions evolving from the work environment.

During the 1990s, the judicial branch continued to adjudicate the issues of reverse discrimination, set-asides, race-based scholarship programs designed to rectify past historical discrimination, and numerical goals. Other legal issues before the Supreme Court and Federal Appeals Courts during the 1990s included race-conscious remedies, consent decrees, and racial preference as well as race-based classifications and strict scrutiny. An assessment of the cases presented in Chapter V during the 1990s revealed that the Courts (Supreme and Appeals) continued to tighten the noose around the neck of affirmative action. The conservative bloc of the United States Supreme Court continued to move in a negative direction regarding affirmative action programs and policies.

The Court continued to rule in the 1990s that racial presumption was a form of racial discrimination as established in *Bakke* (1978). In 1993, the precedent of *Richmond v. Croson* still held in the legal parameters of set-asides. The Court once again reasoned that race-conscious preferential treatment was unconstitutional. In the case of *Podberesky v. Kirwan* (1993), the Court would again confront the issue of reverse discrimination in higher education. The Fourth Circuit Court of Appeals held that the awarding of a race-based scholarship to remedy past effects of discrimination was unconstitutional. Hence, the Court continued to reduce affirmative action programs in universities even when the Court conceded that racial hostility existed.

The federal courts were also confronted with the legality of numerical goals based on race, race-conscious remedies, consent decrees and racial preference during mid-1990s. In *Maryland Troopers Association, Inc. v.*

*Evans* (1993), the Court held that race-conscious relief found in consent decrees violated the guidelines of the Fourteenth Amendment, and therefore were unconstitutional. This case indicated that the federal courts were adhering to the basic guidelines as established by the Supreme Court.

In 1995, the Supreme Court dealt with the issue of race-based classifications and strict scrutiny and affirmative action programs. In a key case involving the legality of affirmative action programs, the Supreme Court held that race-based classifications were subject to strict scrutiny regardless of whether enacted by Congress or other governmental decision makers. The case had a significant impact because the Court continued to establish the parameters of affirmative action cases; this case held that all racial classifications, whether overtly invidious or purportedly benign, were subject to strict scrutiny.

On the Circuit Court of Appeals level, in 1996, the issue of resolving a dispute between a teacher dismissed in support of an affirmative action program and a school district was presented in *Taxman v. Board of Education of Township of Piscataway*. The focal point of the case was the dismissal of a white teacher for the said purpose of an affirmative action plan adopted without remedial purpose designed to diversity faculty and students. The legal issue in this case was racial discrimination. But before the case could be adjudicated before the United States Supreme Court, the case was settled out of court. The case was settled because civil rights groups feared the Supreme Court would use this case to outlaw the widespread use of voluntary racial programs to promote diversity. The decision was predicated on the shifting political and legal consensus in America that demonstrated a movement from affirmative action and toward a policy of neutrality regarding the issues of gender and race.

In 1996, in the State of Texas, the legality of special admissions policies for universities was tested in the case of *Hopwood v. Texas*. As was the case in *Bakke* (1978), the issue was again consideration of race as a factor in admissions--in this case law school. The legal issue of whether racial preferences was a violation of the Equal Protection Clause of the Fourteenth Amendment was again before the courts. The Circuit Court of Appeals, in adherence to the precedent established in *Bakke* held that consideration of race in admission procedures was unconstitutional. This case may have laid the legal foundation for further litigation in other colleges and universities in the United States.

In view of the court cases presented in Chapters IV and V, it can be argued that many public and private entities will question their commitment to affirmative action as well as their approach. The Civil Rights Act of 1991 was an effort to rectify the effects of the sweeping decisions made by the Court during the 1989 term. The struggle between the Court's view of affirmative action and that of the United States Congress continues. Regarding the decisions reached during the 1989-1996 term, the public and private sector must develop strategies for affirmative action in the future that meet the strict scrutiny test, because of the conservative philosophy of the United States Supreme Court in the 1990s.

The methodology of the dissertation was presented in Chapter VI. The methodology for the research utilized, in part, a longitudinal analysis of state government affirmative action employment data. The data were analyzed to assess the impact of affirmative action on employment diversity by assessing the employment hiring and related data of state personnel boards in the seven southern states from the inception of the 1964 Civil Rights Act to 1995. Time-ordered employment data from Arkansas, Georgia, Mississippi, North Carolina, Oklahoma, South Carolina and Tennessee were examined to assess variations over employment periods. The research design allowed for intrastate as well as interstate comparisons to evaluate how states compared with each other, as well as how far each state had come in regard to hiring and promoting African Americans so that they are representative of the state population as a whole.

The data provided statistical information differentiated by job category. The categories were defined by guidelines established by the Equal Employment Opportunity Commission (EEOC), and therefore were uniform across all seven states of the study.

The data supplied by the state of Arkansas covered a time span from 1988 to 1997. The data from the state of Georgia spanned from 1973 to 1995. The state of Mississippi supplied data for the years of 1988, 1989, 1990, 1991, 1993, and 1995. The state of North Carolina provided data for the years from 1977 to 1995. However, the state of Oklahoma only supplied data for the years of 1984, 1994, and 1996. The state of South Carolina gave data for the period of 1987 to 1994. And the state of Tennessee supplied employee data for the years of 1983-1996. All of the data submitted utilized the eight EEO-4 categories.

The methodological section included an assessment of the impact of the 1964 Civil Rights Act and the 1965 Voting Rights Act on employment diversity in the southern states. Political data were obtained for each state during the previously mentioned time periods. The political data included the total population for each state, the total percent of African Americans in each state population, the number of African Americans in the state legislature as a whole, and the respective chambers. The party of the governor was included to determine the effect if any, the governor had on employment practices in each selected state. The analysis included Supreme Court and Circuit Court decisions to determine what effect the judicial decisions at this time had on state government employment.

In examining the progress of African Americans employed in southern state governments, comparisons were conducted based on the longitudinal time frame for the years in which the states supplied data. Arkansas over a nine year period had an increase of 4% in the total number of African Americans in state government (1988-1997). In the case of Georgia, which supplied twenty-years of data, overall employment for African Americans increased nineteen percent. This increase in the state of Georgia represented more than a fourfold increase covering the time period of 1973-1995. Mississippi experienced a six percent increase in the total employment gains for African Americans employed in the state government workforce. The increase for African Americans employed by the state of North Carolina over an eighteen year time frame was five percent going from 22% to 27%.

However, an accurate assessment over a long period of time of employment gains for African Americans employed by the state of Oklahoma was limited. As previously noted, Oklahoma only supplied data for 1984, 1994, and 1996. Based on the data supplied, the state of Oklahoma experienced a precipitous decline in African Americans in state government. The number of African Americans in state government for Oklahoma was 3,777 (11%) in 1984, decreasing to 3,728 (11%) in 1994 and as of 1995, there were only 3,564 (10%) state government employees. Unlike Oklahoma, over a seven year time period African Americans in South Carolina state government increased two percent. The number of African American employees began with 18,638 (35%) in 1987 and reached 21,319 (37%) in 1994. In Tennessee, over a thirteen year period, the total African American employee state workforce increased by one percent from 6,709 (19%) in 1983 to 8,309 (20%) in 1996, but demonstrated a net increase of 1,600. In Arkansas over a nine year period, the total African American employee state workforce increased four percent from 4,045 (21%) in 1988 to 5,952 (25%) in 1997. The number of African Americans in state government for Georgia was 7,438 (18%) in 1973, and increased to 30,714 (37%) in 1995. This demonstrated an increase of 19% for African Americans employed in the Georgia state government. In Mississippi, the number of African Americans employed as state government employees in 1988 was 6,283 (30%) and there were 8,507 (36%) in 1995. Mississippi demonstrated a six percent increase in African Americans employed in state government for the years data were collected.

An interstate comparative assessment of employment regarding the progress of African Americans in state government was conducted based on the years that demonstrated either substantial increases or decreases for African American employment in the selected states. The years of 1988, 1991, 1994, and 1995 demonstrated time periods in which African American state level employees in the Old Confederacy had either attained increased employment or experienced a reduction in state level employment. This was the selected time frame used to assess the impact of employment hiring practices for African Americans in the selected states.

In summarizing the totals for 1988 (except Oklahoma) the data revealed that South Carolina had the highest percent of African American state employees with thirty-six percent. Tennessee had the lowest reported percent of African Americans in the state total workforce with twenty percent. Five of the six states of the Old Confederacy had a higher percent of African Americans in the state workforce than the population as a whole. Arkansas and South Carolina led with 6% more African American workers than African Americans in the state population. Mississippi was the only state with a lower percentage of African American state government employees than the population as a whole, with a -5%. Oklahoma which supplied data for 1984 but not for 1988, also had a negative relation between the percent of African Americans in state government and the state population, with a -4% at that time.

In summarizing the totals for 1991, the data revealed that in Arkansas there was a close relationship with the number of African Americans employed by the state and the actual African American population for the state with a plus 5%. Like all of the other states of the Old Confederacy, Tennessee had a higher percentage (5%) of African Americans employed by the state than the number of African Americans comprising the state population. Mississippi, which had a negative relationship between

African American state employees and the state population in 1988, became the lead state in government employment of this group in 1991 with African Americans comprising 37% of state workforce. Mississippi also experienced the highest percentage increase (12%) since 1988 in African Americans in state government. Because Mississippi had such a large African American population (35%) in 1991, it was also worth noting that they had the closest positive relationship between African American state employment and the state population, a difference of only 2%. Georgia had the largest difference (7%) between the percent of African Americans in the public sector and in the state population in 1991.

In assessing the totals for 1994, the highest percentage of African Americans employed in the public sector was in South Carolina with thirty-seven percent, followed by Georgia with thirty-six percent. Oklahoma was the state with the lowest percentage of African Americans in state government at all levels in 1994. Georgia led the southern states with the highest percentage difference between African Americans employed in the public sector (36%) and the corresponding percent of state population (27%), constituting a difference of 9%. Arkansas and South Carolina were both second with 7% more African Americans employed in state government positions than the population as a whole, followed by Tennessee with 5%.

It was noted that after 1994, 1995 was the only other year in which five of the seven states could be compared to detect employment trends for African Americans, even though this was only a one year interval. After 1995, the data submitted were inconsistent. Those states submitting data for 1995 were Arkansas, Georgia, Mississippi, North Carolina, and Tennessee. During this time period, the state of Georgia exhibited the highest percent of African Americans employed in state government with thirty-seven percent followed by Mississippi with thirty-six percent. North Carolina (27%), Arkansas (24%), and Tennessee (20%) followed in that order. It must be kept in mind that differences reflect to some extent the different levels of African Americans in the state population and labor pools.

Of the states that supplied data, Georgia was the most progressive with regard to African Americans in state government. Georgia began with a total African American workforce of 7,438 (18%) in 1988 and increased to 30,714 (37%) by the year of 1995 quadrupling the 1988 numbers and more than doubling the percent over seven years. The African American workforce for state employees for the state of Georgia increased 23,276 over a twenty-two year time period. In this respect, Georgia was the most progressive of the states studied in the research. Mississippi demonstrated an increase of African American state government employees of 6% during this same period from 1988 to 1995. North Carolina exhibited a 5% increase and Arkansas a 4% increase for African Americans employed by the state. South Carolina experienced a 2% increase while Tennessee demonstrated a 1% increase in employment for African Americans in the total state labor force. While Georgia experienced the greatest gains in percent with 19%, Oklahoma was on the opposite end of the continuum, experiencing a 1% decrease.

In assessing the progression of African American administrative-officials in southern state government, the years of 1988, 1991, 1994, and 1995 demonstrated the years in which there were periods of either substantial gains or reductions in African American administrative-official state government employees. In 1988, South Carolina had the highest number of African Americans employed as administrative-officials with 246 (11%) compared to the other selected states. The state of North Carolina was shown to have the second highest number of 145 (9%) African Americans employed as administrative-officials. Mississippi had 135 actual African Americans employed in the administrative-official category. However, it was noted that Mississippi had the highest percentage (12%) of African Americans employed as administrative-officials for 1988 among the seven states. Georgia exhibited the lowest number of African Americans that were employed as administrative-officials with 68 (8%).

For the year of 1991, South Carolina again had the highest number of African American employed in the position of administrative-officials with 328 (13%). At this time, Mississippi had the second highest actual number of African Americans employed as administrative-officials with 203 but the highest percentage with 16%. Arkansas had the lowest number of African Americans employed as administrative-officials with 113 (11%) employees. The lowest percentage (8%) of African Americans with the actual number of 159 employed as administrative-officials in 1991 was in Tennessee.

A summary review of 1994 revealed that South Carolina continued to have the highest number of African Americans who were employed as administrative-officials with 378 (15%). North Carolina had the second highest number with 239 (13%) African Americans employed as administrative-officials. The lowest number of African Americans employed as administrative-officials was shown in Oklahoma with only eighty-one (5%). In the absence of data from Mississippi in 1994, South Carolina had the highest percentage (15%) of African Americans employed as administrative-officials and Oklahoma had the lowest with 5%.

In 1995, North Carolina had the highest actual number (257) of African Americans employed as administrative-officials among the selected seven states. Mississippi had the second largest number (228) of African Americans employed as administrative-officials. Mississippi once again had the highest percentage (16%) of African Americans employed as administrative-officials among the seven states. The state of Arkansas had the lowest number 134 (13%) of African Americans employed as administrative officials. Tennessee had the lowest percentage (8%) of African Americans employed as administrative-officials in 1995.

An assessment of the progression of African Americans in the occupational category of professionals in southern state governments was also undertaken. The years of 1988, 1991, 1994, and 1995 were most useful for this analysis as well. In 1988, South Carolina had the highest percent of African Americans employed as professionals with 21%. However, Georgia had the largest number of African Americans with 4,444 (20%). Mississippi had 17% with the actual number of African Americans employed as professional state governmental employees at 1,056. Tennessee had 2,198 (16%) African Americans employed in the professional category. Arkansas and North Carolina both had 14% of the African Americans employed in state government as professionals.

In 1991, Georgia continued to have the highest actual numbers (6,112) of African Americans employed as professionals in state government. South Carolina had the second highest actual number (4,410) of African Americans who were employed as professionals in the public sector. The state of Arkansas, with 1,371, had the lowest number of actual employees who were African American employed as professionals and working for the state. During this same time period, on the one hand South Carolina had the largest percentage (23%) of African Americans employed in the category of professionals in state government. North Carolina, on the other hand, with fourteen percent, was the state with the lowest percent of African Americans employed as professional workers in the workforce.

In 1994, the state of Georgia still had the largest number of professionals (7,067) who were African American in professional positions among the seven states. The state of South Carolina had the second largest number of African Americans employed at the professional level with 4,846. Georgia and South Carolina also had the highest percent (24%) of African American professionals among the selected states. The lowest percentage (7%) of African Americans professionals was found in the state of Oklahoma.

The data revealed that in 1995 Georgia, as in the previous years cited, again had the largest number (7,693) of actual African American employees that were classified as professional employees. The state of North Carolina had the next largest number (2,632) of African Americans employed by the state classified as professional employees. Arkansas recorded the lowest number (1,700) of African American professionals in state government. Tennessee reported the lowest percentage (15%) of African American professionals in state government. Georgia had the largest percent (25%) of African Americans in professional positions, followed by Mississippi and South Carolina, both of whom filled 24% of the professional positions with African Americans.

A brief summary of those Supreme Court and Circuit Court's of Appeal cases was presented that affected public personnel and state government. The legal issues of those cases relating to public personnel involved, the establishment of a voluntary affirmative action plan, the legality of a *bona fide* seniority system, reverse discrimination, and the problem of historical discriminatory employment practices. During the time period of 1971-1995 the Court also addressed the issues of egregious historical discrimination, sexual discrimination, and consent decrees. The Court was asked to determine when the statute of limitations began in challenging the legality of a seniority system.

As noted, these various court cases demonstrated an adverse effect on affirmative action policies and programs. However, the states of the Old Confederacy continued to progress in spite of the direction in which the judicial branch was moving pertaining to the issue of affirmative action. These cases did not directly address affirmative action in hiring and promotion in the government sector. Consequently, there was no adverse effect on personnel policies. Most of the selected states reflected continuous increases in the hiring of African Americans in state government during the time period from 1989 to 1995 when the courts handed down decisions that were interpreted as having a negative impact on employment and hiring practices for African Americans. Clearly, the southern states in this study were making a collective effort to overcome historical discriminatory employment hiring and promotion practices.

The statistical analysis of the research was developed from a data set that included the actual state population and the number (percent) of African Americans in each of the seven states. The data also included various political factors such as the percent of African Americans in the state legislature as a whole, and the percent of African Americas in the state House and Senate. The party of the governor at the times when the state in question reported data was also included. The impact of Supreme Court and other federal courts were analyzed to determine whether there was a positive or negative policy impact on employment practices for the states included in the study. The complete data set consisted of 747 cases.

The dependent variable for the data set was the actual number of African Americans in the state government labor force for each of the seven states. In developing the statistical assessment for determining the correlates of employment practices in the southern states, a number of independent variables that would have political effects were included in the study. The variables for the political effects included the percent of African Americans in the state legislature, and this represented the total percent of African Americans in the state legislature of each respective state, the percent of African Americans in the House of Representatives, and state Senate, along with the party of the governor. As noted earlier, the unit of analysis consisted of the agency from which the reported data was collected, the year of the reported data, and the state reporting the collected data.

The statistical analysis of the political data was carried out to determine to what extent the 1965 Voting Rights Act had an impact on the increase in African American elected officials and increased African American hiring and promotional practices. The party of the governor was studied to determine the effect that the party of the governor had in either increasing or decreasing African American employment in southern state governments. An analysis of the year was included to determine, if as the years increased, the African American share of jobs in state government increased after controlling for political factors.

The analysis of the court decisions revealed that the cases had nine legal issues pertaining to affirmative action. The impact of those judicial decisions were coded as either a positive one (+1) or a negative one (-1) depending on whether the decision of the court was either pro-affirmative action or anti-affirmative action. The objective was to determine whether a particular legal issue had greater impact or influence affecting the hiring and promotion of African Americans in state government.

At the same time, the percent of African Americans in the overall state population was statistically analyzed to determine if there was a correlation between the state government labor force and the total percent of African Americans in the state population. The numbers were based on the actual reported population data for each year in question.

A bivariate analysis was conducted to determine the impact of each independent variable using the Pearson R with African American government workers as the dependent variable. The results of the bivariate analysis revealed that the most important independent variable was the population (.36) of the state. The African American population of the selected states had the greatest explanatory value in accounting for the increased employment of African Americans. The results of the bivariate analysis suggest that the higher the African American population for the selected state, then the higher the potential labor pool for African American employees. The next important independent variable was that of the number of African Americans in the state legislature, which demonstrated an importance of .29. The party of the governor had a partial effect of .13 on diversity in state government, after controlling for southern sub-regions. In the bivariate analysis, it was necessary to control for year, suggesting that as the years increased, this may or may not have accounted for the increase or decrease in African American employment for the state government. Based on the results of the bivariate analysis, it was suggested that as time went on, the South elected more Republican governors, yet racial diversity increased in the state workforce. However, these two variables did not have a causal relationship.

In assessing the role of the courts and whether its decisions had an impact on the progress of African Americans, a bivariate analysis was conducted. The results of the bivariate analysis indicated that those cases involving racial discrimination had the largest impact (R=.09) with a level of significance of .01. The study suggested that those legal cases involving the issue of racial discrimination had a causal relationship affecting the number of African Americans hired by the state government. The importance of racial discrimination was evident even when controlling for year  presented with a partial effect of .11 with a significance level of .002. The other predictors had counter intuitive effects largely because they were correlated with year.

## The Conclusion

The research from this study demonstrated that affirmative action is still a controversial issue. As the literature suggests, there are those who still confuse affirmative action with quotas, when, in fact, the United States Supreme Court has declared quotas unconstitutional. American society remains divided on the issue of affirmative action. This was demonstrated in the debate on the Equal Opportunity Act of 1995 by Congress. During that particular legislative term, the United States Congress in subcommittee hearings conducted in both chambers debated the Dole-Canady initiative entitled the Equal Opportunity Act. Divisiveness within the American society and Congress caused the issue to die in legislative subcommittee hearings. Some have argued that the issue died due to the forthcoming congressional elections and its potential impact. The Equal Opportunity Act of 1995 was viewed by Congress as being too hot to handle and the conservative legislative element was unable to set forth legislation designed to end all federal affirmative action programs.

Not only has the issue of affirmative action led to confusion in the United States Congress, but as evidenced in this study, the issue has received diverse reactions across the country. For example, the state of California in 1996 approved the California Civil Rights Act, known as Proposition 209. At the same time, the voters in Houston, Texas rejected a proposed initiative to end affirmative action in the city of Houston. Nevertheless, there still remains the issue of race-based classification in college admission cases. In 1996, the Fifth Circuit Court of Appeals declared the use of race as a consideration for admission to colleges and universities in the Texas system as unconstitutional. This decision was handed down in *Hopwood v. State of Texas* (1996). Even though each of the previously mentioned incidents are germane to specific states, they do provide a barometer for the remainder of the United States.

As demonstrated in this study, well planned affirmative action programs are still effective and work. The Supreme Court has consistently ruled that affirmative action programs that are designed to remedy egregious historical discrimination are valid. The affirmative action plan must be flexible and may not trammel unnecessarily the rights of non-African Americans. But even an affirmative action plan that is legal cannot exist forever, and there must be a limit to its duration.

The United States Supreme Court was perceived as a friend of African Americans during the 1950s through the 1960s. However, the conservative Rehnquist Court has been hostile to African American legal concerns. The liberal bloc of Marshall, Brennan, White and Blackmun has been replaced by the conservative justices of Rehnquist, O'Connor, Kennedy, Scalia, and Thomas. The Supreme Court is now viewed as less sympathetic toward the rights and concerns of African Americans. During the period from 1971-1988, the Court handed down decisions that were favorable to employees. From 1989 through 1996, the Court has reversed itself and became employer friendly. It should be noted that sometimes the employer was on the side of affirmative action and those cases were not included during this period. The Court has gone full circle in the area of affirmative action and policy programs.

Even though the Court has become more employer friendly, this study demonstrates that the decisions of the Supreme Court and other lower federal courts have not served as a deterrent in minority employment gains for those states within the Old Confederacy. It can be argued that the Old Confederacy, in spite of its past, is moving in a progressive direction in the area of employment for African Americans as state government employees. The federal level court cases provides some insight with regard to the future and legitimacy of affirmative action, as more cases come before the United States Supreme Court. The recent out of court settlement in *Taxman v Board of Education of Township of Piscataway* (1996) suggests an alternative strategy. It should be remembered that the Civil Rights leaders were afraid that the Supreme Court, if given the chance to review *Taxman,* would have sounded the death tone for affirmative action.

The appointment of Thurgood Marshall brought not only an African American to the United States Supreme Court, but also a philosophical viewpoint from his own experiences and work as an NAACP lawyer. Marshall was viewed as a liberal individual who championed the rights of others. It was Marshall who reminded the Court, in *Regents of the University of California v. Bakke* (1978) decision, that their legal philosophy had set back the progress for African Americans nearly 200 years.

It has been suggested, that Clarence Thomas, the only other African American to serve on the United States Supreme Court, has neither the scholarly background nor ability to influence other justices in the manner and style of Marshall. Some of the Court cases presented in the study clearly outline his view and stance on affirmative action. Justice Thomas, who attended Yale Law School through an affirmative action program, paradoxically refuses to acknowledge the importance of affirmative action programs or policies. Justice Thomas rarely engages in question and answer sessions regarding his philosophical viewpoints before audiences that are hostile to his views. Hence, it has been argued that African Americans no longer have an ally in Thomas.

In the South, given the demographics, African American state legislators will continue to have an impact regardless of affirmative action programs. African American state legislators, as a result of the 1965 Voting Rights Act, have provided influence in the decision making process and over hiring and promotion policies. Based on the evidence presented in the study, African Americans have continued to make progress in state government. Even though gains have been made in the area of state government, progress in key decision and policy-making areas continues to lag behind the remainder of society. The research data suggested that African Americans have attained increased numbers in the overall state government population workforce. However, those gains have been very minimal in top level administrative-officials and professional state government positions. The data suggested that the farther one gets from the top decision making categories, the higher the actual number and percentages of African Americans employed by the State. In view of the statistical analysis presented in this study, it is obvious that African Americans will continue to increase in numbers in various job categories. Since population as a variable has the most influence, African Americans should continue to increase their numbers in state government.

Even with the advent of conservative Republican governors in the South, there is no reason to doubt that as long as racial inequality exists, there will continue to be a movement to remediate the issue of racial inequality and its lasting effects. This view- point was supported by the fact that in spite of the anti-affirmative action Supreme Court and other federal court decisions, the Old Confederacy continues to remain progressive in the area of employment practices for African Americans. As indicated in the data, each of the seven selected states demonstrated gains in the status of African American state government employment.

It can be concluded from the research that the Old Confederacy has risen again. Southern politics has more clout, in part, as a result of southern migration by those moving from the North to the South. At the same time, African Americans have gained a degree of political power never envisioned when the 1965 Voting Rights Act was implemented. The rise in African American political power had occurred concurrently with the rise of the "New South." As more African Americans obtain policy making positions in state government in the South, re-distributive public policies benefitting their constituency are more likely.

The results of the research reveal that the presence of African American state legislators demonstrate a relationship with the increase in employment and hiring practices for African Americans in the Old Confederacy. Thus, the 1965 Voting Rights Act has provided a viable mechanism for African Americans to attain political power to influence the recruitment, hiring, and promotion of African American state administrators. The visibility of African American legislators placed them in a position to negotiate and bargain for jobs for African Americans in state government. The study suggests that the power of the vote has been utilized to provide employment power for African Americans in the selected states of the Old Confederacy. This has not been lost on white politicians in state government, particularly Democrats, who realize the importance of this vote.

In the midst of the rise of the South, it must be kept in mind that Republican governors currently hold office in the selected states of the Old Confederacy. The youthfulness of the Supreme Court, pending some major tragedy or turnabout, will continue to render conservative decisions for some time to come. Yet, African Americans continue to influence and obtain positions of power they never enjoyed in the past.

It is likely that diversity and some form of affirmative action will continue as a way of life. This is particularly true in the South. Both the public and private sector have benefitted in numerous ways from a diverse workforce and a diversified clientele. The market for recruitment of employees into the workforce has expanded due, in part, to a diversified society and clientele as opposed to a segregated one. The essence of government and governmental policies have been altered to strengthen the rights as well as privileges of African Americans and other protected groups. The type of products that are being manufactured by the various companies in the United States have certainly benefitted from a diversified culture. It is too much to be expected that success in the private and public domain will suddenly come to an end. Similarly, the public sector demands for services are more diversified than ever. African Americans have developed the political clout to influence policymaking that affects their lives. African Americans in strategic positions in government serve this end.

It should be noted that if affirmative action is to continue, plans must avoid tokenism and statistical schemes, both of which are irresponsible and create greater harm. Selection criteria and performance measures must be reexamined to ensure that qualified African Americans are not excluded. Rather than lowering the standards to hire based on quotas, affirmative action plans must focus on expanding the pool of qualified applicants to reflect a diversified market. An effective affirmative action plan should provide education and developmental opportunities for all new and existing employees. Acculturation of employees at all levels reinforces the values of fair treatment and validate the reasons for making an extra effort on behalf of African Americans and other protected groups. Governmental entities trying to attract African Americans should examine employment policies to ensure that they are offering applicants an attractive package. Various levels of government should examine their affirmative efforts with those efforts designed to encourage the development of all employees and to increase the cultural diversity of the workforce (Scott and Little, 1991).

# BIBLIOGRAPHY

Abraham, Henry J. *The Judicial Process.* New York: Oxford University Press, 1980.

Abraham, Henry J. and Barbara A. Perry. *Freedom and the Court: Civil Rights and Liberties in the United States.* New York: Oxford University Press, 1998.

Affirmative Action Minority Set-Asides: Future Justification for Implementation at the State and/or Local Government Level." *Mississippi Law Journal* 57 Spring 1989, pp. 189-208.

Agresto, John. *The Supreme Court and Constitutional Democracy.* Ithaca, New York: Cornell University Press, 1984.

Allen, Robert L. "The Bakke Case and Affirmative Action." *Black Scholar* 9,1, September 1977, pp. 9-16.

Amaker, Norman C. *Civil Rights and The Reagan Administration.* Washington D.C.: The Urban Institute Press, 1983.

Amselle, Jorge. "Pro & Con: Should Affirmative Action Polices Be Continued?" *Congressional Digest,* 75, 6-7, June-July 1996, pp. 177-181.

Anderson, George Edward, The Effect of Affirmative Action Programs on Female Employment and Earnings. (Ph.D. diss., University of California, Los Angeles, 1988), abstract in Dissertation Abstracts International 49(1988):09-A.

Andritzky, Frank William, The Development and Transformation of Federal Equal Employment Opportunity Law: an historical analysis into the Evolution and Politics of Affirmative Action, (Ph.D. diss., Claremont Graduate School, 1984), abstract in Dissertation Abstracts International 45(1984):01-A.

Badgett, Mary V. Lee, <u>Racial Differences In Unemployment Rates and Employment Opportunities (Affirmative Action)</u>. (Ph.D. diss., University of California, Berkeley, 1990), abstract in <u>Dissertation Abstracts International</u> 52(1990):04-A.

Ball, Howard, Dale Krane, and Thomas P. Lauth. *Compromised Compliance: Implementation of the 1965 Voting Rights Act.* Westport, Connecticut: Greenwood Press, 1982.

Barker, Lucius J. and Mack H. Jones. *Americans and The American Political System.* New Jersey: Prentice Hall, 1994.

Bearak, Barry. (1997). "Rights Groups Ducked a Fight, Opponents Say." *New York Times, CXLVII, 50, 984, November, 1997, p. B5.*

Becker, Gary, Thomas Sowell, and Kurt Vonnegrut, Jr. *Discrimination, Affirmative Action, and Equal Opportunity.* The Fraiser Institute, 1982.

Bell, Derrick. *Race, Racism and American Law.* Boston, Toronto and London: Little, Brown and Company, 1992.

Belton, Robert. "Reflections on Affirmative Action After *Paradise* and *Johnson.*" *Harvard Civil Rights-Civil Liberties Law Review*, 23, 1988, pp. 115-137.

Benokraitis, Nijole V. and Joe R. Feagin. *Affirmative Action and Equal Opportunity: Action; Inaction; Reaction.* Boulder, Colorado: Westview Press, 1978.

Berry, Jeffrey M., Jerry Goldman, and Kenneth Janda. *The Challenge of Democracy.* Princeton, New Jersey: Houghton Mifflin Company, 1993.

Binion, Gayle. "Affirmative Action Reconsidered: Justification, Objectives, Myths and Misconceptions." *Women & Politics.* 7,1 Spring 1987, pp. 43-62.

Bolick, Clint. *The Affirmative Action Fraud.* Washington, D.C.: Cato Institute, 1996.

Bowen, Erie Jean, <u>Affirmative Action Employment Programs in Mississippi Public Universities: 1972-1979.</u> (Ph.D. diss., The University of Mississippi, 1981), abstract in <u>Dissertation Abstracts International</u> 42 (1981):11-A.

Brown, William H., <u>Affirmative Action Programs and the Impact of Recent Court Orders on Alabama College System Administrators (Employment, Promotion, Women, Minorities).</u> (Ph.D. diss., The University of Alabama, 1996), abstract in <u>Dissertation Abstracts International</u> 57(1996):06-A.

Burnstein, Paul. *Equal Employment Opportunity.* New York: Aldine DeGruyter, 1994.

Carter, Stephen L. "Affirmative Action Harms Black Professionals." *Reflections of an Affirmative Action Baby.* New York: Basic Books, 1993.

Cohen, Carl. "Pro & Con: Should Affirmative Action Policies Be Continued?" *Congressional Digest,* 75,6-7, June-July 1996, pp. 181-187.

*Congressional Digest* 75,6-7, June-July 1996, pp. 162-171.

*Congressional Quarterly Almanac.* "104th Congress: 1st Session-1995." 51, 1995, pp.24-26.

*Congressional Quarterly Almanac.* "104th Congress: 2nd Session-1996." 52, 1996, pp. 37-38.

Connor, Lyman Alexander, <u>The Impact of Affirmative Action on The Employment Practices in Pennsylvania's State System of Higher Education; 1974-1984 (Blacks, Administration, Minorities, Faculty).</u> (Ph.D. diss., University of Pittsburgh, 1985), abstract in <u>Dissertation Abstracts International</u> 46 (1985):11-A.

Curry, George E. *The Affirmative Action Debate.* Reading, MA: Addison-Wesley Publishing Company, Inc., 1996.

Davidson, Chandler and Bernard Grofman. *Quiet Revolution in the S South: The Impact of the Voting Rights Act 1965-1990.* New Jersey: Princeton University Press, 1994.

Diubaldo, Donald V. The Effects of a Four Year Affirmative Action/Employment Program upon Gender Attitudes of Academic Staff and The Effects Upon the Occupational Distribution of Academic Women in an Urban School Board in Ontario, Canada. (Ph.D. diss., Wayne State University, 1991), abstract in Dissertation Abstracts International 52 (1991):12-A.

Eastland, Terry. *Ending Affirmative Action.* New York: Basic Books, 1996.

Edmond, Beverly Cheryl, The Impact of Federal Equal Employment Opportunity and Affirmative Action Policies on the Employment of Black Women in the Higher Grades (1982-1986) (Federal Employment). (Ph.D. diss., Georgia State University, 1990), abstract in Dissertation Abstracts International 51(1990):06-A.

Elazar, Daniel J. *American Federalism: A View from the States* (2nd ed.). New York: Thomas Y. Crowell Company, 1972.

Elazar, Daniel J. *The American Mosaic: The Impact of Space, Time, and Culture on American Politics.* San Francisco: Westview Press, 1994.

Eskridge, William, D. Farber and P. Fickey. *Constitutional Law: Themes for the Constitution.* St. Paul, MN: West Publishing Company, 1993.

Espinosa, Dula Joanne, The Firm Revisited: An Investigation of the Link Between Changing Work Arrangements and Changing Employment Outcomes (Affirmative Action). (Ph.D. diss., University of California Santa Barbara, 1991), abstract in Dissertation Abstracts International 52(1990):04-A.

Ezorsky, Gertrude. *Racism and Justice.* New York: Cornell University Press, 1992.

Farber, Daniel A., William N. Eskridge, Jr. and Philip P. Frickey. *Constitutional Law: Themes For The Constitution's Third Century*. St. Paul, MN: West Publishing Co., 1993.

Farley R. (1977). "Trends in Racial Inequalities: Have the Gains of the 1960s Disappeared in the 1970s." *American Sociological Review*, 42, April 1977, pp.189-208.

Farrell, John A. (1997). "Cash Settles Affirmative Action Lawsuit." *The Boston Globe*.

Fields, Cheryl M. "U.S. Congress urges Supreme Court to Send Bakke Case Back to California." *Chronicle of Higher Education*, 15, 4, September 26, 1977, pp.9-12.

Fisher, Jeanne B. (1978). "Bakke Case: Part I - The Issues." *Journal of College Student Personnel*, 19,2, March 1978, pp.174-179.

Fisher, Jeanne B. (1979). "Bakke Case: Part II - An Analysis and Implications." *Journal of College Student Personnel*, 20,3, May 1979, pp.264-270.

Fleming, John E., G.R. Gill, and D.H. Swinton. *The Case for Affirmative Action for Blacks in Higher Education*. Howard University Press, 1978.

Fullinwider, Robert K. *The Reverse Discrimination Controversy: A Moral and Legal Analysis*. Totowa, N.J.:Rowman and Littlefield, 1980.

Glazer, Nathan. *Affirmative Discrimination: Ethnic Inequality and Public Policy*. New York: Basic Books, 1975.

Goodwin, Felix Lee, Affirmative Action and Equal Employment Opportunity at the University of Arizona from May 1966 to December 1976. (Ph.D. diss., The University of Arizona, 1979), abstract in Dissertation Abstracts International 40 (1979):09-A.

Greene, Kathanne W. *Affirmative Action and Principles of Justice*. New York: Greenwood, 1989.

Greenhouse, Linda. "Justices Bolster Race Preferences at Federal Level." *New York Times, 1990.*

Greenhouse, Linda. (1997). "New Jersey School Move Leaves Affirmative Action in Limbo." *The New York Times, CXLVII, 50, 984, November 1997, p. B4.*

Higgins, James Michael, <u>A Partial Application of an Inventory Model Social Audit of Equal Employment Opportunity Programs in Selected Commercial Firms from Two Urban Areas: with Special Emphasis on Recruitment, Selection, and Affirmative Action Programs</u>. (Ph.D. diss. Georgia State University, 1974), abstract in <u>Dissertation Abstracts International</u> 35 (1974):11-A.

Hudson, Charles Kenneth, <u>The Employment of White Males Before and After Affirmative Action</u>. (Ph.D. diss., University of Louisville, 1994), abstract in <u>Dissertation Abstracts International</u> 33 (1994):01.

Hudson, J. Blaine. "Simple Justice: Affirmative Action and American Racism in Historical Perspective." *The Black Scholar, 25,.3, 1995,* pp.16-23.

Hyman, Harold M. and William M. Wiecek. *Equal Justice Under Law: Constitutional Development 1835-1875.* New York: Harper & Row, 1982.

*Information Please Almanac.* Atlas and Yearbook, 47th Edition. Boston & New York: Houghton Mifflin Company, 1994.

*Information Please Almanac.* Atlas and Yearbook, 48th Edition. Boston & New York: Houghton Mifflin Company, 1995.

*Information Please Almanac.* Atlas and Yearbook, 49th Edition. Boston & New York: Houghton Mifflin Company, 1996.

*Information Please Almanac.* Atlas and Yearbook, 50th Edition. Boston & New York: Houghton Mifflin Company, 1997.

Johnson, Jean Thomasena Jackson, Affirmative Action Employment Programs: How Blacks Employed at Michigan State University and Vocational Rehabilitation Services Understand the Program and Perceive it as affecting their Careers. (Ph.D. diss., Michigan State University, 1976), abstract in Dissertation Abstracts International 37(1976):06-A.

Joint Center for Political Studies. *Black Elected Officials: A National Roster* (1984). Washington, D. C. University Press of America, Inc.: Lanham, MD.

Joint Center for Political Studies. *Black Elected Officials: A National Roster* (1985). Washington, D.C. University Press of America, Inc.: Lanham, MD.

Joint Center for Political Studies. *Black Elected Officials: A National Roster* (1986). Washington, D.C. University Press of America, Inc.: Lanham, MD.

Joint Center for Political Studies. *Black Elected Officials: A National Roster* (1987). Washington, D.C. University Press of America, Inc.: Lanham, MD.

Joint Center for Political Studies. *Black Elected Officials: A National Roster* (1988). Washington, D.C. University Press of American, Inc.: Lanham, MD.

Joint Center for Political Studies Press. *Black Elected Officials: A National Roster* (1989). Washington, D.C. University Press of America, Inc.: Lanham, MD.

Joint Center for Political and Economic Studies Press. *Black Elected Officials: A National Roster* (1990). Washington, D.C. University Press of America, Inc.: MD.

Joint Center for Political and Economic Studies Press. *Black Elected Officials: A National Roster* (1991). Washington, D.C. University Press of America, Inc.: MD.

Joint Center for Political and Economic Studies Press. *Black Elected Officials: A National Roster* (1992). Washington, D.C. University Press of America, Inc.: MD.

Joint Center for Political and Economic Studies Press. *Black Elected Officials: A National Roster* (1993). Washington, D.C. University Press of America, Inc.: MD.

Joint Center for Political Studies. *National Roster of Black Elected Officials*, 4, April 1974, Washington, D.C.

Joint Center for Political Studies. *National Roster of Black Elected Officials,* 5, July 1975, Washington, D.C.

Joint Center for Political Studies. *National Roster of Black Elected Officials,* 6, August    1976, Washington, D.C.

Joint Center for Political Studies. *National Roster of Black Elected Officials,* 7, July 1977, Washington, D.C.

Joint Center for Political Studies. *National Roster of Black Elected Officials,* 8, 1978, Washington, D.C.

Joint Center for Political Studies. *National Roster of Black Elected Officials,* 10, 1980, Washington, D.C.

Joint Center for Political Studies. *National Roster of Black Elected Officials,* 11, 1981, Washington, D.C.

Joint Center for Political Studies. *National Roster of Black Elected Officials,* 12, 1982, Washington, D.C.

Jones, Elaine R. "Race and the Supreme Court's 1994-95 Term." *The Affirmative Action Debate.* Ed. George E. Curry. Reading, MA: Addison-Wesley Publishing Company, Inc., 1996.

Kahnlenberg, Richard. "Society Needs Affirmative Action Based on Class, Not Race." *Affirmative Action.* San Diego: Greenhaven Press, 1995.

Karst, Kenneth L. *Civil Rights and Equality*. New York: MacMillan Publishing Company, 1989.

Kellough, James and Susan Ann Kay. "Affirmative Action In The Federal Bureaucracy: an Impact Assessment." *Public Personnel Administration*, 6,2, 1986 pp. 1-13.

Kennedy, Randall. *Racial Preference and Racial Justice*. New York: Aldine DeGruyter, 1994.

Kinsley, Micheal. "The Spoils of Victimhood." *New Yorker*, March 27, 1995.

Kull, Andrew. *The Color-Blind Constitution*. Cambridge: Harvard University Press, 1992.

Lee, Sheila Jackson. "Pro & Con: Should Affirmative Action Policies Be Continued?" *Congressional Digest*, 75,6-7, June-July 1996, pp.176-182.

Lewis, Gregory B. "Equal Employment Opportunity and The Early Career in Federal Employment." *Public Personnel Administration*, 6,3, Summer 1986, pp.1-18.

Long, Robert Emmett. *Affirmative Action*. New York: The H.W. Wilson Company, 1996.

Loury, Glenn. *One by One from the Inside Out: Essays and Reviews on Race and Responsibility in America*. New York: Free Press, 1995.

Mandelbaum, Leonard B. "Affirmative Action Preference Systems: The Case For Human Resource Development." *Public Personnel Administration*, 3,2, Spring 1983, pp.1-14.

Manifold, Edward Moye. Implementation of Affirmative Action Plans for Equal Employment Opportunity in Public School Districts of the Commonwealth of Pennsylvania. (Ph.D. diss., University of Pittsburgh, 1980), abstract in Dissertation Abstracts International 41(1980):07-A.

Marable, Manning. "Staying on the Path to Racial Equality." *The Affirmative Action Debate.* Ed. George E. Curry. Reading, MA: Addison-Wesley Publishing Company, Inc., 1996.

Mathis, Robert L. and John H. Jackson. *Human Resource Management.* Minneapolis: West Publishing Corporation, 1994.

Mead, Linda and Brian H. Kliener. "What The New Civil Rights Law Will Mean to Organizations." *Labor Law Journal,* October 1995, pp. 627-631.

McClelland-Cooper, Pamela. Kansas State Government: Employee Trends (1973-76) and Employee Perceptions of the Impact of Equal Employment Opportunity and Affirmative Action. (Ph.D. diss., Kansas State University, 1977), abstract in Dissertation Abstracts International 38 (1977):09-A.

Mitchell, John Albert. The Impact of Equal Employment Opportunity and Affirmative Action Legislation on Virginia Public School Divisions as Perceived by School Personnel Officials. (Ph.D. diss., The College of William and Mary in Virginia, 1982), abstract in Dissertation Abstracts International 45 (1985): 09-A.

Molinari, Susan. "Pro & Con: Should Affirmative Action Policies Be Continued?" *Congressional Digest,* 75,6-7, pp. 173-175.

"NAACP Statement on Implications of the Bakke Decision." *Crisis,* 86, 41, February 1979, pp. 41-43.

Nava, Roberto. An assessment of Affirmative Action Employment Programs in selected California School Districts and an Analysis of Environmental Factors Affecting the Implementation of Affirmative Action Programs in California Public Schools. (Ph.D. diss., University of the Pacific, 1982), abstract in Dissertation Abstracts International 43 (1982):07-A.

Norton, Eleanor. "Affirmative Action in the Workplace." *The Affirmative Action Debate.* Ed. George E. Curry. Reading, MA: Addison-Wesley Publishing Company, Inc, 1996.

Odezah, Sunday. The Search for a Representative Bureaucracy in Oklahoma State Government: Equal Employment Opportunity, Affirmative Action. (Ph.D. diss., The University of Oklahoma, 1993), abstract in Dissertation Abstracts International 54 (1993):04-A.

Patrick, Deval. "Pro & Con: Should Affirmative Action Policies Be Continued?" Congressional Digest, 75,6-7, June-July 1996, pp. 172-176.

Patrick, Deval. "Standing In The Right Place." The Affirmative Action Debate. Ed. George E. Curry. Reading, MA: Addison-Wesley Publishing Company, Inc., 1996.

Phillips, Robert Hansbury. Equal Employment Opportunity, Affirmative Action, Mayoral Initiatives and Bureaucratic Responses: The Case of Detroit, Michigan. (Ph.D. diss., Wayne State University, 1987), abstract in Dissertation Abstracts International 49(1987):04-A.

Puddington, Arch. "Affirmative Action Should Be Eliminated." Affirmative Action. San Diego, CA.: Greenhaven Press, 1996.

Raskin, Jamin. "Society Needs Affirmative Action to Fight Discrimination." Affirmative Action. San Diego, CA: Greenhaven Press, 1996.

Rice, Mitchell F. "Government Set-Asides, Minority Business Enterprise and the Supreme Court." Public Administration, 51,2 March/April 1991, pp.114-122.

Scott, Dow K. and Beverly Little. "Affirmative Action: New Interpretations and Realities." Human Resource Planning, 14,3, 1991, pp.179-182.

Shafritz, Jay M., Norma M. Riccucci, David H. Rosenbloom and Albert C. Hyde. Personnel Management in Government. New York: Marcel Dekker, Inc., 1992.

Shulman, Steven and William Darity Jr. The Question of Discrimination. Middletown, Connecticut: Wesleyan University Press, 1989.

Sowell, Thomas. *Black Education: Myths and Tragedies*. New York: McKay Company Inc., 1972.

Sowell, Thomas. *Civil Rights: Rhetoric or Reality?* New York: William Morrow and Company, Inc., 1984.

Sowell, Thomas. *Preferential Policies: An International Perspective*. New York: William Morrow, 1990.

Sowell, Thomas. *Inside America Education*. New York: The Free Press, 1992.

Spratlen, Thaddeus H. "The Bakke Decision: Implications for Black Educational and Professional Opportunities." *Journal of Negro Education*, 48,4, 1979, pp. 449-456.

*State Elective Officials and The Legislatures 1987-88*. The Council of State Governments: Lexington, Kentucky.

*Statistical Abstract of the United States 1982-83*. National Data Book and Guide to Sources (103rd Edition). United States Department of Commerce. Bureau of the Census.

*Statistical Abstract of the United States-1994*. National Data Book and Guide to Sources. United States Department of Commerce. Bureau of the Census.

*Statistical Abstract of the United States-1995*. The National Data Book and Guide to Sources. United States Department of Commerce. Bureau of the Census.

*Statistical Abstract of the United States-1996*. The National Data Book. (116th Edition). United States Department of Commerce. Economic and Statistics Administration. Bureau of the Census.

*Statistical Abstract of the United States-1997*. The National Data Book (117th Edition). United States Department of Commerce. Economics and Statistics Administration. Bureau of the Census.

Steele, Shelby. "Affirmative Action: The Price of Preference." *Taking Sides*. Ed. George Mckenna and Stanley Feingold. Connecticut: The Dushkin Publishing Group, Inc., 1994.

Swain, Carol. *Race versus Class: The New Affirmative Action Debate*. New York: University Press of America, Inc., 1996.

Swanson, Kathryn. *Affirmative Action and Preferential Admissions in Higher Education*. Metuchen, N.J. : Scarecrow Press, 1981.

Taylor, Bron Raymond. *Affirmative Action at Work: Law, Politics, and Ethics*. Pittsburgh, PA: University of Pittsburgh Press, 1991.

*United States Civil Rights Commission*. "The Voting Rights Act: Unfulfilled Goals." The U.S. Commission on Civil Rights: Washington, D.C. 1981

Wallace, Phyllis A. *Equal Employment Opportunity and the AT&T Case*. Cambridge: The MIT Press, 1976.

West, Cornell. "Affirmative Action In Context." *The Affirmative Action Debate*. Ed. George E. Curry. Reading, MA: Addison-Wesley Publishing Company, Inc., 1996.

Whitehead, John Clark. The Development of a model for establishing and maintaining an Affirmative Action Employment Program for Public Institutions of Higher Education (Ph.D. diss., University of Utah, 1972), abstract in Dissertation Abstracts International 33(1972):03-A.

Williams, Linda. "Tracing the Politics of Affirmative Action." *The Affirmative Action Debate*. Ed. George E. Curry. Reading, MA: Addison-Wesley Publishing Company Inc., 1996.

Wilson, Theodore B. *The Black Codes of the South*. University: University of Alabama Press, 1965.

Zashin, Elliot. (1978). "The Progress of Black Americans in Civil Rights: The Past Two Decades Assessed." *Daedalus* 107,1, Winter 1978, pp. 239-26.

# INDEX